REGION AND RENAISSANCE

Reflections on planning and development in the West Midlands, 1950-2000

REGION AND RENAISSANCE

Reflections on planning and development in the West Midlands, 1950-2000

Edited by

David Chapman

Clive Harridge

Janet Harrison

Graham Harrison

Bob Stokes

Picture editor: **Sandra Newton**

Published to celebrate the Golden Jubilee of the
West Midlands Branch of the Royal Town Planning Institute.

BREWIN
BOOKS

Dedicated to all those planners who have helped shape the region, but are no longer with us.

First published by Brewin Books Ltd.
Studley, Warwickshire B80 7LG in 2000.

British Library Cataloguing in Publication Data
A catalogue record for this book is available from
The British Library

ISBN: 1 85858 155 9

Typeset in Plantin
and made and printed in Great Britain
by Warwick Printing Company Limited,
Theatre Street, Warwick, Warwickshire CV34 4DR.

Contents

The views expressed in this book are those of the individual authors and not necessarily of the editors, the Royal Town Planning Institute or its West Midlands Branch.

Acknowledgements

We should like to thank all the authors, without whose articles there would have been no book, and all those who generously supplied photographs, illustrations, maps and other material. We would also like to record our special thanks to Sandra Newton who, as picture editor, painstakingly sought the most appropriate material.

We are very much indebted to Birmingham City Council, Bournville Village Trust and the Croft Trust for their generous grants towards the publication cost and, not least, to the Royal Town Planning Institute West Midlands Branch which expressed its faith in the project by agreeing to underwrite most of the cost. We are also grateful to those who supported us by ordering pre-publication copies and whose names appear in the back of the book. Here we would wish to thank Mike Beazley for his help in promoting the publication nationwide, Sheena Terrace for allowing the Planning Aid office to become a post-box and Sandra again for collating all the orders.

We would like to thank all members of the Branch's Executive Committee for their help and support and, in particular, the Secretary, Paul Harris, for the original inspiration for this book. In Brewin Books, we were fortunate to find someone prepared to publish a specialist book with a limited print run and we are grateful for all the help and guidance we have received from them. Finally, we should all like to thank our families for their encouragement and forbearance over the past eighteen months.

The Editors

All illustrations, including maps, are reproduced by courtesy of the following:

Architectural Press 6,25; Birmingham City Council 3,24,65,91,92,119,123,125,162,165; Bournville Village Trust 32,34; Centro 93,96; Coventry City Council 17,19,20,217(b); Coventry Evening Telegraph 15,22; East Staffordshire Borough Council 74; English Partnerships 149; Clive Harridge 45; JV & GR Harrison 30,37,58,63,66,88,102,107,114,127,131,132,134,146, 151,152,177,180,182,189; John Madin Design Group 68; The Millennium Point Trust 217(t); Jim Newton 169; Sandra Newton 47,139; Harry Noble 42; Graham Reddie 55; Redditch Dev Corp 54; RTPI West Midlands Branch 142; Sandwell MBC 116,159,172, 174; Sandwell Dept of Housing 46; City of Stoke-on-Trent 110(t&b); Telford and Wrekin Council 49,53; Urlan Wannop 76,81; Warwickshire County Council 10 (t&b); West Midlands Local Government Association and Staffordshire County Council xii,61,179; West Midlands Planning Aid Group 195,197, 204; West Midlands Planning and Transportation Sub-committee 86; Wolverhampton MBC 170; Worcester City Council 105(t&b).

Illustrations on pages 9 and 10 (centre) are Crown copyright, reproduced with the permission of the Controller of Her Majesty's Stationery Office. All maps are based upon the Ordnance Survey map by permission of Ordnance Survey on behalf of the Controller of Her Majesty's Stationery Office, © Crown Copyright MC 100031258.

Data for 'Signs of the Times' were derived from the *Census*, *Annual Abstract of Statistics* and *Regional Trends*.

Foreword

It gives me great pleasure to write this Foreword to *Region and Renaissance*. Ever since my great grandfather, George, commenced the building of his garden village at Bournville in 1895, my family has been associated with planning in the West Midlands. My grandfather, George Cadbury Junior, a member of the Birmingham Town Planning Committee, wrote a book on the subject in 1915, with special reference to Birmingham schemes. Three more family members, including Paul who acted as Honorary Secretary, were on the West Midlands Group on Post-war Reconstruction and Planning that produced the widely acclaimed publication *Conurbation* in 1948. More recently, my father, Christopher, was a member of the Telford Development Corporation and my cousin, Sir Adrian, was chairman of the West Midlands Economic Planning Council from 1967-1970.

Reading this book, I was taken by the way in which some of the early pioneering concepts have developed over the past fifty years. For example, the New Towns very much reflect the original aim for Bournville of a village in green countryside, though naturally on a very much larger scale. Then there was the massive redevelopment of Birmingham, which was foreseen in *Conurbation*.

Many town planners from the West Midlands have become nationally known and respected members of their profession and the articles that follow stand as testimony to their efforts to improve the lives of many. Sadly, some who would willing have contributed to this book are no longer with us. In particular, I would like to pay special tribute to Professor Gordon Cherry, my predecessor as Chairman of the Bournville Village Trust from 1992-1996. He was also a Past President of the Royal Town Planning Institute and was held in very high esteem by the planning profession.

Two major changes are apparent to me. Firstly, there has been a gradual transition from 'planning for people' to 'planning by people'. Fifty years ago, we were mostly content to have our surroundings planned for us, but today we rightly expect to be active participants in what happens to our environment. This was brought home to me recently when, as Chairman of the Bournville Village Trust, I was involved in a 'planning for real' exercise.

Secondly, the environment itself has now emerged as a priority alongside people and the economy. The key theme at the start of the new Millennium is sustainable development. To deliver this, we need to have a far greater understanding and respect for our natural environment. For too long we have managed to destroy our natural surroundings, whereas to live in harmony with nature is far more demanding, but more rewarding. My hope is that the planners of the future will take up this challenge.

Indeed, the Bournville Village Trust's combined Millennium and Centenary Project is to develop a second Bournville at Lightmoor, in Telford, based on urban village concepts, which include economic, social and environmental sustainability, hopefully learning some of the planning lessons from the past 50-100 years.

So, against this background, I am particularly interested in this publication to celebrate the Golden Jubilee of the West Midlands Branch of the Royal Town Planning Institute and in its conclusion which, based on a fascinating analysis of the past fifty years, promotes the continuing importance of planning for the future.

Roger Cadbury

Introduction

Compiling a book on planning and development in the West Midlands region over fifty years and looking forward to future prospects seemed a suitable way to mark the Golden Jubilee of the Royal Town Planning Institute, West Midlands Branch. It is also appropriate at the start of a new Millennium, when thoughts are very much on past reflections and future aspirations.

The West Midlands is situated right at the heart of England and is unique in being the only land locked standard region in Britain. It measures 160 km (100 miles) from north to south, 145 km (90 miles) from east to west and covers 13,000 km² (5,000 square miles) comprising Herefordshire, Shropshire, Staffordshire, Warwickshire and Worcestershire as well as the West Midlands and North Staffordshire conurbations. Renowned as the manufacturing heartland of Britain, it is home to over five million people.

We invited some thirty authors to write about their experiences of this diverse region and, in bringing together their various contributions, we have been continually struck by the realisation of all that has been done in the past fifty years. In charting this progress, we have also become acutely aware of how much we are having to neglect in this current volume.

The West Midlands has been in the forefront of planning from the time of the post-war comprehensive redevelopment of Birmingham through to its emergence as an international city, and with projects as far apart as the reconstruction of Coventry and the reclamation of derelict land in Stoke-on-Trent. The concept of a green belt to constrain urban sprawl, with new and expanded towns beyond it, served the region well during the rapid growth of the 1960s, with Redditch and Telford both major successes. Since then, the urban development corporations and city challenge have stimulated urban renewal in the Black Country and Birmingham Heartlands during times of recession. In the countryside, a network of country parks has been established and progressively more consideration has been given to conserving both our built heritage and natural environment.

The region has pioneered new approaches to planning, ranging from the techniques developed by regional and sub-regional studies of the 1970s to the regional planning conference of the 1990s. Equally significant, but less well known, has been the contribution made by the West Midlands Branch of the Royal Town Planning Institute to environmental education and planning aid.

Of course, not everything has been a success. As the authors frankly admit, there have been failures too, particularly with the high-rise flats of the mass housing programme and the empty shops following the property boom. But to make a fair assessment, one needs to understand the social, economic, environmental and political circumstances of the time at which decisions were taken. It is from this that the structure of the book evolved.

We decided to devote a chapter to each decade and then to conclude with a final chapter that looks into the new Millennium. The chapter titles reflect a key theme for each decade, while the chapters themselves begin with an overview that sets the scene and provides an introduction to the feature articles that follow. Many of these features, of course, span more than one decade, but we have generally tried to include them at the time when they first sprang to prominence. After all, this is the period and background against which they should be judged. By following this approach, we hope our readers will have a clearer understanding, not only of what happened, but why it happened and that this will lead to a deeper appreciation of what was achieved.

We have made extensive use of acronyms, but have generally put the title followed by the acronym in brackets the first time it appears in each chapter, or when it has not appeared for some time. For example, the Royal Town Planning Institute (RTPI) becomes RTPI thereafter. References to the Branch refer to the RTPI West Midlands Branch. Readers should also be aware that the RTPI was the Town Planning Institute (TPI) prior to receiving its Supplemental Royal Charter in 1971. We have also given both imperial and metric measurements, with the former first in the 1950s and 1960s and the latter first thereafter. This reflects the change to metric measurement that occurred around the early 1970s. We have also fully referenced all principal sources, but not some of the more ephemeral ones.

Through the richness of their contributions, which reflect their individual styles, thoughts and experiences, our authors have skilfully recorded how planners have responded to the region's needs from the days of post-war optimism to the renaissance of recent years. The achievements between times have shown many tangible successes. But there are perhaps many more, though far less obvious results. These may be easier to appreciate if we try to imagine what the region might have been like had there been no planning in place over those fifty years.

The Editors

The West Midlands Region

Chapter 1:

The 1950s – Planning for a Better Future

Overview

Janet Harrison

Post-war Britain presented a strange mixture of austerity and optimism. The after effects of the war lingered well into the 1950s, with rationing of certain foods and fuels and building restrictions persisting into the decade. Yet hopes were high and almost everyone felt they could aspire to a better future. To a large extent this optimism was fuelled by the radical programme of legislation introduced by the new Labour Government, which promised reform of the education system and the introduction of the National Health Service and the welfare state. Amongst this ambitious programme was the Town and Country Planning Act 1947, which, though subsequently much amended, remains the foundation of planning in Britain today, as John Holliday later explains when he traces the development of planning from 1950 onwards.

After years of enforced separation for married couples, there was a post-war 'baby boom', with birth rates 20% higher than in the pre-war years. This exacerbated the housing shortage and the priorities of the day were to provide people with homes and to get the economy moving again. Many parts of the West Midlands had suffered from bomb damage, but none more so than Coventry, where the city centre and St Michael's cathedral were largely destroyed on the night of November 15th, 1940. The air raids also damaged over 50,000 houses in the city. In his article, Terence Gregory describes the subsequent re-building of the city centre, with its pedestrianised shopping precinct and Basil Spence's new cathedral, both of which were landmark achievements, with the cathedral especially still drawing visitors from around the world.

But bomb damage was only part of the problem. Much of the housing was also sub-standard and this provided the opportunity for local authorities to think about comprehensive redevelopment of the inner city areas. The West Midland Group (1948) reported that one-third of the houses in the conurbation should be replaced as soon as possible. To appreciate the full significance of this state-ment, it is important to remember just how poor housing conditions were by contemporary standards. Less than half had bathrooms and many only had outside toilets. Telephones and refrigerators were the prerogative of the rich and freezers and washing machines were almost unheard of. Serious over-crowding was also a problem.

Birmingham, especially, rose to the challenge these conditions posed by taking advantage of earlier legislation to embark upon an ambitious programme of inner city renewal in five Comprehensive Development Areas. The powers conferred by the 1944 Town and Country Planning Act were used to sweep away the slums, where houses stood back-to-back to one another and cheek-by-jowl with heavy, polluting industries, and to replace them with a pattern of segregated land uses and attractive new housing. The process of this massive undertaking is explained by Alan Geeson and Colin Rodgers. A major problem was density. So many people had been crammed into the inner cities that redevelopment inevitably meant accepting high-rise blocks of flats in the rebuilding schemes. At the time, no one foresaw the social problems that this would eventually create. Even with the high-rise blocks there were still insufficient homes to accommodate all the displaced families, so there had to be a parallel programme of large peripheral council estates, such as those at Quinton and Lea Hall. Other bodies, such as the Bournville Village Trust, helped by working in conjunction with the City Council and Alan Shrimpton outlines how their own estates were expanded at an accelerated rate and a higher than usual density.

Whilst comprehensive redevelopment would be unacceptable today, at that time it seemed far more acceptable. People generally were looking for leadership and seemed much happier to accept the new ideas emanating from the Government and their local councils than they are today. Indeed, the general mood of the day was to go for all things modern and to sweep away much of the past. For their part, local authorities were charged with providing solutions quickly. During the war there had been no building, but considerable destruction, so there was an enormous need for houses in particular. Moreover, with priority given to repairing war damaged buildings and to constructing the new schools and hospitals required under the Government's welfare state policies, serious shortages of materials and labour caused building costs to escalate. Many local authorities responded by putting up prefabricated houses in gaps in street frontages and on other small areas of open land, but not on sites earmarked for permanent housing. These prefabs, as they became known, were intended to be a short-term measure until proper, permanent homes could be built. Somewhat optimistically, they were given an expected life of ten years. Yet fifty years on some can still be found in Birmingham, where they have survived to become listed buildings.

Gross under-estimates of how long it would take to recover from the effects of the war were a feature of the time. For example, the region's infrastructure had suffered years of intensive use combined with neglect and under-investment and it took much longer than expected to recover. Narrow boats were still carrying goods along the canals, but the bargees' trade did not last long in the face of competition from rail and road. The railways, of course, were still steam powered and were the lifeblood of the region's industry. Without proper maintenance and

Prefabs – temporary post-war housing, given a life of ten years, but some have survived to become listed buildings.

investment, however, they became increasingly unreliable and never regained their pre-war eminence. This applied especially to passenger traffic, with Birmingham, unlike other cities, having relatively few rail commuters. Road transport was very much in the ascendancy and congestion was becoming a serious concern for industry. Only the wealthy owned cars, however, so the vast majority of people were dependent on trams and buses to go about their daily business. As an example, surveys at two Birmingham factories showed 60% of the workforce travelling by train, tram or bus and only 14% by car (West Midland Group, 1948). The transport priority of the time was seen as better road links to London and the ports.

Manufacturing industry, particularly of vehicles, dominated the economy and employed over half the region's workforce in a plethora of factory buildings ranging from ramshackle sheds and small workshops to large, efficient installations. Working conditions were frequently dirty, smoky, smelly and noisy and these polluting elements often spread beyond the factory into the surrounding residential streets. During the war, many factories had switched to producing armaments as part of the war effort and now their owners had to revert to traditional products and find new markets in a world with very little spending power. Nevertheless, the region remained prosperous, with high activity rates and full employment. Indeed, the unemployment rate for the decade was only

Signs of the Times

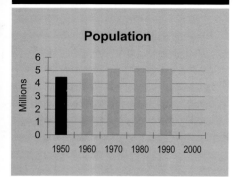

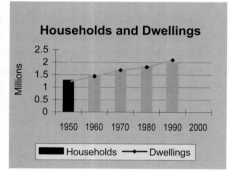

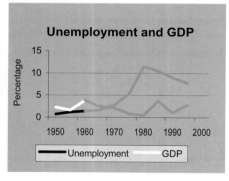

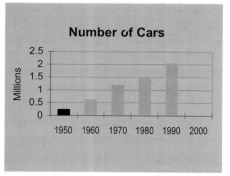

around 1%. There had also been a major shift in social attitudes to work. Many of the women who had first been recruited into factories during the war to replace the men serving in the armed forces stayed on afterwards to replace those men who sadly were never to return. Thus the constitution of the labour force was irreversibly changed.

Though very different, circumstances in rural areas were not necessarily better. Even in the late 1950s many villages were without sewerage and some residents still had to draw their water from wells. Indeed, at Kinver people were still living in sandstone caves into the 1950s. Agriculture was the dominant industry, employing half the workforce in parts of Herefordshire, Shropshire, Warwickshire and Worcestershire. The work was hard, the hours long and the wages low and many young people chose to forsake the country life in favour of what they perceived to be better opportunities in the towns and cities. As a consequence, the composition of the rural population gradually became older.

Although planning controls existed in certain areas before the war, the inauguration of comprehensive planning by the Town and Country Planning Act of 1947 marked a significant milestone. For the first time development everywhere became subject to planning control and, barring a few exceptions, no landowner could develop his land without first obtaining planning permission. As well as having to administer this control over development, local planning authorities were also required to produce development plans within three years and thereafter to review them every five years. The purpose of these plans was to show how the land in an area could be used. All these extra responsibilities created new jobs and the few professional planners there were in those days soon found themselves engaged in one way or another with implementing the new system.

With insufficient qualified planners to meet demand, the profession found itself having to fight to maintain standards and to ensure that planning became recognised as a separate discipline rather than an adjunct to architecture or engineering. These concerns arose largely because the local councils of many towns and cities chose to add their new planning functions to those already administered by architects, engineers or building inspectors. Only in the shire counties, where there had been very little prior involvement in planning, were separate planning departments under qualified chief officers established. As John Holliday also explains, there was an immediate need to increase the opportunities for planners to train and qualify. In the West Midlands, this culminated with the establishment of the Birmingham School of Planning in 1957. Under the charismatic leadership of the late Leslie Ginsberg, the school quickly established a high reputation and was granted formal recognition by the then Town Planning Institute in 1961.

For most of the West Midlands this was a prosperous decade during which the life styles of many families improved significantly, with better housing, full employment, better education and greater mobility. There were drawbacks nonetheless. The population was growing, both through natural increase and immigration, and this was fuelling congestion. The age structure was also changing. Retired people were escaping to the more pleasant environments of the countryside and coast, while young people were being attracted into the cities and towns even from beyond the region. There were also changes within the cities and towns themselves as people moved away from the core areas to the periphery. Industrial unrest also began to manifest itself through strikes and these were later to become the bane of the region's economy. Nevertheless, the Prime Minister, Harold Macmillan, was probably right in 1957 when he said "most of our people have never had it so good."

Fifty Years of Development Planning

John Holliday

Laying the foundations

"I like to have a plan" said Mr Palliser, "and so do I" said his wife – "if only for the sake of not keeping it." So wrote Trollope in 1864 in *Can You Forgive Her?* In the 1870s Joseph Chamberlain and Birmingham had led the country in the first great planning adventure after the Industrial Revolution. Now in the 1950s another plan was needed.

During the Second World War there had been a belief amongst all parties that planning could solve many problems and afterwards came legislation to back it up, including the Distribution of Industry Act (1945), the New Towns Act (1946), the Town and Country Planning Act (1947) and the National Parks and Access to the Countryside Act (1949). The depressed regions would be re-vitalised, the industrial cities renewed, new towns built and the countryside protected.

Patrick Abercrombie, the leading planner in the UK, had much to do with all this and had a direct involvement with the West Midlands, when he and Herbert Jackson of Birmingham were asked by the Ministry of Town and Country Planning to prepare a plan for the region. This was done but never published. There was a large gap between the thinking of Abercrombie and the outlook of Birmingham. The regional plan proposed a green belt and new towns. Birmingham's stance, expressed to the Barlow Commission on Distribution of the Industrial Population in 1939 (of which Abercrombie was a member) was that towns grew, as they had always done, at their edges. There was some independent evidence that Birmingham and the Black Country could solve their own problems in a self contained way. This was in a valuable study *Conurbation*, produced by the West Midland Group in 1948.

A typical scene, evocative of the conurbation after the war.

The 1947 Act required all planning authorities to prepare development plans and to control new development and changes of use, except for some categories of permitted development such as operational land for major industries. The financial provisions were all important and included a Central Land Board to make a 'once and for all' payment to settle claims for lost potential development value and to allow for the collection of betterment, that is the increase in value given to land by development which was permitted. The ability to acquire land without paying excessive compensation was a major provision. This was an apparently ideal position for planning, which could thus become fair and rational for the public good, allocating land for new houses, schools, their playing fields and public buildings. The development plans comprised a written statement of proposals and maps, drawn at 6" to the mile scale for town maps and 1" to the mile for counties. They were also accompanied by a substantial written analysis. These plans were to span twenty years and be reviewed every five. Nearly all the West Midlands planning authorities had submitted their plans by 1950-52, but only three had been approved by 1955.

One of the unique achievements in the Black Country was the reclamation of derelict land; there were 9,300 acres (3,800 ha) of it estimated in *Conurbation*. Deep holes were filled, tips levelled and housing and industry built over the sites. This was a leading technological achievement, although the ultimate designs were unimaginative. It was also an early notable victory in the battle to save green fields and use brown, or black, land (Oxenham, 1966).

Meanwhile the private market in land virtually stopped, partly because the betterment levy allowed for no profit, partly because the control on building materials allowed for very limited building. By 1951 a Conservative Government had been elected and during the decade the unfair compensation payment and the betterment charges went. Only the extinguishment of development rights remained.

Were Development Plans working?

In the 1960s the mood changed. The market came to life and central areas were redeveloped (Holliday, 1973). In 1963, apart from the war-blitzed cities, the Bull Ring in Birmingham became the first major central area redevelopment to open outside London. The Second City was still showing what could be done and *The Birmingham Post*, describing the development, inserted a "Note for Londoners: The Centre's 140 individual shops .... would stretch from Oxford Circus to Marble Arch." Population and economic activity were growing and whilst architect planners and their schemes prospered, the early excitement of development plans had declined. The great experiment in central planning was failing. The demand for housing and land continued to grow, but in 1955 Duncan Sandys had produced his famous green belt circular (MHLG, 1955). The counties surrounding the conurbation were quick to girdle it with a green belt, so that the question of housing demand and new sites arose again, culminating in the famous Wythall Inquiry and the clash between Birmingham and the counties of Worcestershire and Warwickshire over a site for 50,000 people.

Under the Distribution of Industry Act, relocation from the prosperous West Midlands to development areas was a continual thorn in the side of Birmingham industry, where linkages were close and where not even the idea of nearby new towns was welcomed. Nevertheless, some industry was moved, but it was a venture of doubtful use.

The expansion period of the 1960s coincided with some disillusion over the development plan system, which was seen as too slow, too detailed, too inflexible and subject to inappropriate and tedious Government scrutiny. The plans also failed to deal with design quality, whether in high-rise building, private estates or central areas. In the counties the achievement of quality was easier, dealing as they were with a prosperous agriculture, attractive landscapes and small settlements. Villages were protected, scattered housing stopped and care was taken over the routing of new roads and overhead electricity lines. There were special procedures and maps to deal with mineral working. By the early 1960s, however, the population and housing demands in the region were to lead counties into agreements for expanded and new towns and to the emergence of regional studies.

Since the war, an attack on poor quality building design had been led by the architectural press and Gordon Cullen in his vivid townscape illustrations, while John Betjeman did much to raise the profile of architectural conservation. In 1960 *The Observer*, acknowledging Leslie Ginsburg of the Birmingham School of Planning, published *Must Britain be a Mess?* In 1967 a Civic Amenities Act was passed and amongst its other effects was a switch, in Birmingham, from the over emphasis on road schemes to a central area conservation scheme, which hinged round the Colmore Row Decision (Borg, 1973).

A new pressure was the increase in car ownership and the search for recreation in the countryside. The 1968 Countryside Act gave powers for the creation of country parks, in part to act as honey-pots for trippers, and several of these were opened. The counties were becoming busier, although the march of agricultural and forestry operations continued to develop and alter the landscape without any planning control.

In the meantime, dissatisfaction with the development plan process led Richard Crossman, Minister of Housing and Local Government and a Coventry MP, to set up the Planning Advisory Group (PAG). The Report of the Group in 1965, *The Future of Development Plans*, drew attention to the fact that planning was as much about the quality of the environment as about land use. Its main criticism of development plans was that they were unresponsive to changes in population, traffic growth and other social and economic changes. It stressed the relationship between traffic and land use; the redevelopment of town centres by private enterprise; regional patterns of development; problems of environmental quality; and finally over centralised procedures and delays. PAG recommended that urban and county structure plans, as primarily statements of policy, should replace existing detailed plans, but with the use of action areas and local plans where comprehensive development was needed. Scope for public participation was anticipated and this was later enlarged upon by the Skeffington Report, *People and Planning,* in 1969. There was an appendix to Skeffington, written by Audrey Lees of Coventry, outlining the city's experience in the 1960s, which had anticipated a good deal of what was needed.

Sketch from People and Planning, the Skeffington Report (1969) on public participation.

The New Development Plan

The structure and local plan proposals were accepted as a basis for the Town and Country Planning Act of 1968 and became the new development plan. They are still in use today. At the same time, pressures in Coventry, Warwickshire and Solihull gave rise to a sub-regional study published in 1971, the first in the region to make full use of computer technology. Following this, the three authorities simultaneously produced their structure plans. All three were then considered at the first Examination in Public (EIP) to be held in the country, a procedure set up under the Town and Country Planning Act 1971. The EIP was very informal after the old, stiff quasi-legal planning inquiry and three quotes help to make the point.

The first comes from the panel which conducted the EIP and is the words of Trollope quoted at the outset. The second is also from the panel: "We see no valid reasons why the preparations and consideration of structure plans should be a predominately male operation and plenty of reasons why it should not." This now looks a little quaint. The third quotation comes from Neville Borg, City Engineer, Surveyor and Planning Officer of Birmingham: "One of the greatest

Evolution of the Development Plan

The Development Plan comprises a written statement supported by a map or diagram.

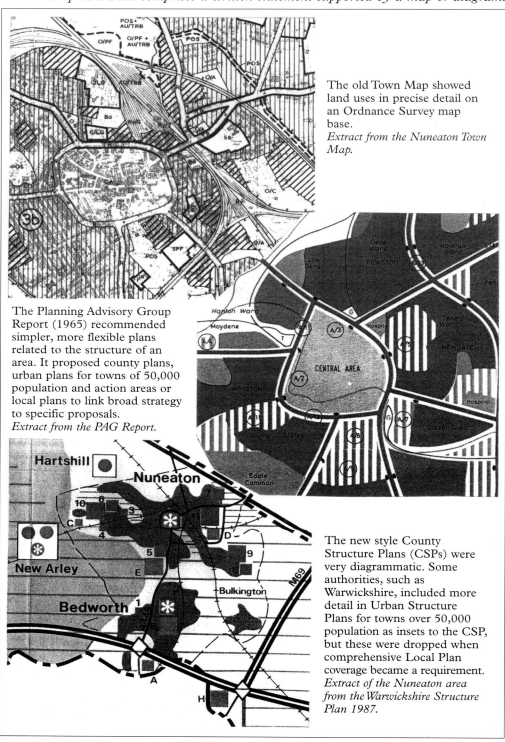

The old Town Map showed land uses in precise detail on an Ordnance Survey map base.
Extract from the Nuneaton Town Map.

The Planning Advisory Group Report (1965) recommended simpler, more flexible plans related to the structure of an area. It proposed county plans, urban plans for towns of 50,000 population and action areas or local plans to link broad strategy to specific proposals.
Extract from the PAG Report.

The new style County Structure Plans (CSPs) were very diagrammatic. Some authorities, such as Warwickshire, included more detail in Urban Structure Plans for towns over 50,000 population as insets to the CSP, but these were dropped when comprehensive Local Plan coverage became a requirement.
Extract of the Nuneaton area from the Warwickshire Structure Plan 1987.

dangers in structure planning is to be satisfied in answering for one's earlier misjudgements by pleading flexibility." Perhaps there are certain philosophical relationships between these three quotations.

The structure plans produced by the constituent authorities of the West Midlands Conurbation were the first set in the country to be ready for the new metropolitan county councils established in 1974. Much of the credit for this goes to William Ogden, then in charge of planning at the government regional office, and a persuasive advocate of regional and metropolitan strategies. The Examination in Public into these plans took place in 1975. In its report, the presiding panel raised the question of the relationship between structure plans and corporate plans. The latter had been strongly developed in Coventry and studied at the University of Birmingham. Should the main task of local authorities be to fit all their policies to the resources available, perhaps subsuming structure planning within it? Or alternatively should the structure plan be a corporate plan for an authority?

The panel concluded that the structure plan must be strategic in nature and related to land use; it was not a corporate plan. The question of the key diagram also caused some problems. If too detailed it did not illustrate general policy, which it should. If too general and not well related to future needs, such as safeguarding major road lines, it was not very useful. The panel urged the Department of the Environment to give further guidance on key diagrams, but to some extent they remain a problem.

A Fresh Direction

The late 1960s and early 70s marked a turning point for planning, which now changed from a purely technical exercise into a highly political one. Public participation questioned basic assumptions about housing, roads, social provision and other major concerns. Public consultation over plans and the wide nature of the EIP allowed this; in fact the conurbation EIP panel innovated a discussion on social impact.

A number of changes followed on greater public and local involvement. Widespread housing clearance gave way to housing improvement under the 1969 Housing Act and the 1974 Housing Act created housing action areas where disadvantaged groups were given priority. The old centralised plan approval was ended, leaving local planning authorities free to hold inquiries into their own plans and to subsequently adopt them. They could also prepare action areas and subject plans. Whatever was done, however, the inner cities showed how social and economic forces underlay planning problems. In 1977, a white paper *Policy for the Inner Cities* led to a series of national community development projects and that for Coventry was the first to be formally processed under planning law.

By the end of the 1970s, one person and a global problem had important effects on planning. The person was Prime Minister Margaret Thatcher and the problem a growing realisation that the global environment was under threat. In a sense planning was under threat from the deregulation measures introduced by various legislation in the 1980s to alleviate the worst effects of recession and unemployment. It became a dirty socialist word in Whitehall, where market philosophies ruled, though later the 1990 Town and Country Planning Act was to reassert the development plan and the plan-led system. The new environmental threats, though, were no respecter of either urban or national boundaries, as pollution and the destruction of wildlife spread across the world. British planning, far from being a panacea for society's problems as it had seemed in 1945, had now settled to a less ambitious role. To be sure development plans began to contain more to do with natural environment, and environmental impact assessment became a European Union directive. But one of the biggest impacts on the environment was the development of agriculture, which had never come under planning scrutiny or control.

Development plans, although continuing today from the foundations set in earlier decades, still treat the development of urban building separately from the development of rural land. The latter may be protected, but its major land uses of agriculture and forestry are outside planning jurisdiction and, in an age of much wider environmental concern, it may be time to reconsider planning from its roots.

Meeting the Demand for Planners

The few qualified town planners of the 1950s soon found their skills very much in demand and it quickly became apparent that more were needed. Moreover, better education was required to stimulate new thoughts on planning, not simply train for what was being practised. Professor Patrick Geddes thought through the connections planning makes across society and the environment and, through his advocacy of survey and analysis before plan, influenced the regional plans of Professor Patrick Abercrombie from the 1920s onwards. Patrick Abercrombie and Herbert Jackson with their West Midlands plan, together with the influential *Conurbation* study (1948), drew together all the strands which were to influence practise in the West Midlands at the outset, although the clash with Birmingham, as a leader in the old style of civil engineering planning, gave rise to an exceptionally wide debate over the first decade.

The West Midlands in 1950 was one of the few regions without a planning school, despite interest from Birmingham University. Lewis Silkin, father of the 1947 Act, set up the Schuster Committee, which reported in 1950 on the qualification of planners. The Institute, led in its early years by architects, engineers and surveyors, was now faced with Schuster's view that a wide variety of social and arts graduates should enter the profession, a view justified by events. But Schuster was wrong in his doubts about undergraduate education. Both Durham and Manchester had begun full-time undergraduate degrees at this time and they were to be followed by many others. Meanwhile, the West

Midlands had to prepare development plans with inadequate staff. The county councils appointed chief planning officers, but the boroughs were all led by engineers, except for Coventry which had appointed Donald Gibson, an architect/planner, who brilliantly produced the first pedestrian town centre in Europe in tandem with Rotterdam's Lijnbaan.

The absence of a planning school led to one being set up in 1957 at the College of Art in Birmingham. The head of the School was Leslie Ginsberg and the courses run were a part-time certificate for non-graduates and a diploma course for graduates. Apart from Leslie, all teaching staff were part-time until I joined in 1960 before moving on to establish another new school in Coventry in 1964, with support from the City Council which sponsored ten full-time students. The Town Planning Institute (TPI) recognised the courses at Birmingham in 1961 and Coventry in 1965 as exempting students from the Institute's external examinations. The Birmingham and Coventry Schools established full-time courses and eventually they became part of the universities of Central England and Coventry.

At Birmingham University, Professor Barry Cullingworth set up the Centre for Urban and Regional Studies (CURS) and published in 1964 the most successful planning text book ever, *Town and Country Planning in the UK* (Cullingworth and Nadin, twelfth edition 1997). He was succeeded in 1973 by Professor Tony Travis, a former lecturer at the Birmingham School, with Gordon Cherry as his deputy. Also at the University, David Eversley led the New Towns Society in arguing the case for sound economic and social research into population, employment and housing problems.

With the high demand for planners, old arguments about education reappeared. The Town Planning Institute's Council advocated shorter ways to increase the supply quickly through direct membership for experienced staff of different disciplines – specialists – and quicker education for other specialists. This brought the Council into confrontation with those who had been building the discipline through undergraduate and postgraduate courses. The proposals split the membership and were heavily defeated at an extraordinary general meeting in January 1965. Town and country planning as a discipline in its own right had come of age. Although the future course of the Institute was settled, arguments about the nature of planning went on.

Coventry was now operating corporate planning and the Institute of Local Government Studies (INLOGOV) at Birmingham University was running courses on the subject. In 1973, the Centre for Environmental Studies in London (note the new word environment) published the Report of a Working Group on Education for Planning, under the chairmanship of Jim Amos. The West Midlands was well represented in this group by Professor Gordon Cherry and John Stewart from CURS and INLOGOV respectively, and myself from Coventry Polytechnic. Three core areas of knowledge were identified as being essential for planning: community and environment knowledge, organisation knowledge and operations knowledge. The interests of 1973 have greatly expanded and there are now specialisms which have developed from the core discipline of town and country planning as well as planning taught as part of a related discipline. Environment, design, management, land economy, tourism, conservation, housing and information systems all feature in the current planning education scene.

The Way Ahead

For over fifty years planning has developed enormously with a hiccup over the Thatcher years. Its modern origins were in the Industrial Revolution, but its foundations, upon which it still rests, were laid in the 1940s and this must raise questions about its superstructure. The revolutions in the structure of society, in the economy, including agriculture, and in the technological advances in communications and the biological field all suggest that it is time for a fundamental rethink about the place of planning in the environment. Perhaps 21st century planning will leave the old development plan system behind?

Reconstruction of Coventry

Terence Gregory OBE

The Early Plans

The reconstruction of Coventry's city centre was one of the great achievements of post-war British town planning. The mediaeval 'cross-roads' city centre, constrained by the remains of the town walls, urgently needed redevelopment to provide more services and relief from traffic congestion. This had been recognised even before the war, with the appointment in 1938 of Donald Gibson as City Architect. The following year, he prepared a model of comprehensive redevelopment for 40 acres (16 ha) around the 'old' cathedral. Meanwhile, the City Engineer, Ernest Ford, who was also responsible for town planning, studied more achievable highway developments. The question was how could all this be realised with a patchwork of freehold interests and many legal and financial constraints?

Tragedy created an opportunity which could not have been foreseen! Mass bombings in November 1940 and April 1941 caused widespread destruction in the city centre, killing 1,029 people and damaging the cathedral, public buildings and 400 shops. The cathedral was now a roofless shell, but the focal points of the 'three spires of Coventry' still stood proud as emblems of spirit and resilience.

Mass bombing caused widespread destruction in Coventry city centre.

Gibson's Plan of 1941, showing land-use zonings, three-dimensional building forms, open spaces and a reorganised road pattern, but retaining the focus of the 'cross-roads' at the centre, was adopted by the City Council. A Redevelopment Committee was established to implement this, with Government encouragement at the time to plan 'with bigness and boldness'. The plan included a surface level Inner Ring Road to distribute through traffic; severing the east-west road across Broadgate to create a formalised, pedestrian shopping precinct, with a grand vista up to the Cathedral spire; and a cleared parkway around it and Holy Trinity church and spire. Buildings were to be generally 'low height' to protect views to the Cathedral, with offices above shops, and car parks off-street, some up to three storeys. An 'exhibition model', produced in 1942, later influenced professional planning techniques and the provisions for comprehensive development in the 1944 and 1947 Town and Country Planning Acts.

Under the new legislation, progress was slow. In 1947, after a public inquiry into objections, the Minister approved an 'Area of Extensive War Damage' with a 'Declaratory Order' of 275 acres (111 ha). This allowed land to be acquired through Compulsory Purchase Orders for redevelopment, including the Inner Ring Road, when it was considered 'ripe' for development. This protracted procedure involved making 99 Compulsory Purchase Orders for 180 acres (76 ha); spending £31m on land, roads and sewers; and preparing sites for buildings. To avoid becoming outdated, plans had to accommodate changing public, political, social, commercial, economic and technological resource factors. For example, car registrations rose by 55,000 in twenty years from 1950. The plans included civic design and traffic management studies to reconcile the human environment, vehicular access and pedestrian and highway circulation.

Such factors caused the original Gibson proposals to be amended. Traders' concerns in 1945 for car and bus access to shops resulted in a new road, Smithford Way and Market Way, running north-south across the east-west pedestrian shopping mall (Upper and Lower Precincts). Rear parking and service areas became fragmented; amenity areas close to the cathedral were reduced when the public resisted the potential loss of significant heritage buildings; and a park near Pool Meadow, north of the Cathedral, proved impracticable. At the time, commercial demands also precluded a parkway from Broadgate to the railway station. More old streets, with their less formal layout and higher density, were retained, open space was dispersed and there was less residential use. The central area was to be a business zone, with public services to the east and light industry to the west. This amended plan was approved by the Minister in 1949 as a basis for redevelopment, 'subject to such improvements as further study and experience showed to be necessary.' It was then incorporated into the city-wide *Development Plan 1951*, as a proposal to be implemented in the next 20 years.

Progress depended upon site availability and the orderly planning of compulsory purchase orders as areas became 'ripe' for development. The Development Plan proposals; current use; possible relocations, especially of businesses; and the readiness of new development projects all had to be considered. Dealing with objections to the orders, negotiations and public inquiries could be very time consuming! Site purchases offered the City Council the opportunity to assemble and redevelop land. It could then fulfil its own municipal programme, accommodate occupiers displaced from elsewhere, such as the area of the Inner Ring Road, and build where private developers could not. One such development was Broadgate House, which set the scale and pattern of civic design. Thereafter, private enterprise co-operated in viable projects, the Council offering ground leases subject to planning briefs and building agreements. Examples were the Hotel Leofric, a major store in Broadgate and the Upper Precinct shops. Freehold disposals were rare, except to government agencies such as the Crown Courts. The flexibility of this complex planning, land and financial system sustained the central area redevelopment programme over some 30 years. In this way, the Council built up a 'bank' of developed land and the citizens benefited from its profitability. Wilfred Burns, Principal of the Planning Division, made a major contribution towards achieving these plans.

Donald Gibson continued his department's implementation role from war damage to temporary shops and municipal development programmes. The civic area provided sites for a library, college of art and technology, swimming baths, police headquarters, magistrates' courts and council offices. Elsewhere, there was a civic theatre, central bus station and privately-sponsored art gallery. Adjacent to the city centre, the Comprehensive Development Areas of damaged, obsolete housing at Spon End and Hillfields provided housing, schools and social projects to help the city accommodate its ever-growing population.

The City Engineer retired in 1949 and Donald Gibson became City Architect and Planning Officer, the first of four people to hold this post. His responsibilities now included city-wide town planning and civic design as well as architecture, landscape architecture and quantity surveying. A Land Resource Programme Unit within the planning division initiated site acquisition and relocations and programmed development projects in liaison with clients and other chief officers. The Town Clerk, Sir Charles Barratt, serviced the Policy Advisory Committee and chaired regular inter-departmental progress meetings – an early example of local authority corporate management!

Turning Plans into Reality

The Coventry story now moved on, with the opportunity to turn plans and models into reality! Donald Gibson's brief in 1938 had been 'to provide public buildings reflecting the city's status as a growing sub-regional centre'. He achieved this by setting the pattern, scale and 'Festival of Britain' style of the new Broadgate civic square and buildings, with weather protected frontages also

Coventry's shopping precinct, with its original vista to the Cathedral, was amongst the first pedestrian town centres in Europe.

opening into the Upper Precinct. Here were two-level shops, with an upper gallery surrounding the pedestrian mall and ready access to car parking behind. Within the mall, flowering trees, seats, sculptures and a water feature provided restful pleasure amidst all the bustle. The plan maintained views to the Cathedral. Its horizontal and vertical axes are marked by the levelling stone and the Coventry standard, with the City's coat-of-arms, which overlooks the Lady Godiva statue in Broadgate. The latter was originally set in a garden for which the Dutch people, also victims of bombing, gave shrubs and bulbs as a mark of friendship and peace. A resurgence in community pride was engendered. The first blocks of the new Council Offices and the Art College were built in 1954 and the Market Way and inner ring roads were started. New pedestrian areas, with three-dimensional civic design and vehicular segregation, provided the basis for subsequent evolution. These concepts pioneered city rebuilding at the time, influenced redevelopment techniques and raised international interest. At this point Donald Gibson moved on, the originality of his ideas later contributing to a well-deserved knighthood.

The Council and traders were then persuaded by the next City Architect and Planning Officer, Arthur Ling, to pedestrianise the north-south route along Smithford Way and Market Way and link into Shelton Square and the City Arcade of smaller shops. This created a 'giant cross' of pedestrian shopping, its extremities served by buses and later linked by circulatory covered ways. This had been in the Development Plan approved in 1957, which, however, still retained two-way traffic in Broadgate. A circular retail market was opened in 1959, with roof-top car parking and links over shops to further roof-top and multi-storey parking. The Lower Precinct provided a pedestrian environment of 'Festival of Britain' style, three-storey galleried shops with coloured neon-light tableaux of local industry and a circular glazed café. As a counterpoint to the cathedral spire, the vista along the Lower Precinct was closed by a 17-storey tower of flats and a restaurant. In the 1960s, other 17-storey blocks of municipal flats were erected outside the ring road to mark radial routes into the city.

Arthur Ling was also responsible for further public buildings, including civic offices with a quiet courtyard, the Mecca Dance Hall, the first post-war civic theatre, named the Belgrade after Coventry's twin city, the striking international swimming baths and the College of Technology, later the Polytechnic and now the University. He also designed the controversial, 19-storey halls of residence, using a light-coloured material to contrast with the cathedral opposite. The cathedral and university entrances have the potential for a well-landscaped civic square. South of the College, a new Art Gallery and Museum was gifted by Sir Alfred Herbert, a local industrialist, in 1959. In 1962, British Rail rebuilt the obsolete railway station in a contemporary style, with an impressive glazed concourse. Offices, with a focal high-rise block, surrounded the station square. Arthur Ling left Coventry in 1964, having enthused colleagues with his concern for civic design, increased pedestrianisation, introduced interesting point blocks and initiated a review of the development plan.

The controversial University halls of residence contrast with the Cathedral opposite.

The Cathedral as a Symbol of Peace and Unity

Rebuilding the war-damaged Cathedral was of international interest. In 1946 the Royal Fine Art Commission did not approve 'rebuilding plans' in the Gothic style. Two options were either to retain the ruins, or to clear them, except for the medieval tower and spire, and redevelop the site. Following a major competition, (Sir) Basil Spence's design was selected in 1951. The ruins became a monument to the futility of war, but offering reconciliation, while a porch linked across St Michael's Way to a majestic 20th century style new Cathedral in sandstone, glass and copper. Consecrated in 1962, the north face mass dominated the valley of Pool Meadow, with the circular light-structured chapel of industry looking outward to human activity and a seat of learning. Inside, the skills of contemporary artists lifted the spirit through sculpture, tapestry and mosaic. The angels soaring against images of ruin on the great 'west' screen and the dazzling and dim coloured glazing all add to the human experience for peace, unity and international understanding. Continuity, symbolised for centuries by the surviving spire, completes a world-wide attraction.

As the third City Architect and Planning Officer, I consulted Sir Basil Spence and the Royal Fine Art Commission about the pedestrianised Cathedral Square to the north. This was to be flanked to the west by an eight-storey De Vere Hotel of horizontal emphasis and to the north, facing the Cathedral, by contrasting linked units of halls of residence, raised on columns along Fairfax Street to allow views into the square. Opposite the Cathedral, the Polytechnic, now Coventry University, together with some of its departments further afield, create a pleasant environment of scale and vitality, together with continuing employment, economic and social contributions.

The old and new Cathedrals stand side by side as symbols of peace and reconciliation.

Conserving for Future Generations

Views hardened against destroying old buildings, but the lack of resources meant disrepair. In 1966 F.W.B. Charles, a consultant architect, carried out a survey of the once dominant, medieval timber-framed buildings and found only 34 remaining, due to pre-war slum clearance, war damage and road improvements. The largest 'townscape group' was in Spon Street, a former through route, but now a cul-de-sac. I sought restoration and also obtained support from the Historic Buildings Council in 1967, later endorsed by the Minister, to import similar buildings affected by redevelopment elsewhere into Spon Street as 'an archeological exercise of considerable potential interest value'. From 1970, several relocations were added to earlier restorations, creating 'a living museum' of medieval buildings. A successful approach was made to the Minister in 1969 to save the derelict, half-timbered Cheylesmore Manor to house the Registry of Marriages and the Whitefriars Monastery was also restored as a museum in 1970. In addition, to conserve the city's craftsmanship, shop premises were adapted into the now renowned Museum of British Road Transport.

The Civic Amenities Act 1967 and Town and Country Planning Act 1968 were used to designate four Conservation Areas, at Spon Street; Hill Top/Cathedral; Greyfriars Green; and Lady Herbert's Gardens. Later, the first *Structure Plan*, submitted in 1973, continued the visual policies for city centre development with its focus on views of the spires, whilst seeking to achieve character and variety in the urban form.

Between 1960-1972 the Civic Trust recognised the 'contribution made to the appearance of the local scene' by central area projects, namely two landscape schemes, three shopping developments, three timber-frame restorations and the Lanchester College (now University) administration/union blocks. More recently, several reconstruction projects have been recognised nationally for their civic design contribution and some post-war buildings have been listed as being of architectural and historical interest under the 1990 Town and Country Planning Act. These include the new Cathedral, Railway Station, Belgrade Theatre and Central Swimming Baths.

The Final Stages

Public participation came more to the fore and once again Coventry's systems became exemplars of corporate and community planning. As part of the *Development Plan Review* (1966) submission, three exhibitions were held, attracting 11,700 visitors, 5,100 people attended 80 public meetings and 2,000 comments and 410 final objections were received. A public inquiry was held in 1968 and the amended plan approved in 1972.

Meanwhile, multi-level junctions were provided on the inner ring road and sections were elevated to segregate it from pedestrian and local traffic routes. With car parking beneath some elevated sections, the overall central area provision was increased to 10,000 spaces. Three new links, Fairfax Street, New Union Street and Greyfriars Road, extended the inner circulatory road round the cathedral, university and civic areas. This enabled the removal of through traffic from Broadgate and the pedestrianisation of Hertford Street in 1969. A twin tower office block closed the Market Way vistas and a 15-storey civic block, built by 1973, housed the Department of Architecture and Planning, a major evolution from the original Gibson plan. All this, together with tree planting, improved the environment of the City Centre.

Harry Noble became the last City Architect and Planning Officer in 1973. After legislative delays, some remaining gaps from the 1951 Development Plan were completed, namely the new County and Magistrates Courts, the Central Fire Station and a bus station building. The recession then ended significant city growth and reduced municipal building programmes, so that the teams of architects and quantity surveyors were no longer viable. It was time to review the department, as the priority now was to attract developers. The above post was therefore redefined in 1986 and Harry Noble was appointed Director of Economic Development and Planning.

The reconstruction of Coventry generally enjoyed the continuity of a bi-partisan political approach and it is important to give credit to those who maintained the political and financial imperatives behind it. Two of these were Alderman Sidney Stringer CBE and Alderman Gilbert Richards CBE, both

Alderman Hodgkinson alongside the City Centre Plan.

leaders of the City Council at various times, but the politician who perhaps made the most direct contribution was Alderman George Hodgkinson OBE. Chairman of the Planning Committee three times, he said his reconstruction aims had been "adherence to a master plan comprehensively developed, provision for vehicle separation, a public share in the equity of development and planning for people's environment by participation." He showed forthright leadership and partnership with the professional officers and was conferred Honorary Membership of the Royal Town Planning Institute in 1977.

Walter Bor CBE, a Past President of the RTPI, wrote in 1974 "The most striking feature of Coventry case history is the continuously changing and improving process of planning it so clearly illustrates in evolution of the 1940 design through to the 1971 city centre Structure Plan."

Finally, echoing its memorable story of peace and reconciliation, the Cathedral easily won a poll conducted in 1999 by English Heritage and Channel 4 television to find the '20th Century's Best Loved National Building'. For the future, the challenge will be to control the environmental impact of major commercial developments! But an immediate Millennium excitement is a heritage excavation to unearth remnants of the great Benedictine Coventry Priory, or 'first cathedral', destroyed by King Henry VIII!

Comprehensive Redevelopment in Birmingham

Alan Geeson and Colin Rodgers

The built-up central area of Birmingham prior to the First World War was a legacy of the rapid industrialisation of the city in the late-19th and early 20th centuries. Workers had to live within walking distance of their place of employment and this resulted in the densely packed network of streets, with small terraced and back-to-back houses. Factories were intermixed with dwellings, and the problem was accentuated by the conversion of houses into small factories and workshops. The population almost doubled in forty years, from 230,000 in 1851 to 429,000 in 1891 before the extension of the boundaries. This increase resulted in over-crowding and congestion, which often produced social and health problems that local and central government could not ignore. Successive legislation was consolidated in the Housing Act of 1936, which made provision for local authorities to define Clearance Areas, Improvement Areas and Redevelopment Areas. In 1937, the City Council declared a Redevelopment Area at Duddeston and Nechells, where the Medical Officer of Health had already condemned a considerable number of houses as unfit for human habitation.

From the experience of small-scale clearance and rebuilding, which took place up to the outbreak of the Second World War in 1939, it became obvious that this process would never result in the complete renewal and regeneration of whole neighbourhoods to a new and improved layout. The opportunity to carry out more radical rebuilding schemes came with the powers contained in the Town and Country Planning Act of 1944. This provided for the compulsory acquisition and redevelopment of areas of extensive war damage, or of bad layout and obsolete development.

The City Engineer and Surveyor at that time, (Sir) Herbert Manzoni, had been a member of a committee appointed by the Government to advise on legislative and other measures required to deal with post-war problems. He was therefore well placed to produce proposals for redevelopment and, in addition to the already mentioned designation of 267 acres (108 ha) at Duddeston and Nechells (later renamed Nechells Green), four further redevelopment areas were declared at Newtown, Ladywood, Lee Bank and Highgate. In total, they covered nearly 1,400 acres (550 ha) of which 1,000 acres (400 ha) were largely unfit

Birmingham's five Comprehensive Development Areas

REFERENCE

RESIDENTIAL — — — — — — —
INDUSTRIAL — — — — — — —
PUBLIC OPEN SPACE — — — — — —
SHOPS & PUBLIC BUILDINGS — —
PRINCIPAL BUSINESS — — — — — B
EDUCATIONAL USE — — — — — E

SCALE—MILES

SIR HERBERT J. MANZONI, C.B.E.
CITY ENGINEER & SURVEYOR,
CIVIC CENTRE,
BIRMINGHAM 1.

properties. The City Council made a Compulsory Purchase Order in February 1946 and, after a public inquiry, this was confirmed in June 1947. It included new powers to expedite the acquisition of such properties, whereby Notice to Treat was deemed to have been served and ownership could be transferred by means of Vesting Declarations. The Council was thus empowered to acquire all the property within the areas covered by the Order, which included some 30,000 houses, 2,650 shops and 2,300 industrial and commercial premises as well as pubs, churches, cinemas and other buildings. The ownership of this vast amount of property presented a major problem of administration, which was dealt with by the Central Areas Management Committee set up for this purpose.

By January 1958, 27,863 dwellings and 5,488 other properties had been taken over by the Council. A Housing Management Committee was established to manage all municipal housing, with the Estates Committee being responsible for industrial and commercial property only. The Central Areas Management Committee, having served its purpose, was then dissolved. These actions simplified both the management and re-housing of tenants. At least 90 per cent of the houses required some degree of attention. As soon as possible after acquisition, work was carried out to make them wind and waterproof, particularly by repairing roofs with a covering of hessian and tar. More extensive renovations were carried out on houses not included in the first five-year demolition programme. By the end of 1957 some 14,200 houses had been temporarily repaired. This repair work was not carried out with the intention of delaying demolition, but only to make properties more tolerable until they could be replaced.

Typical courtyard of back-to-back houses cheek by jowl with industry.

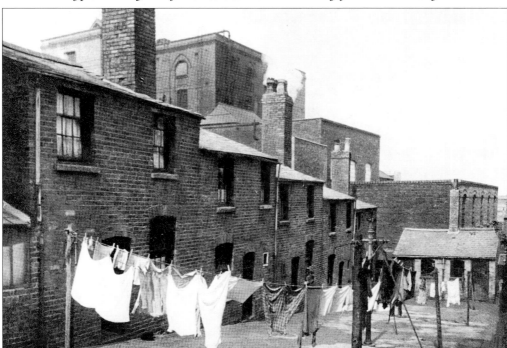

In retrospect it seems incredible that the members of the City Council in 1946 were prepared to undertake the enormous responsibility of purchasing such a vast area of land and property and, in effect, to take a leap in the dark so far as the financial implication of their action was concerned. Apart from the charismatic nature of Herbert Manzoni, there is little doubt that the 'slum clearance' aspect of the project was in the forefront of the decision. After all, many members had personal experience of life in back-to-back houses and courts and were anxious to end that sort of housing, which in the context of post-war aspirations could not be allowed to continue. Indeed one such member, who later attained some prosperity in business, put in a bid to purchase the street lamp used as a wicket when he and his fellow urchins played cricket during the war years!

Just how bad conditions were may be appreciated from a committee report of the City Engineer in 1937, later reproduced in the Uthwatt Report (1942), which catalogued the actual conditions in the 267 acres (108 ha) of Duddeston and Nechells as follows:

- Nearly 11 miles of existing streets, mostly narrow and badly planned.
- 6,800 individual dwellings, the density varying locally up to 80 to the acre.
- 5,400 of these classified as slums to be condemned.
- 15 major industrial premises or factories, several of them comparatively recent in date.
- 105 minor factories, storage buildings, workshops, industrial yards, laundries, etc.
- 778 shops, many of them hucksters' premises.
- 7 schools.
- 18 churches and chapels.
- 51 licensed premises.

Many miles of public service mains, water, gas and electricity, including over a mile of 42-inch trunk water main, nearly all laid under carriageways and consequently in the wrong places for good planning. Add to these a railway viaduct, a canal, a railway goods yard and a gas works, and you have a beautiful problem in redevelopment.

If the overall conditions seem grim, the living conditions for the majority of families must have been horrific. The worst houses were the small two up, one down back-to-backs, with a living room/kitchen, two very small bedrooms and a cellar. The rear properties were approached by a covered entry to a court also containing back-to-backs, shared WCs and a wash-house. Many courts also provided access to other courts or to small factories or business premises. A quarter of the back-to-back houses had no separate water supply. Bathing was either at the local washing baths or in a tin bath in front of the range, which was also used to heat the water. Despite these conditions, some of the courts were tidy, with spotless WCs and there were even 'little palaces' where ranges were black-leaded every week and the edges polished like silver. After all, this was their home and some had lived there all their lives. They were loathe to move away from these close communities, but just wanted new houses with kitchens and bathrooms.

The twenty-year clearance programme was based upon estimates of the number of homes that could be allocated to disturbed tenants. At each stage, it was necessary to ensure a balanced development of housing, shops, schools, open space and industrial sites. Mixed uses abounded prior to redevelopment, but the new plans were based upon the principle of separating the main land uses, such as housing or industry, into well-defined zones. This was because industry then was mostly noisy, smelly and dirty. Now, of course, with heavy traffic congestion, mixed uses are back in vogue. Housing was grouped into residential neighbourhoods with social and shopping facilities forming centres of interest. The road layout was designed to encourage through traffic to remain on main roads and to restrict traffic in residential areas to that having business there. Public open space was included at a standard of four acres per thousand residents and was intended to form a continuous parkway system with good provision for pedestrians and cyclists independent of main roads.

Providing land for public open space, school playing fields and other amenities, meant reducing gross densities by nearly a half. Moreover, the old houses often contained more than one family, so only approximately 56% of the original population could be accommodated after redevelopment, leaving a surplus of 49,000 to be housed elsewhere.

Land Use in the Five Comprehensive Development Areas

Redevelopment Area	Acres	Ha	Population	Dwellings		Education		Industry		Open Space	
				No	per Acre	Acres	Ha	Acres	Ha	Acres	Ha
Nechells Green											
Before	267.0	108.1	19,072	5,885	30.7	8.0	3.2	63.3	25.6	3.9	1.6
After			12,537	3,635	26.7	27.0	10.9	62.4	25.3	41.7	16.9
Newtown											
Before	398.5	161.4	28,125	9,349	35.9	12.9	5.2	118.5	48.0	6.4	2.6
After			15,400	4,467	24.9	39.9	16.2	118.7	48.1	60.4	24.5
Ladywood											
Before	289.0	117.1	24,418	7,558	34.2	4.6	1.9	61.6	24.9	1.9	0.8
After			12,448	3,609	23.8	25.3	10.2	62.1	25.1	49.8	20.2
Lee Bank											
Before	192.0	77.8	14,797	4,492	31.2	3.4	1.4	44.2	17.9	0.2	0.1
After			6,531	1,894	16.5	12.7	5.1	39.7	16.1	24.7	10.0
Highgate											
Before	236.0	95.6	16,484	4,886	29.3	6.0	2.4	53.4	21.6	9.7	3.9
After			10,080	2,924	25.5	32.1	13.0	50.3	20.4	39.0	15.8
Total											
Before	1382.5	560.0	102,896	32,170	32.7	34.9	14.1	341.0	138.1	22.3	9.0
After			56,996	16,529	23.7	137.0	55.4	333.2	135.0	215.6	87.4

Notes:
1. Area of the Compulsory Purchase Order was 981.0 acres (397.3 ha).
2. Number of unfit dwellings before redevelopment was 24,670.
3. Residential density is net of other major uses.
4. The number of schools remained more or less the same.

Source: Derived from Birmingham City Council data.

The clearance programme was rather like a large Chinese puzzle, or series of puzzles, where a vacant space is needed to carry out the next move. However, an added complication was that development had to take place in order to re-house tenants or relocate businesses before the next move could occur. In the interim, temporary accommodation often had to be found. This was particularly upsetting for families if they were moved into houses in a later clearance stage, or to businesses that might require temporary premises for some time because they were proposing to rebuild on Council land awaiting clearance. Progress was slow at first, but gradually gathered momentum. Whilst every endeavour was made to provide alternative accommodation, it was inevitable that, as people moved out and clearance took place, many small businesses would close.

Wherever possible properties were demolished as they became vacant, but it was debatable whether it was better to have an occupied property surrounded by void buildings or standing isolated in the middle of a cleared site. Demolition was noisy and dirty. Services had to be cut off beforehand and the stability of adjoining premises taken into account. It was quite common to find that the adjoining property had only a $4^{1}/_{2}$" (112mm) wall, or no wall at all! Drains had to be stripped and sealed at the sewer connection to prevent rat infestation; cellars emptied of rubbish and rubble and then refilled to provide solid ground; and wells properly filled. It certainly was not pleasant to be the last one to leave. If demolition did not take place immediately and void property was boarded up, it was then broken into – 'tatting' was a way of life. It still is!

Because the layout of the redevelopment areas was being completely remodelled, many administrative and legal matters had to be resolved before new development could take place. To create the new street pattern, many existing streets had to be closed or diverted. This meant close co-operation with the statutory undertakers, since their mains were mostly within the highway and many had to be removed or re-routed. At the same time they had to maintain supplies to existing properties and serve new ones. The larger mains were all part of the city network and, being too costly to move, had to be accommodated in the layout and protected during development. It really is easy to black out half the city! The statutory road closure procedure required time for advertising, objections, subsequent negotiations, possible public inquiries and detailed discussions with the emergency services and public transport operators. A considerable amount of time was also needed for negotiations on compensation for changes to existing mains and the provision of new services, so all procedures had to be started well before actual clearance dates. Temporary lamps and barriers indicating road closures and diversions became a normal part of the street scene. The demolition programme, and the resultant reduction in population, involved closing a considerable number of public houses. The consequent negotiations with the brewery companies over the disposal of surplus licences were another somewhat tedious task.

With so many council committees and statutory undertakers being involved, working parties became common practice (woe betide anyone who lagged behind!).

However, there was an enthusiasm to get on with the job now that the war was over. To do so, it was essential that each player knew exactly what their role was, the timescale to be achieved and the current position at all times. Computers were not available! All information was recorded on plans, schedules and progress reports. Basic plans to a scale of 1:2500 showed the Compulsory Purchase Order, clearance programme and overall layout for each of the five redevelopment areas; a schedule of properties and detailed 1:500 scale plans were kept for each phase of the clearance programme; and a master set of plans recorded information and progress from all departments and statutory undertakers. Progress was monitored monthly and reported to the various committees and working parties. The system worked very well. Everyone used it, understood it and knew their job, but of course there were problems – they occurred each and every day! Whilst the clearance programme was able to proceed in annual stages, new development was not so easily programmed. To give contractors complete control of viable plots without any encumbrance, sites often had to lie idle until adjoining land in later stages was cleared. This applied particularly to low-rise development and schools, where the buildings were spread out across the site. Land not required immediately would often be used as contractors' depots, but nevertheless large areas of land were vacant at times.

Considerable thought and discussions had taken place both prior to and after the Second World War with regard to the building of flats to re-house people from the slums. Early experiments before the war with maisonettes and three-storey flats were fairly well received, so far as the internal accommodation was concerned. There was, however, criticism of the number of stairs, long corridors and numbers of people living in close proximity. The higher rents were also a problem for many. In 1935 an open competition produced a further experimental scheme of concrete four-storey balcony-access flats in Highgate. These were completed in 1939.

It was not until 1950 that work actually started on the rebuilding in Nechells by the erection of a block of 12 storey flats, with lifts, on a site partly cleared as a result of war damage. This block, of brick and steel construction, was the first of a group of four to be sited alongside 'The Parkway', a landscaped dual carriageway road dividing the area into two separate communities! Most of the 66 flats had two bedrooms, a living room, fitted kitchen, bathroom, central heating and a balcony for drying clothes. The refuse disposal system enabled everything to go down the sink! These flats were luxurious for the time and unlike some subsequent designs have survived the ravages of time.

The residential areas generally were designed with a mixture of housing types providing a range of accommodation to meet the needs of each community. Alternative methods of construction were used as well as traditional ones, which helped to overcome the shortage of building materials. A conscious effort was made to retain the existing community groups within the new environment, but this was very difficult in practice. The close, friendly atmosphere of the old courts had changed and it took time for the new communities to settle down.

The four earliest high-rise blocks of flats at Nechells have survived the ravages of time and the picture shows more recent landscaping.

The design of park layouts and planting schemes amounted in total to a formidable programme of work. In particular, the desire to produce a sympathetic environment from the start of redevelopment necessitated planting large numbers of semi-mature trees and a special nursery was established in one of the City's suburban parks to supply trees as required. One result of this enterprise was to form a Tree Lovers League among local schoolchildren, which encouraged their interest in trees. They took part in planting ceremonies and competitions for collections of leaves. A notable entry in one competition showed a photograph of a youngster proudly displaying his black eye received 'while protecting our trees from vandals'.

The Council recognised its responsibility to maintain the industrial and commercial prosperity of the city by making every endeavour to relocate those firms displaced during redevelopment. In the industrial zones, firms were given the opportunity to lease sites for rebuilding. The most imaginative proposal, however, was to build 'flatted factories' with units of various sizes to let. Two such buildings were erected, one in Nechells Green and one in Lee Bank. The first, completed in November 1957 in Dartmouth Street, was known as Nechells House and had a lettable floor-area of 177,000 square feet (16,500m^2) in 46 units. The second, opened in June 1958 at Holloway Head and known as Lee Bank House, had a lettable floor area of 73,000 square feet (6,800m^2) in 42 units. Each self-contained unit had floors designed to sustain heavy loading and was provided with gas, water, drainage and electricity. Toilet facilities, goods and passenger lifts and loading bays were common to all tenants.

In assessing the results of the comprehensive redevelopment scheme, due weight must be accorded to what was removed as well as to what was created. The thousands of unfit houses and large number of obsolete factories and workshops could never have been cleared away in an orderly fashion without the complete ownership obtained through the 1947 Compulsory Purchase Order. Similarly, the redesign of the street pattern and the creation of large areas of parkland depended upon overall control through unified land ownership. Thousands of previously unhappy people were re-housed in modern accommodation with sanitation; hundreds of small firms made a fresh start in up-to-date premises; and various swathes of parkland were created, with trees that have now matured. Together these constitute a positive asset to the inner area of the city.

There can be no doubt that the post-war 'leap in the dark' must be recognised as a major achievement to improve the standard of life and the environment of the City of Birmingham.

Post-war Expansion at Bournville

Alan Shrimpton

The decision of brothers George and Richard Cadbury to move their chocolate factory four miles from the centre of Birmingham into the countryside at Bournbrook was a landmark in early town planning. Although the move was stimulated by practical and economic considerations, George especially had philanthropic concerns and believed his workers and their families would benefit from decent homes with gardens.

So, in 1879, they began the village of Bournville by building their new factory and sixteen cottages for key workers. Gradually the concept of a 'garden village' emerged, but soon the nearby suburbs were threatening to engulf it. So, to preserve its rural aspect, George took the bold step of turning his estate into a charitable trust. Thus, the Bournville Village Trust was founded in 1900 with 313 dwellings set in 330 acres (134 ha) (Henslowe, 1984).

Between the two world wars, Bournville continued to grow, with 360 rented homes and 1,101 houses for sale built between 1919 and 1939. Then all house building came to an abrupt halt, but even as the storm clouds gathered, plans were being prepared for a return to building. The Trust itself commissioned research, which led to the publication in 1941 of a report called *When we build again*. This contained a comprehensive analysis of the living and working conditions of the city and also suggestions for quite new development patterns for reconstruction. These were to prove influential in the planning of extensive residential and industrial redevelopment areas after the war.

Also during the Second World War, the Government, through its Ministry of Health (later the Ministry of Housing and Local Government), was planning for the future. Meanwhile, the City of Birmingham marked time on its redevelopment proposals. All knew that, after the hostilities, there would be great pressure to provide the promised 'homes fit for heroes' by replacing both bomb-damaged properties and those demolished to make way for redevelopment. Looking further ahead, new family homes would also be needed after the inevitable baby boom.

On the national scene, the Dudley report *Design of Dwellings* (GB Central Housing Advisory Committee, 1944) had been published, its terms of reference being to report on "the design, planning, layout, standards of construction and equipment of dwellings for the people throughout the country." This led to the *Housing Manual* of 1944 (Ministry of Health, 1944).

The Government allocated the number of homes that each council could build and issued licences for individual owners and developers to build, but bodies such as Bournville Village Trust had to comply with the Manual and obtain the local authority's agreement to use some of its allocation. Not surprisingly therefore, the standards between the City Council and the Trust became very similar.

Housing at Bournville contrasts with the high-rise blocks of flats in Birmingham's Redevelopment Areas.

The Trust used two basic house types, one with the living and dining rooms combined and the other with them separate. All dwellings had three bedrooms and were built at the upper limit of the size allowed in the Manual, which was 800-900 square feet (74-84m^2) until a revised Housing Manual in 1949 increased it to 900-950 square feet (84-88m^2). It was assumed the need for smaller units would be met by prefabricated dwellings. The new homes were larger and better equipped than the pre-war types, with ground-floor toilets, built-in wardrobes and improved heating, electrical supplies and sound and heat insulation. The Trust was able to let a first contract for 56 houses in 1946. These were not dissimilar to the pre-war properties, the most noticeable differences being a change of brick type and the adoption of metal window-frames, both caused by restrictions on materials.

By 1952, matters were moving on a pace and several initiatives were tried. In the Yew Tree Farm area, the Trust made land available to small contractors who could obtain the necessary building licences. The result was mostly three-bedroom, semi-detached houses, which sold at between £1,250 and £1,800. Meanwhile, the Trust's own building department continued to complete the Weoley Hill Estate. Houses and bungalows, many of them larger one-off types, were built for individuals who had themselves obtained a building licence.

On the initiative of a Trustee, Edward Cadbury, a group of bungalows for retired professional people had been built in 1949. This was done on the basis that such people would be an advantage to the balance of the village community. Two other special needs developments were then undertaken by the Trust, in conjunction with the Copec Housing Society (now the Focus Housing Association). The first was Brook House, a terrace of 20 flats built in 1951 for single women, who at that time generally earned less than their male counterparts and frequently had difficulty in obtaining a mortgage. Bryony House, for the elderly and infirm, followed in 1955.

A new form of housing development was also tried when the Trust made a considerable area of land available to self-build groups. The Trust designed the houses, undertook to train those involved for a period of time and acted as a 'supervising officer'. Under this initiative, some 124 houses were underway by 1955, with two groups of mainly Cadbury employees, one group from Joseph Lucas and one from the Austin Motor Company building their own homes in their spare time!

The largest growth area was yet to come. The Trust owned several farms in Bournville, which had been a significant source of food production during the war. Now their future came under intense pressure. Back in 1950, the Trust produced a plan for the development of the Shenley Fields Neighbourhood and, in order to discuss this more widely, a model was made. Negotiating with the City Council proved difficult and, during discussions, mention was even made of compulsory purchase. Eventually compromises were reached in order to provide accommodation at a density of 50 persons to the acre (125 to the hectare). To achieve this, the final scheme embodied a considerable number of three-storey, walk-up flats and maisonettes over flats. In further discussions, the Trust felt it had been successful, despite the fact it would be building homes without gardens for the very first time.

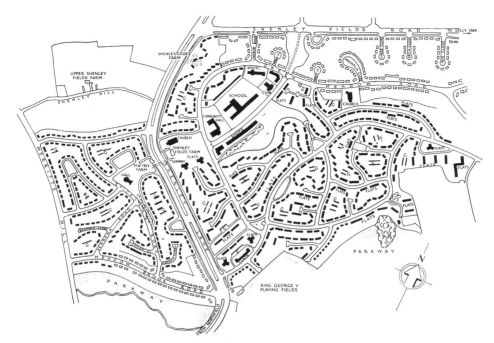

The 1953 Plan of the Shenley Fields Neighbourhood at the higher density of 50 persons per acre.

With the benefit of hindsight, this is perhaps the least successful part of the estate. It is certainly holding back the declaration of the whole estate as a conservation area. So far, two areas have been declared and a third is being contemplated. Most significantly, Shenley is where the Trust is contemplating redevelopment for the first time – and not for the 100 year-old housing, which goes from strength-to-strength, but for parts of the 1950s estate. But at least Bournville managed to avoid the problems of multi-storey flats or system-built dwellings faced by many others.

In addition to housing, the Shenley Neighbourhood also included shops, community halls, schools and a church, along with incidental open space and one larger area of public open space. Whilst the restrictions on building resulted in a more bland form of design, the topography of the area at least offered new opportunities. In typical Trust style, existing forest trees were retained and much more use was made of curves and bends in the roads to follow the undulating ground. This is in marked contrast to the early form of housing in Bournville, which tended to be confined to straight roads. Additional trees and landscaping were also provided in reasonable Trust traditions.

In conclusion, much was achieved during the 1950s despite the restrictions on building. Perhaps, looking back, the style of architecture was not of a golden age. There was, of course, a rush to modernise, yet the properties of the 1950s have not withstood the inevitable march of progress as well as most of the pre-war houses that have a timeless charm. After all fashion comes and goes, but taste and style last forever.

Chapter 2:

The 1960s – The Development Boom

Overview

Graham Harrison

The early years of the 'Swinging Sixties' were generally ones of prosperity and growth. Freed at last from the shackles of wartime restrictions, many people found themselves enjoying an improved quality of life. It was a decade for fashion and 'pop', when the young had the spending power and called the cultural and social shots. Politically, the major milestone was the Government's decision in 1961 to apply for membership of the Common Market, now the European Union (Heald, 1992).

The region's economy remained buoyant throughout the first half of the decade. Indeed, because of its success the Government had long viewed the West Midlands as a source of manufacturing employment and during 1945-65 almost 70,000 jobs were exported to depressed regions (Development Areas), such as Merseyside, through the Industrial Development Certificate policy (WMRS, 1971). Many planners questioned the wisdom of this policy, fearing it would eventually have dire consequences for the region, but the Government persisted with it nonetheless. Not unnaturally, the workforce also demanded its share of the buoyant economy and this led to several notable strikes and an unenviable reputation for militancy.

By the mid-1960s, half the region's workforce was still engaged in manufacturing industry, with many skilled and semi-skilled blue-collar workers at assembly lines, on the shop floor or in workshops. With fewer than average unskilled workers, wages were above the national average and household incomes were higher even than those of London and the South East, being 13% above the national average in 1963. Activity rates were also above the national average, while unemployment was generally below 2%. At this time, too, just over half the jobs and just under half the population were concentrated within the conurbation (DEA, 1965).

However, in 1962 came an early warning that all was not well. Unemployment rose and a 'pay pause' was imposed as we failed to match the economic performance of Germany and Japan. Then, in 1966, the economy deteriorated further, forcing the Government to impose a freeze on pay and dividends and the Prime Minister, Harold Wilson, to announce "the time has come to call a halt" to runaway inflation. The manufacturing sector, for so long the mainstay of the region, stopped growing and even began to contract. Unemployment rose above 3%, exceeding the national average for the first time in years, and strike action against redundancies closed all the British Motor Corporation's (now BMW) factories. The following year brought a credit squeeze as labour troubles, a massive foreign trade deficit and a heavy run on sterling forced the Government to devalue the pound. Finally, in 1969, a White Paper *In Place of Strife* proposed legal action to combat strikes, but the Prime Minister was ultimately forced to abandon the consequential legislation because of opposition from cabinet colleagues and the trade unions. Overall, the region lost 40,000 jobs between 1967-1970.

Notwithstanding these economic set backs, the first development plans began to emerge and, with improved supplies of building materials and new types of construction, development boomed. Housing remained the priority and Harry Noble provides a very personal insight into the mass housing programme which saw 35,000 new homes a year being built during the first half of the decade.

Even so, the demand seemed to be insatiable. With the birth rate high and considerable immigration from overseas, the region's population increased by 8% from 4.38 million to 4.74 million between 1951-1961. Many of the immigrants came from Ireland and the Commonwealth, notably the West Indies, India and Pakistan, thereby laying the foundations of today's multi-cultural society. Not unnaturally, they formed their own communities to try and preserve their individual languages and cultures. Most had little money and were forced by the housing shortage to share accommodation, even to the extent of shift workers sharing the same bed, but at different times of the day and night! Integration was an uphill struggle with, for example, planning objections to the use of dwellings for religious purposes, but gradually many lively, respected and vibrant communities have been established and these contribute greatly to the region's culture and achievements.

By 1966 the population had risen a further 4% to 4.91 million, despite the Commonwealth Immigrants Act of 1962. These rates were markedly above the national average as the region's favourable economic climate encouraged indigenous youngsters to remain and attracted young immigrants as well. Many elderly people, though, retired to the coast. In consequence, the regional population was much younger than the national average, with half the inhabitants under the age of 45, and the Office of Population Census and Surveys forecast it would increase to 5.7 million by 1981 and 7.0 million by 2001! (WMRS, 1971). These projections inevitably created widespread consternation, fuelled in part by Enoch Powell's infamous anti-immigration speech in Birmingham in 1968, and raised the perennial question of where was everyone going to live?

Significant movements were already occurring, with non-manual workers drifting southwards from the conurbation and skilled manual workers moving from the older mining districts in the west towards the better job prospects in the Coventry 'belt' from Nuneaton to Warwick. This set the foundations of wealthy commuter belts around the towns and cities, leaving unskilled, low-income groups caught in the inner city poverty trap. Whilst this was recognised at the time, the subsequent consequences of social polarisation were not foreseen.

Following the emergence of the first development plans and planning inquiries into major housing developments at Wythall and Chelmsley Wood, where a peripheral settlement for 50,000 people was approved in 1964, the media began for the first time to view planning as a topical issue. Central to the debate was whether the conurbation should continue to grow peripherally, or whether growth should be dispersed to new and expanded towns. In the event, both proved necessary because of the magnitude of the problem. Two new towns were designated, at Dawley (later renamed Telford) in 1963 and Redditch in 1964 and their development is described by Michael Barker and Graham Reddie respectively. Additionally, town expansion schemes were agreed for Droitwich in 1963 and Tamworth in 1965.

The Kingfisher Centre at Redditch, with its palm trees, was one of the first shopping centres outside the USA to be fully enclosed.

Signs of the Times

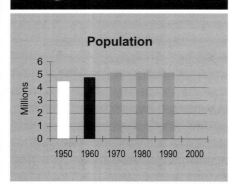

Population

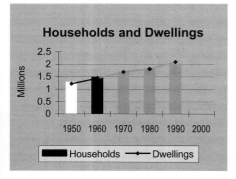

Households and Dwellings

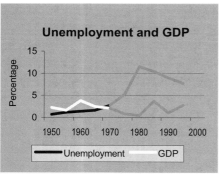

Unemployment and GDP

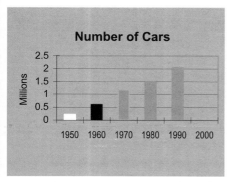

Number of Cars

Allied to the concept of new and expanded towns, proposals to contain urban sprawl with a West Midlands Green Belt were first submitted in the early 1960s, though it was 1975 before the Secretary of State for the Environment finally confirmed them. As Michael Law explains, the green belt quickly became the best known and liked planning concept. Although the 1947 Planning Act was named Town and Country, it was not until the late 1960s that countryside planning began to emerge. Hitherto, most development plans showed the countryside as 'white land', where the existing uses were to remain undisturbed.

Now planners began to appreciate the intrinsic value of the countryside and the wisdom of planning town and country as an entity. Over 70% of the region was still farmland, but, with agriculture less labour intensive, alternative employment was needed for those forced out of farming. By the mid-1960s, 60% of the region's population was living and working in 5% of its area. In theory this left plenty of room for future growth, but avoiding constraints such as good quality agricultural land, green belts and areas of outstanding natural beauty limited the options significantly (WMRS, 1971).

Good communications, particularly improved roads to London, the South East and the major ports, were considered vital to the land-locked West Midlands. Gradually these began to emerge with the opening of the M1/M45 in 1959, followed by the M5/M6 and the electrification of the West Coast railway line in the 1960s. All of these helped to strengthen the region's position as the hub of the national communications network. New motorways aside, however, the region's roads were straining under increasing traffic. Commuting into the conurbation rose by 14% in the first half of the decade and 60% of all trips were by car, making this the most car-dependent conurbation in Britain. Moreover, they were predicted to double between 1966-1981 (WMRS, 1971). Even this early, it was recognised that no conceivable road network could accommodate the forecast traffic. Yet, in an economy founded on vehicle manufacture, increasing car ownership was inevitable and it was predicted to more than double by the end of the century. At the same time, bus patronage declined by a quarter and the Government's rationalisation programme saw many railway lines and stations fall victim to the 'Beeching axe'. Meanwhile, air travel remained a novelty, with Birmingham Airport handling less than half-a-million passengers a year compared with over five million by 1996.

One contentious issue was whether to redevelop or rehabilitate central areas. Early on, public opinion favoured the new rather than the old, with the highly acclaimed traffic-free precinct at Coventry very popular. Towns throughout the region sought to emulate this by proposing inner by-passes to allow the main shopping streets to be pedestrianised, whilst in Birmingham and Coventry the city centres were totally enclosed within ring roads.

Before refrigerators, shopping was a daily activity. Now a retail revolution began in response to once-a-week shopping by car. Towards the end of the decade, supermarkets began to appear along the High Street, but soon they were ousted by even larger hypermarkets outside town centres. Retailing acted as a barometer of prosperity and rival towns often competed to attract new shopping facilities, resulting in many empty shops after the economic downturn. There was also a boom in office development, which led the Government to impose restrictions on building in Birmingham. The volume of work kept consultancies busy and, whilst this book is primarily about what happened in the West Midlands, Lewis Jones, in describing the work of one practice, reminds us that through their work the region's planners were building reputations across the world.

Arguably the 1960s was the era when planning changed from an art to a science. Hitherto, it was largely a social and civic design activity, but now, as the economy wavered, economic considerations began to loom large. The Department of Economic Affairs published *The West Midlands – A regional study* in 1965 and the West Midlands Planning Authorities' Conference, concerned about population growth, stresses in the industrial structure and the thrusting development of the conurbation, then set up the West Midlands Regional Study to produce a clear, incisive strategic framework within which these issues could be resolved. This was followed in 1969 by Coventry, Solihull and Warwickshire Councils jointly setting up a Sub-Regional Study.

During the decade, mathematical modelling became the vogue in planning. Initially the techniques were primarily used for transport and retail planning and the TPI West Midlands Branch itself made a significant contribution to this with its publication *Predicting Shopping Requirements* in 1967. Subsequently their use was broadened and further developed in the regional and sub-regional strategies referred to above, but that is something to be discovered in the next chapter.

Mass Housing Development – One Man's View

Harry Noble OBE

When asked to write this article, I said "yes". After all, I had been totally immersed in the process of house building during the 1960s, both in Yorkshire and the Midlands. I was involved in the expanded towns of Droitwich, Tamworth and Daventry and in the major peripheral housing projects at Chelmsley Wood and North Worcestershire. I recalled the swinging sixties as being the most exciting, productive and rewarding time of my life.

Being the fiftieth anniversary of the RTPI West Midlands Branch, I assumed I was required to blow a trumpet for the achievements of planners in that era. It did, after all, represent one of the greatest if not *the* greatest building period in the history of the United Kingdom. Wasn't it the time when, once and for all, we would wipe out homelessness and the 19th Century slums and provide, as Clement Atlee had promised in 1945, "homes fit for heroes"?

The sixties gave town planners, architects, engineers and everyone involved with mass housing and its associated developments an opportunity to reshape society for the better, to build those homes fit for heroes and to create a world we would be proud to hand on to our children and their children's children. I have to tell you, we blew it. Far from being the decade when planning had its finest hour, the sixties were when the world discovered that planners did not have divine guidance, nor had they been ordained by God. If only we could have provided such lasting pleasure as the Beatles, or shown such design sense as Alex lssigonis with the mini. If only .... Instead we were too busy with threshold theories, mathematical modelling and the teachings of that misguided journalist, Le Corbusier, to realise we were planning and playing with people's lives and aspirations.

So how did the mass housing development of the sixties come about? One can trace its origins to Lord Beveridge's report of 1942, when he referred to the five great evils of 'want, disease, squalor, ignorance and idleness'. The problems stemming from no housing or poor housing loom large in all these 'great evils'. Against that background, it is not surprising that promises of new and improved housing featured large in the Labour Party Manifesto of 1945, as it did in respect of all political parties from that time through until the seventies.

In 1945, seventy percent of our national housing stock dated from the nineteenth century and was often sub-standard. Moreover, the 1939-45 War had seen many dwellings damaged or destroyed. No new houses had been built during the war years and right through until the early fifties there was a shortage of building materials and craftsmen. Despite the massive backlog, only 800,000 dwellings were built in the six years from 1945-1950, of which 157,000 were prefabs. Because of these shortages, the size and type of dwellings were also seriously restricted. In 1950, for instance, local authorities could only approve one private dwelling for every four public sector ones – a proportion changed to 50:50 by the Conservative Government in January 1953 (Marwick, 1990).

By 1951, the national shortfall in dwellings was estimated at 1.5 million and many of those that did exist were far from adequate. It is not surprising, therefore, that, once the building material shortage ended in the early fifties, a massive drive began to improve the size and quality of our housing stock. In 1955, the Government found it both necessary and possible to provide the resources to build new houses, with the first priority being to clear away the designated slums. Such was the emphasis on slum clearance, and the loading of grants towards this, that housing authorities (all 1,367 of them) were judged not by the number and quality of the dwellings they were building, but by the number they were knocking down! So great became the enthusiasm for demolition, and so attractive the grant regime, that many dwellings of character and quality, which could have been rehabilitated, disappeared under the bulldozer. So the housing drive of the sixties began in the mid-fifties. It finally ended in 1974, when local government reorganisation reduced the number of housing authorities to manageable proportions just at the time when there became no housing programme to manage.

I joined local government in 1955, just as the housing development boom was about to begin, and three years later started the town planning course at Leeds School of Planning. Here I was taught that all, or nearly all, new housing should be stuck in the air, leaving the ground free for roads, garages, parking and, in moments of inspiration, somewhere for children to play. Armed with the teachings of Le Corbusier, we were brain washed into the belief that high-rise was wonderful and low-rise so very bad. My problem was that I worked in an area of mining subsidence, so I could only build two-storey, semi-detached dwellings. Making models of our housing schemes was mandatory – low-rise had no sex appeal, whereas the concept of high-rise may have been flawed, but the development created wonderful pieces of pure sculpture – the vertical garden city.

Building only semis was frustrating and I began to get a complex. I concluded that, as soon as I got my planning diploma, I should move to an enlightened authority, which would let me build my monument – my vertical city. So it was that in 1963 I was appointed deputy chief architect to Droitwich Town Development. Unfortunately, they didn't tell me at my interview that Droitwich was affected by salt subsidence and, in consequence, low-rise development was the order of the day. So my desire to build a high-rise monument was again frustrated. But many young planners were not so afflicted. Although most of the new towns and many smaller housing authorities continued to build sensible, low-rise attractive houses, which owed more to Unwin, Welwyn Garden City and Louis de Soisson than Le Corbusier, in the larger urban authorities, where big meant beautiful, high-rise, high density development began to be the order of the day. By 1966 over 25% of new dwellings were in blocks of five storeys or more. Since the private sector could only build what would sell, that meant something like 40% of all new public sector dwellings were high-rise. This was a remarkable statistic. Traditionally, the British are not flat dwellers and before the Second World War only 5% of the population lived in flats (40% in London).

The author's desire to build high-rise flats was again frustrated in Droitwich, where only low-rise housing was permitted.

Birmingham, being by far the biggest authority in the West Midlands, built the most high-rise flats, with 85% of its new housing in 1961 being of this type. This statistic was even more remarkable, as Birmingham had absolutely no tradition for high-rise living. Indeed, Joseph Chamberlain, reporting to the Royal Commission on the 'Housing of the Working Classes' in 1884, remarked "No, we have no flats and no cellars", while *The Birmingham Gazette* on May 24th 1930 reported: "There is a Birmingham prejudice against flats and it is not confined to any one class. It springs, we believe, from something deep in the civic life. Indeed it is, probably, one expression of the independence of character which has done so much for Birmingham."

Even so, as early as 1957, 75% of all new dwellings in Birmingham were flats, which caused John Macey, the Housing Manager, to tell his Committee in November 1958 that "80% of flat dwellers dislike their homes and wish to move into a normal house." But still the architects and planners in their arrogance and doctrinal beliefs planned and built high-rise, high-density dwellings. In spa towns like Leamington, country towns like Kidderminster and county towns like Worcester high-rise blocks sprang out of nowhere. I think we planners called it vertical punctuation. We justified our actions by the argument, to quote Mark Twain, "They don't make land any more", so it was obviously important to conserve it by building high-rise, high density. However, this myth was dispelled by the then London County Council's study into the proposed Hook New Town early in the 1960s, which showed that higher density housing would only have a marginal effect on overall land needs. If saving green fields was the issue, why was it that a large percentage of cleared land remained vacant through the sixties and for that matter the seventies? It took the Black Country Development Corporation of the eighties and nineties to tackle many of the derelict sites in this region.

Whenever events do not work out as intended, we excuse ourselves by claiming to be 'only obeying orders'. In the case of high-rise, naturally, the Government was to blame. It is true the Government did encourage higher densities and even gave them higher subsidies. Nevertheless, it frequently advised against flats for families with children. The 1949 Housing Manual, which was the housing bible until 1969, made this abundantly clear. Even Sir Keith Joseph's publication of 1962, *Residential Areas: Higher Densities* cautioned against "inappropriate high-rise development for families" despite the fact that he was predicting the need for six million new homes over the next 20 years. Since the Government paid the piper, one could argue that they could have called the tune. It should, however, be appreciated that we started the sixties with 16.6 million dwellings in the UK and, despite slum clearance and massive demolition for road construction, finished the decade with 19.2 million – no mean feat.

In fairness to Birmingham, the majority of its high-rise flats were for two or three people and seldom resorted to balcony accesses or highly complicated plan forms. Throughout most of the sixties, though, the planning and architectural press was extolling the virtues of unusual and complex housing solutions to simple housing problems. Invariably, these solutions were high-rise, high density. It was, therefore, somewhat out of character when the *Architectural Review* published a damning article by Nicholas Taylor in November 1967 entitled 'The Failure of Housing' in which he states that "More slums are likely to be built in the next five years than in the past twenty."

On May 16th 1968 a high-rise block of flats in east London, Ronan Point, collapsed killing four people. That signalled the beginning of the end for the boom in high-rise development and for many industrialised housing systems, which appeared to use materials that had seemingly not been invented and constructional systems that were not fully understood. In 1969, Councillor Beaumont Dark, Chairman of Birmingham's Housing Committee, announced that the City would not contract the building of any more high-rise flats – a decision echoed by most other authorities in the West Midlands over the following months.

From the very outset of the housing drive, the Government recognised that it would be difficult to achieve the rate of building necessary to provide the required homes using conventional methods and materials alone. The brick was then, and still is, the standard module of construction. The wheelbarrow was, and still is, the standard method of on-site transportation. Initially, the Government tried friendly persuasion, but when that did not work, it established the National Building Agency (NBA) in 1964 to encourage the development of industrialised housing systems. Hundreds of companies, many never before involved in the building industry, were encouraged to produce systems and were awarded NBA certificates in consequence. This allowed them to sell to the 1,367 housing authorities previously mentioned. It goes without saying that every authority, despite dealing with the same basic problems and issues, had to have something different. What with that and the fact that the NBA issued certificates like confetti, the exercise could best be described as an unmitigated disaster. Some companies never won a single contract. Some won contracts, but never made a single penny and wished they had never been involved. Others built systems in large quantities and with large failures and then the recipient housing authorities wished that they had never been involved.

The trouble was that many of the industrialised systems were designed without consideration for such basic issues as condensation, cold bridging or thermal movement. When many of these systems failed, or proved to be inadequate, the NBA washed its hands of the problem, saying its certificate did not imply any kind of warranty – it was wholly a matter for the respective housing authority to resolve. Thus we had to add to the often inappropriate high-rise developments, euphemistically called 'difficult to let', the often inappropriate industrialised units, euphemistically called 'difficult to repair'. When we had inappropriate high-rise developments built in inadequate industrialised systems they were euphemistically called 'impossible to let'. By the nineties, most of them were simply called 'rubble'.

The West Midlands faired better than most regions in respect of industrialisation. Many of its housing authorities, including Coventry, Stoke-on-Trent and Redditch Development Corporation, formed themselves into the Midlands Housing Consortium which, under the leadership of Fred Lloyd Roche, produced its own timber-framed industrialised housing system linked to a standardised range of well considered designs. This resulted in attractive dwellings, which have stood the test of time. Birmingham was also fortunate in that the majority of its industrialised dwellings were either no-fines concrete, or Bryant's pre-cast concrete panels, which being brick-clad looked and behaved like traditional dwellings.

In 1967, Ernie Bond, Chairman of Birmingham's Housing Committee, persuaded me that I was silly building houses in Droitwich for people on Birmingham's housing waiting list. I should cut out the middleman, so to speak, and work in the City Architect's Department. Birmingham built high-rise flats – I could see my ambitions being fulfilled. The A38 from Droitwich to Birmingham

By the 1990s, most tower blocks had been reduced to rubble.

turned out to be the road to Damascus. I arrived in Birmingham just after the Housing Manager had advised Committee that Chelmsley Wood was then 48% high-rise flats and he wished this percentage to be drastically reduced as he was having difficulty letting them. His preferred percentage was nil. I arrived in Birmingham just as the Housing Ministry introduced Housing Cost Yardsticks (Circular 36/67) and indicated that, from the end of 1968, all new dwellings must conform to Parker Morris space and equipment standards. I arrived in Birmingham just as the Council had discovered that, despite building 48% high-rise flats, densities on Chelmsley Wood were falling below prediction.

In consequence of all that, David Leyland, Barry Price and myself were instructed to set about designing low-rise, high density schemes for four areas of Chelmsley Wood, using new house types to full Parker Morris standards and of a form capable of industrialisation and prefabrication. That was our brief from Bill Reid, the Deputy City Architect. The City Architect, Alan Maudsley, gave further directions. "Don't talk to the Housing Manager, he's only a rent collector."

"Don't talk to the City Engineer and Surveyor. Whatever I build he'll put a road over it, under it or through it."

"Whatever the Housing Manager says, we are going to have some more high-rise flats at Chelmsley Wood. We need them to meet our building targets. He can't blame us if he can't let them. By the way, with all these houses, its time we had a Gold Medal."

I did secretly visit Mr Atkinson, the Housing Manager, to find out what he and the tenants wanted and, hopefully, to persuade him to support my high-rise monument. He said he couldn't understand why anyone brought up in a home with a garden and a door at ground level needed to ask what was wanted. "What you need to do", he said, "is build dwellings where people do not have to live, but where they want to live." "How do I find that out?" I asked. "Simple", he replied, "When they have been in their new homes a little while, pop round, knock on the door and tell them you are the architect. If they like what you have done, they will offer you a cup of tea."

"And if they don't?"

"I'm told that the Queen Elizabeth Hospital is very good!"

He then spelt out very clearly why I shouldn't build high-rise flats. He convinced me. I think all town planning courses should have visiting housing managers.

I also went to see Neville Borg, the City Engineer. I don't know if he was planning any roads through my housing creations, but I do know he was always a perfect gentleman. He had the ability to make you think you were being totally unreasonable when you knew all the time it was he - a great guy to have on your side at a public inquiry.

Not long ago, I went to the Black Country to see a sixties high-rise block of flats being demolished. The demolition contractor said he would have to bring

1960s tower blocks at Sandwell being demolished.

the block straight down so as not to damage the surrounding houses. These were refurbished Victorian terraces, which were originally scheduled for demolition in the fifties to make room for yet another block of high-rise flats. The contractor was not expecting any problems as he had "demolished hundreds of these things."

I was 65 in 1999 and so time to hang up my drawing board and clean up my golf shoes. To mark the occasion, I decided to take the Housing Manager's advice, visit someone who lived in a house that I had designed and tell them I was the architect. Thirty-two years is a long time, but I eventually found Chelmsley Wood just where I had left it. It was a glorious day and the place looked more attractive and much better maintained than I had expected. Plenty of people were out gardening or just chatting over the fence. They were retired people – people who would have moved into the houses when they were first built. I walked up and down the pedestrian ways hoping that someone would engage me in conversation, but nobody did. I got back into my car with the intention of departing. "No", I said, "I have got to do it now." I went back down the pedestrian way where I had seen an elderly man repairing his garden fence.

"Do you like living here?" I enquired.

"Why do you ask?"

"I was the architect for this estate." Silence.

He walked slowly into the house. He came back even more slowly with his wife. "This man", he said, "was the architect for the estate. He designed our house."

"It's wonderful here", she said.

I then got the whole history, her daughter now had a house on the estate, but her son had a good job so he lived in Solihull. At the end of all that she offered me a drink. It wasn't a cup of tea it was a small German lager. The world moves on, but I suppose Mr. Atkinson would have considered it to be an acceptable alternative and I now have an empty lager bottle in my study as a monument to myself!

After thirty years, the architect returns to find out what the residents think of his creation!

The New Towns Experience

Michael Barker and Graham Reddie MBE

The new towns are a landmark of British town planning and nowhere demonstrates their achievements better than the West Midlands. The odds against success were formidable, making the scale and quality of their achievements all the more remarkable.

The origins of the West Midlands new towns lie in national and regional planning initiatives of the late 1940s and 1950s. The post-war aim of containing the growth of the West Midlands Conurbation included plans to house overspill population in economically and socially balanced new communities beyond the green belt. Various locations for new towns were considered, but only Dawley, later renamed Telford, and Redditch were eventually designated.

Both were commitments to create new self-sufficient settlements through the town planning process, but the failure to designate them sooner meant their early growth was hampered by a deteriorating economic climate. Redditch, in the pleasant north Worcestershire countryside and only 15 miles (24 km) from Birmingham, had some advantage as a satellite town. Dawley, later Telford, had the harder task. It was twice as far from Birmingham and had to contend with the legacy of industrial decline and dereliction that had overtaken the 'birthplace' of the industrial revolution.

The task of creating the new towns was given to Development Corporations, controlled by a board of Government appointees with multi-disciplinary professional staff. Each Corporation's financial resources and its extensive acquisition and development powers went beyond normal town planning provisions and caused some tension with the local authorities. The indigenous population also received the new towns with mixed feelings, some welcoming the new jobs and houses they would bring, but others regretting the older settlements being engulfed by extensive new buildings and new neighbours.

Telford, situated on the former East Shropshire coalfield, includes the Ironbridge Gorge. Here, by the mid 18th century, the local industries had risen to national importance and the landscape had been transformed by sprawling settlements, mines, spoil mounds, industrial buildings, canals, roads and railways. From the mid 19th century, the coalfield and its associated industries were in decline and by the end of the 1950s 5,000 acres (2,000 ha), or 27 % of the new town area, lay derelict. There were 3,000 known mineshafts, with probably many more unrecorded, and 120 miles (200 km) of abandoned railways and canals.

Thus, Telford had two planning objectives:

- To accommodate overspill population from Birmingham; and
- To regenerate an area of dereliction and decline.

Re-housing Birmingham people at Dawley began under the Town Development Act 1952 and one hundred dwellings were provided between 1958-1961. Compared with the scale of the problem, however, this was too slow. In 1961, a year after the Government had rejected an expansion plan by the City Council, the Midlands New Town Society suggested a new town and the concept began to receive serious consideration.

Designation followed in 1963, with the intention that Dawley would take 50,000 people from the conurbation, then grow to around 70,000. John Madin & Partners prepared the Master Plan in 1965. However, later that year the new *West Midlands Regional Study* (DEA, 1965) identified the planned expansion of Wellington and Oakengates as a necessary part of the strategy to disperse people from Birmingham and the Black Country. So, in 1966, a Continuity Plan was published to enable the development of Madeley to proceed whilst John Madin prepared a new plan for Dawley, Wellington and Oakengates. At this stage the viability and economic prospects of the new town were being questioned and, in response, Sir Frank Price was appointed the new chairman of the Development Corporation. Changes to the scale and planning of Madeley rapidly followed and investment to reclaim some of the worst dereliction in the Dawley area was postponed. Developments at Wellington and Oakengates were also delayed while proposals for the new town were being reconsidered.

Telford in 1990

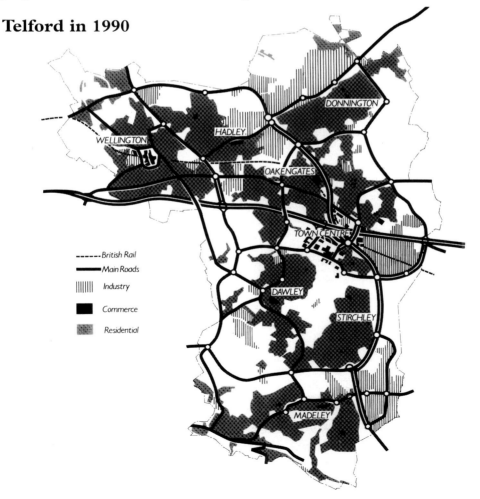

Unfortunately all this coincided with the local and national economies slowing down. Up until the early 1960s, there had been few job losses, even in coal mining, and the Dawley plan had envisaged economic independence for the new town based on the continued prosperity of the Wellington-Oakengates area. But employment there was heavily dependent on manufacturing and during the 1960s and 1970s the established industries began to fail. Between1960-68, the rate at which manufacturing jobs were being created declined by 20%.

As the economic situation worsened, Birmingham's interest in the new town also waned as it resumed peripheral expansion. The City's mass housing programme of the late 1960s over-shadowed all the overspill schemes put together and by 1968 it was clear that population and industry were moving to Dawley primarily from the Black Country rather than Birmingham.

Despite the poor economic outlook, the Government decided in 1968 to expand the new town. Wellington and Oakengates were included, the town was renamed Telford and a new Basic Plan was produced in 1971 to accommodate an additional 50,000 overspill and subsequent growth to around 220,000 by 1991. Now doubled in area, Telford was to accommodate a population three times that originally proposed for Dawley.

The major task for the Development Corporation was to turn an area of scattered existing settlements into a cohesive town with a logical structure. The initial aim was to create a series of residential districts, each with its own identity but linked to industry, the town centre, open land and green areas. Residential areas were to include schools, shops and health, recreational and social facilities.

To begin with, the majority of houses were for rent, but from the late 1970s a higher proportion were for sale. This, together with the 'right to buy' legislation of the 1980s, further increased the proportion of owner-occupied houses. Since then, low-cost housing has been built by collaboration between the Development Corporation, the Commission for New Towns (now English Partnerships) and housing associations.

By the late 1970s, the Government was concentrating on inner city regeneration and in 1977 it announced lower population targets and the winding-up of New Town Corporations. In the same year, the Development Corporation produced a ten-year strategy to guide the town through its final phase of growth. By 1983 Telford's population was just under 108,000 – the combination of falling birth rates, economic recession and reduced migration having contributed to the downward revision of its target population. The Development Corporation had never included high-rise building in its plans and the low densities being achieved indicated an eventual capacity of around 180,000. These changes resulted in less growth around the edges of the town and more green space than might otherwise have been the case. Today Telford's strong network of linked green space occupies almost 30% of its urban area.

The first three Development Corporation estates reflected the Radburn principle developed in the USA in the early 1930s by Clarence Stein from the earlier neighbourhood concept of Clarence Perry (Hall, 1975). Dwellings were grouped around culs-de-sac within a 'superblock' encircled by a perimeter road. Access roads linked the culs-de-sac to the perimeter road and there were no through roads. Industrialised forms of building were used for these estates, with extensive landscaping to reduce their monotony. The more expensive private housing was usually outside the superblock and separated from the rented housing by the perimeter road. Later estates moved away from these initial design principles, with more traditional dwellings and smaller areas designed as a unit. From 1979, houses for sale and rent both followed similar patterns of layout and design, led by developers whose primary aim was to sell their properties. Within the early estates, pedestrians and vehicles were segregated by a network of footpaths and cycle-ways running through the green areas away from the roads, with under-passes at crossings. Development of this network continued as the town grew, but remains to be completed.

Telford and Redditch were the first new towns to be planned following the publication of *Traffic in Towns* (Buchanan, 1963). This, together with the experience of the master planners elsewhere, meant they were planned around a strong road network to cater for high levels of car ownership and use. Given its shape, the basic plan for Dawley proposed a U-shaped urban motorway, with the open, northern end ultimately being closed by the proposed A5 bypass (now M54). From this primary route, distributor roads served the residential and industrial development areas, with local distribution and estate roads leading off them. The plan was designed to ensure travel between any two points in the town within ten minutes – an interesting concept in today's circumstances!

Throughout Telford the private car undermined the economic viability of public transport. With over 30 square miles (78 km²) of scattered settlements, profitable bus services were unlikely before the planned population was achieved. In a town planned for the motor vehicle, people without access to a private car would inevitably be at a disadvantage.

In contrast with the planned development, a small area at Lightmoor was allocated for a new self-build community. This was intended to fulfil the dream of the garden city movement and the Town and Country Planning Association for an alternative community, offering people the freedom to build what they wanted, in their own way. The 14 families on their 23 acres (9 ha) were allowed to build individually designed houses and set up their own, home-based enterprises either in workshops or their houses. This, together with the half-acre plots, allowed them room to keep livestock and grow food. Built and completed by residents, this now famous community exemplifies how 'non-planning' also contributed to the development of Telford.

Early in the 1980s, the Development Corporation's life was extended and the specified target population gave way to growth dependent on the demand for private housing. The aim now was to achieve a long-term balance between publicly rented and privately owned and occupied housing. This marked the end of the public rented housing programme; it also saw public investment restricted to the minimum necessary for growth.

The effect of these changes is most noticeable in the central part of Telford. Initially, Gordon Cullen's conceptual plan for the new town centre was promoted, but by the 1980s planning changes and commercial pressures had restricted development to the north and west of the centre, which was now some ten years old. This broke the town's physical cohesion and weakened the centre's urban surroundings.

Work on planning the central area had already begun when the Basic Plan for Telford was produced. The centre was intended to be a covered, pedestrianised shopping area, on one level and with parking for several thousand cars. Two further phases of development followed the initial building of the Carrefour hypermarket (now ASDA), which was the first of its kind in Britain, and Telford now has a regional shopping centre with over 120 shops that attract more than 300,000 visitors per week. There are also commercial and administrative facilities, but neither the potential integration with surrounding residential districts, nor the creation of a true centre, with an evening economy and a range of cultural and leisure facilities, has yet been achieved.

Major areas of open space were integral to planning the new town, with the landscape policy aiming to provide functional, as well as visual, links between developed areas. Acknowledging the importance of structural planting, the 1971 landscape plan proposed a 'forest town'. Around 20 million trees and shrubs were planted between 1968-1991 and, by the early 1990s, there were some 2,500 acres (1,000 ha) of woodland within the designated area, around half of it planted by the Development Corporation. The landscape plan also aimed to produce a network of green corridors and spaces to link the centre of the town with the surrounding countryside, provide a wooded edge to built development and contain the primary road network. This Green Network now has statutory protection within the district-wide Local Plan for Telford and the Wrekin. At its heart is the 450 acre (180 ha) Telford Town Park, which was planned as a recreational area for the whole town. Together with the woodland of the Green Network, the park is a defining feature of the new town.

No description of Telford New Town would be complete without reference to Ironbridge and the Ironbridge Gorge Museum Trust. The Museum Trust was established in 1967, with support from the Development Corporation, to preserve, restore, improve and enhance features and objects of historical, domestic and industrial importance. Since its foundation, the Museum has won many awards and the Trust has played a key part in saving the industrial heritage that spawned the settlements around which the new town has grown. In 1986 the Ironbridge Gorge became a World Heritage Site, one of only a handful in the UK to be recognised by UNESCO.

The Gorge is now a major tourist attraction, making a significant contribution to the economy of the area, while the world's first iron bridge, erected in 1777, provides a powerful symbol of Telford's innovation and achievement. The birthplace of the industrial revolution has been transformed into a new town at the forefront of planning development. At times this process made Telford the largest reclamation project in Europe, but the result is an attractive, thriving town, which is the largest, and probably the greenest, in Shropshire. Above all, though, Telford is renowned for attracting inward investment. There are now over 2,000 firms, 130 of them from the European Union, Asia and North America, and twice as many jobs as before.

Despite its early difficulties, Telford has become very successful in attracting inward investment.

While Telford took time to earn its accolades, Redditch was a run away success from the start. Proximity to Birmingham and good road, rail and bus connections encouraged employers and home-seekers to move whilst retaining contact with friends and relatives. When designated as a new town in 1964, Redditch was a small industrial town known for the manufacture of needles, springs and fishing tackle. Sir Hugh Wilson prepared the Master Plan for expansion from 35,000 to 70,000 population by 1981, with natural growth to 90,000 by 2001 (Wilson and Womersley, 1966). The plan had a number of unusual features, such as a ladder of dual-carriageway roads capable of extension in any direction and a segregated figure-of-eight public transport route linking all the residential and employment zones with the town centre to the north and the hospital to the south. It had residential 'beads' 'strung' along the bus route and also employed Radburn principles as in Telford, with segregated footpaths radiating from each local centre. Unlike Telford, the bus service was a success due to rapid speed, frequent headway, cheap season tickets and effective promotion.

The Basic Plan for Redditch New Town, 1965

Implementation of this plan lay with the Development Corporation, especially the Department of Architecture and Planning under Brian Bunch. Nearly all the design work was done in multi-disciplinary teams. Thus planners were involved in everything from major tasks, such as the overall design of a 'bead' comprising homes, workplaces, local shops, schools, play areas and open spaces; down to considering planning applications for individual houses or footpaths through nature trails.

One such team worked on the town centre. Its first task was to consider whether to have a new centre near the heart of the designated area, or to expand the existing. The latter was chosen. The hilly site enabled the access road, service roads, car parks and all pedestrian areas to be segregated from each other. The surveyors favoured a new bus station near the main shops, whereas the planners wanted it beside the railway station even though this was at the end of a branch line, threatened with closure and 100 feet (30 m) below the main shopping level! The latter option eventually prevailed, with escalators to the main shopping level. The railway line was saved and has since been electrified as part of the cross-city line through Birmingham. The Corporation's air-conditioned shopping centre, without shop entrance steps or doors, won awards from organisations for the disabled and delighted wheel-chair users. It was perhaps the Development Corporation's greatest innovation, being largely enclosed and fully pedestrianised at a time when this seldom happened outside the USA.

Innovation was again to the fore when the Development Corporation won its first award. This was for an upside-down housing scheme on very steep land, hitherto considered un-developable. Views of the Worcestershire countryside from the first-floor living room windows were spectacular! Another award-winning developer's scheme had back-to-back houses – though not in the Victorian fashion. A development of four-storey flats, set in groups of eight and stepped up the steep hillsides of Headless Cross, also gave commanding views, this time across the town to Warwickshire.

Good use was made of a sloping site at Redditch by building four-storey flats with commanding views across the town to the Warwickshire countryside.

The Corporation built two more unusual estates of rented houses in Church Hill, following the principles of *Design Bulletin 32: Residential Roads and Footpaths* (DoE/DTp, 1977) which recommended the creation of 'moving roads'. Here, local distributor roads were restricted to nine feet (2.7m) width, allowing no parking, but providing passing places adjacent to housing culs-de-sac. These layouts reduced road costs, created extra land for buildings and gardens and increased safety by lowering speeds. Despite these advantages and such excellent examples, the concept has not been widely adopted.

As well as purpose-built factories, the Corporation designed advanced unit factories from 400-50,000 sq. ft. (37-4,650m^2) area, built and let prior to completion, with a policy which allowed occupants to move to larger or smaller units with ease as their progress required.

Travelling through Redditch, one is barely aware of the new development, due to the extensive landscaping. In addition to extensive shrub planting, well over three million trees had been planted by 1982 and many are now approaching full height. Another major feature is the 27 acre (11 ha) lake, central to the 840 acre (340 ha) Arrow Valley Park, which links the countryside to the north of the town with that to the south, along the River Arrow.

Of course, Redditch had its share of planning battles, such as changes to local authority boundaries, resisting expansion to the north-west and seeking expansion to the south, all of which involved the planning section. As intimated earlier, it is people who make a town. Redditch was fortunate in its appointed Board Members and its chief officers and staff. The eight initial Board Members, under Sir Edward Thompson, stayed together for 10 years, with no sudden change of personnel or policy. The chief officers remained much the same for some 15 years and this continuity brought great strength of purpose, essential in pushing forward a new enterprise swiftly and coherently. This unity also kept the staff contented and dedicated and many still regard their time at Redditch as among the happiest in their lives.

To sum up, the greatest achievement of Redditch Development Corporation was the creation of a town where the vast majority of the 80,000 inhabitants are contented and enjoy all the necessities of a good life – good homes, workplaces, shops, schools, leisure facilities and open spaces – all in the space of 21 years. That is no mean thing.

Green Belts in the West Midlands

Michael Law

No story of planning in the West Midlands would be complete without some examination of the region's green belts. For almost forty years our main urban areas – Birmingham, the Black Country, Coventry and Stoke-on-Trent – have all had their land use, social, economic and environmental futures influenced by this mighty sword in the planners' armoury.

So what is this magic weapon? Certainly it figures amongst the earliest concepts used to control development. As early as 1580 Queen Elizabeth I decreed that new building should be forbidden on any new site within three miles of the city gates of London. Again, in 1657, James I proclaimed that there should be a limit to the amount of building within 10 miles of London. So we can see the green belt has for many years been recognised in one form or another as a crucial element in the 'planning package'. As a concept, it is much loved by the man and woman in the street, who see it as a means whereby 'they' (the authorities) will protect the open country around the city where they live.

But what is it? The dictionary defines it as "a zone of farmland, parks and open country surrounding a town or city, officially designated as such and preserved from urban development." Coming more up to date with a recent legislative reference, *Planning Policy Guidance Note 2* (DoE, 1995) confirms that the essential characteristic of green belts is their permanence.

However, those wielding this weapon in their planning armoury come up against the inevitability of change in all aspects of our society and our environment. There is no such thing as for ever – even 20 years is a very long time – and this sits uncomfortably with our concept of permanence for the green belt. Change acts as a primer of so much planning activity, but at the same time is an irritant in the context of 'the good life, stability and certainty'. In the wider scheme of things, planning, including green belt policy, is just one cog or mechanism, so perhaps any attempt to describe our region's green belts and their evolution needs to start by looking at the historical and socio-economic framework within which they have been set. In particular, we need to think about the long-term significance of designating one belt of open land as green belt as opposed to, say, a more loosely-drawn area of containment and protection. A look at the settlement pattern of our towns and cities, and how they evolved and affected land use, can help us to understand the *raison d'être* of our designated green belts.

Burgeoning Urban England

As industries developed and the population of Birmingham, the Black Country, Coventry and the Potteries grew in the 19th and 20th centuries, so too did the demand for space for new and better housing and for expandable industrial sites. Periods of prosperity increased these demands, health care increased life expectancy and there were great strides in personal mobility – initially by public transport, then by the dramatic increase in car ownership, which provided total freedom of movement.

Where did this take Midlanders in the 1920s up to the 1950s? In increasing numbers they sought new homes just outside the towns and cities. They were mobile, but not so very affluent, and they wanted to be within easy commuting distance of existing centres of employment. However, there were many thousands who couldn't move from their urban homes, or who chose not to flee to the suburbs. Surely their quality of life and environment deserved equal consideration. By the 1950s we were in the era of the 'Brave New World' and planners were housing increasing numbers in high-rise, high-density blocks. Yet still demand exceeded the supply of land. Urban authorities saw it as natural simply to extend their development limits – after all that is what had happened for the past century or so. Only now the authorities surrounding each major conurbation began to resist further outward growth. The shire counties, especially, saw this expansion not only as a potentially limitless incursion into their countryside, but also as a challenge in terms of political control. Further influences were the new towns, which brought about wholesale population redistribution, and also more sophisticated forecasting of population change, employment and housing demand.

The green belt stops further encroachment by Birmingham into the Worcestershire countryside.

During the early part of the century, social evangelists sought healthier, cleaner and more salubrious living environments through the Garden City Movement. The Second World War came with just a few examples in existence, but enough to demonstrate the potential of this type of solution to housing pressures. At the same time the statisticians started to tell the politicians what was rapidly becoming apparent – we were a very fast growing post-war nation with demands which, when translated into land use terms, were of massive proportions. It was just beginning to be clear, in addition, that moving all these people around could not be achieved in the old ways.

Green Legislation

The evolution of green belt policy began in the 19th and early 20th centuries, when those industrialists and developers with a more visionary approach saw the case for containing urban sprawl and planning new settlements. Whilst healthier environments were beginning to feature, for example Bournville in this region, there was an absence of legislation and no real ground swell of public concern to guide and to drive the planners into more drastic land use policies. Planning predecessors had, in the Greek City States, the Roman towns and some mediaeval examples, created urban communities with firm city limits, usually for defensive reasons. Consciously or unconsciously, they had recognised the distinctiveness of town and country. By the 20th century, defence was no longer a constraint, but now there was a new reason to protect land outside city limits, namely to guarantee physical and mental recreational space for those living within the city.

The 1938 Green Belt Act was largely a response to pressures in Greater London and its provisions applied only to that region. Nonetheless, it was becoming clear that other urban regions were exhibiting similar symptoms, albeit on a different scale. The later years of the war produced many expert reports and particularly Acts of Parliament, culminating in the New Towns Act 1946 and the Town and Country Planning Act 1947. These laid down the basic tenets of planning, recognising that, if we were going to improve the quality of life for millions of urban dwellers, more drastic solutions had to prevail.

On the fringes of many cities, including Birmingham, authorities had been acquiring large tracts of land to protect them from development. But this was an expensive solution. The new post-1947 planning system gave local authorities the power to refuse permission for the development of such sites. Despite that power, by the 1950s urban fringe authorities were starting to incorporate green belts in their plans in some form. Issuing the Green Belt Circular 42/55 (MHLG, 1955), the Minister of Housing and Local Government, Duncan Sandys, said "I am convinced that, for the well-being of our people and for the preservation of the countryside, we have a clear duty to do all we can to prevent the further unrestricted sprawl of the great cities."

In the West Midlands, the more enlightened had long realised that some limits to outward expansion had to be established. The problems of not doing so were beginning to be recognised, reluctantly by many, and by the early 1960s proposals emerged for a green belt around Birmingham and its adjacent urban areas.

Agreeing to the principle of a green belt to constrain urban expansion was one thing. Finally approving and implementing its limits was quite a different matter. This was political and Political, a matter for the 'Voice of the People'. On the one hand were those desperate for homes, or for better, more spacious living, and on the other those who urged protection of their wider environment, fearing that peripheral growth *ad infinitum* would inevitably bring congestion and threaten their nearby breathing space.

Applying the Principles

It is all too easy to apply a simplistic approach when assessing the place of green belts in the planning of post-war Britain. Regarding the political dimension, rural residents and their local authorities are apprehensive of their immensely powerful urban neighbours. Big urban authorities carry power and political clout and the degree of ruthlessness and self-interest they sometimes show creates a perception of inevitability that is not easily dispelled by logical argument. Planning, whether in green belts or anywhere else, has to demonstrate realism alongside altruism: it has to address real world issues not just what we would like to see.

In determining the outer limits of urban expansion – where perhaps the green belt may begin – there are big influences associated with affluence, new technology and the movement towards independence in locational terms. Then there are the wider issues of pollution and global warming, all of which influence our land use policies to varying degrees. How far down the path of better roads should we go? Given greater affluence, how far down the American path of dispersed urban development should we go?

A further issue of considerable importance, linked in some ways with the density of urban development, is the degree to which urban containment policies, including the green belt, can influence the redevelopment of outworn inner urban areas, decaying industrial sites and low-grade residential environments. The value of putting pressure on private and public institutions to invest in these potentially important inner areas, as opposed to 'easy' peripheral sites, is recognised. More recently has come the realisation that stoking up too much pressure to build and rebuild in the existing urban areas can itself irreparably damage the environmental qualities for those living in and using our cities. These and many other factors consciously, or subconsciously, influenced professional and political planners at local, regional and national levels as they assessed the validity of green belt provision round the major urban areas in the West Midlands. The degree to which a sound balance was reached has to be an assessment for future generations as the effects work through the urban fabric.

Statutory Plans

Between 1960-62, the proposed West Midlands Green Belt was included in amendments to the county development plans. The problem was establishing their precise limits. Even the most politically sensitive recognised the need to bite the bullet and mechanisms were established to finally resolve the arguments surrounding such definitions – but doing so took time.

Then came the West Midlands Regional Study and the Coventry-Solihull-Warwickshire Sub-regional Study, both proposing locations for future development. Following these, the first structure plans were prepared. Encouraged by the Government, Warwickshire and Worcestershire both proposed substantial southerly extensions of the green belt. With impeccable timing, the Secretary of State for the Environment chose this very moment in 1975, to approve the original green belt proposals that had been submitted some fourteen years earlier! To avoid pre-empting his eventual approval of the structure plans, he devised the Interim Green Belt – a designation unique to the West Midlands. Here green belt policies were to apply until the strategies for future development had been finally determined and precise boundaries defined in local plans. Around a quarter of the green belt was designated as Interim and many developers, not surprisingly, sought to interpret this as second-rate green belt, leading to many arguments at public inquiries, notably that into the proposed business parks around the M42 in 1991.

The Region's Green Belts

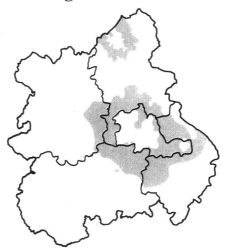

Eventually the approved West Midlands Green Belt was to extend more than 12 miles (20 km) from the edge of the conurbation as far as Telford in the west, Stafford in the north, Rugby in the east and Stratford-upon-Avon in the south, with a small outlier separating Droitwich and Worcester. Meanwhile, the North Staffordshire Green Belt was proposed in 1974 and approved in 1978. This surrounded Stoke-on-Trent and Newcastle-under-Lyme, themselves at the core of a conurbation so much in need of regeneration, with declining industries, growing housing needs and green space already infiltrated by development. Finally, following a boundary change in 1991, Staffordshire inherited some very small areas of the Derbyshire green belt between Burton-on-Trent and Swadlincote.

The New Towns Act, the Town Development Act and Industrial Development Certificates together had a major impact on planning in the region and in turn on the application of green belt policies. These were all macro-influences working alongside local political pressures demanding room for growth. What if there had been no new towns or town expansion schemes – or again what if the providers of new homes had been exclusively the local authorities – could the green belt policies have been sustained? Would the pressures on areas, for example, between Birmingham and Coventry, west of Wolverhampton, south-west through Droitwich towards Worcester or again between Nuneaton, Coventry and Warwick have proved irresistible? Certainly an old Warwickshire County Council map of planning applications showed that, without the green belt, Coventry and Birmingham would have been joined by ribbon development. In North Staffordshire, similar issues affected the open areas between the five towns and Leek, Congleton, Stone and Cheadle. Giving in to the pressures on these areas could have been catastrophic in long term social and communication terms.

All this and much more provided the background to the formulation of the approved green belts. There has, of course, continued to be much debate about precise boundaries, both in sub-regional terms and when examining individual locations. That debate has continued through the structure and local plan processes. Because there is no such thing as an unalterable end state in land use terms, that debate and some variation to the precise edges of the green belt will no doubt continue indefinitely.

Green Belt Land Use

Given the establishment of a green belt, how is all this sternly protected land to be used when, with few exceptions, development is precluded? The predominant uses today remain agriculture and forestry – although often written off, farming *can* subsist in the urban fringe. It also has to be recognised that the location of typical green belt uses such as sports areas, recreational areas and some institutional uses can be beneficial in offering a *cordon sanitaire* between more intensive urban and agricultural activities. It is true that today there are more golf courses and playing fields; the rights of way are becoming better marked, maintained and used; and horse riding for urban dwellers has emerged as a growth activity on the periphery of all our urban areas.

More significantly, perhaps, our green belts are bisected and bordered by motorways and major traffic routes. These not only consume land, they create corridors of noise, pollution and economic pressure for development. Cynics might even suggest that the importance of green belts is to protect land around the periphery of conurbations for future development needs!

Indeed, the West Midlands already provides some classic examples. One concerns premium employment sites. In response to an identified deficiency in the region's portfolio of employment land, the former West Midlands County Council, through its structure plan, successfully secured the release of green belt land east of Birmingham for a business park. A similar need identified by the West Midlands Regional Forum then led to a public inquiry in 1991 into seven proposals for high-quality employment sites along the M42 south-east of Birmingham. Eventually, Blythe Valley Business Park was approved on green belt land in Solihull and is now under construction. Finally, acknowledging the need for further sites, *Regional Planning Guidance Note 11* (RPG 11), (GOWM, 1995) says: "Sites not in the green belt should be considered first. However, in the particular circumstances of the West Midlands, with its tight green belt boundaries and shortage of suitable sites within the built-up area, some sites may, exceptionally, need to be in the green belt." This, like the Interim Green Belt, is another concept unique to the West Midlands and one that has attracted envious glances from elsewhere.

After the incursion into the proposed green belt by the tower blocks of Chelmsley Wood (in distance), the narrow strip of green belt that remained to separate Coleshill from Birmingham was then filled by some 20 lanes of main roads!

Another example is the regional strategy proposal for development along transport corridors as a means of achieving sustainable development. To counteract any potential threat this might pose to the green belt, RPG11 says "... ...only in exceptional circumstances, and if a significant contribution can be made to the aim of reducing the need to travel, should locations (for development) within the currently-defined green belt be identified."

These are examples of the exceptional circumstances in which another policy sometimes over-rides the green belt. Neither circumstance could have been envisaged when the green belt boundaries were first drawn up, but their embodiment in regional planning guidance does cast some doubt onto the concept of a permanent green belt.

Even individual development proposals can be exceptional enough to out-weigh green belt considerations. Examples, again from within the M42 corridor, are the 15,000 houses at Chelmsley Wood, the National Exhibition Centre and the expansion of Birmingham Airport. However, the need for two other major proposals, namely a new superpit at Hawkhurst Moor (west of Coventry) and a regional shopping centre at Stonebridge, was not considered sufficient to over-ride green belt considerations.

One further matter for planners to consider when defining the outer extent of the green belt is the point at which it simply becomes agricultural with no special characteristics. The transition between intense pressure and no pressure is a gradual one and planners have had few magic formulae to apply in their determination of these limits.

Final Thought

It is abundantly clear that green belts have proved to be widely understood and accepted as an important instrument of planning policy. The man or woman in the street might not be able to define it, but the underlying 'goodness' of the concept is understood and generally approved. Some planning concepts come and go as changes in fashion or life-style squeeze and cajole planning authorities into reviewing and modifying their policies from time-to-time. In particular, economic imperatives may lead to land use allocations being varied, or to communication corridors rising or falling in prominence. Yet the roots of our planning – embracing as they do social, economic and land use influences – have a commendable durability.

Until we have learnt to carry through our development in a totally sustainable manner acceptable to society as a whole, then long may the concept of Raymond Unwin and a handful of like-minded individuals over the years remain a belt of verdant green on the map of our impact on the environment.

The Property Boom through the eyes of one Planning Consultancy

Lewis Jones

The 1960s witnessed an unprecedented boom in commercial development as well as housing. Office development had begun in London as soon as building licences were dropped in 1954, but it took several years to reach provincial cities such as Birmingham. The theory was simple. Developers bought and developed parcels of land in city centres, speculating on its value being boosted by inflation and demand. "Since all the money to buy the site was usually lent by the banks, all the cost of construction carried by the contractor or the bank, and the total repaid from a long term mortgage borrowed from an insurance company, the developer seldom had to find any money at all, once his credit was established." (Marriott, 1967). To begin with, the risks were slight and the profits huge, and many people saw this as an easy route to a fortune.

In the West Midlands, the office boom, epitomised by the Rotunda, was largely concentrated in Birmingham, where more floor-space was created than in any other provincial city (Taylor *et al*, 1975). Such was the rate of growth that the Government, concerned about the continuing drift of population to the prosperous South East and West Midlands, introduced the Control of Office Employment Act in 1965. Initially applicable only to London and Birmingham, this sought to regulate building through office development permits (Hall, 1975).

The Rotunda epitomises the 1960s office boom in Birmingham that caused the Government to impose building restrictions.

With new office space restricted and ever more people jumping onto the development bandwagon, competition intensified. So the developers switched to retailing. Local authorities throughout the region had been acquiring land for many years in readiness for town centre redevelopment. For example, when I joined Worcestershire County Council in 1960 there was already a special County Town Centre Redevelopment Committee and work was well advanced on two Comprehensive Development Areas (CDAs) in Halesowen, with Drivers Jonas as advisers. During the next three years, further CDAs were proposed for Kidderminster, Redditch and Stourbridge. Now, inspired by the enclosed environment of Birmingham's Bull Ring and Coventry's traffic-free precinct, the authorities began to enter into partnerships with developers, who themselves were keen to broaden their geographical base. Between 1966-1969, new shopping centres appeared right across the conurbation, from Mell Square in Solihull to the Manders Centre in Wolverhampton, and beyond from the Hanley Centre in the north to Lynchgate (Worcester) in the south and the Swan Centre (Kidderminster) in the west to Bargates (Burton-on-Trent) in the east (Jones, Laing, Wootton, 1999).

Mell Square, Solihull, was one of the more successful town centre shopping developments of the period.

Surprisingly, the Government made no attempt to control retail development. Eventually the boom ended, but not before one or two people became too greedy and corruption crept in, tarnishing the image of developers and a few of the professionals associated with them. The bubble finally burst when the dearth of offices and shops turned into a glut. As the economy wavered, retailers found themselves squeezed between high rents and low profits. Many pulled out, leaving behind a plethora of empty shops. Indeed, a region-wide survey of thirty-six 1960s developments showed a quarter to be vacant and one town centre scheme to be almost half empty five years after completion (RTPI West Midlands Branch, 1977). Even the Bull Ring, described at the time as 'Europe's most advanced shopping centre', did not escape and traders were offered concessionary rents to boost the occupancy for the official opening in 1965. Notwithstanding this, Councillor Beaumont Dark still described it as the biggest white elephant in the history of Birmingham (Marriott, 1967).

The boom created plenty of work and brought to prominence two Birmingham architects, John Madin and James Roberts. Each pursued a different course. James Roberts became associated, through his work for developers, with Smallbrook Ringway, the Rotunda and the initial designs for the Bull Ring. John Madin, starting in 1952, rose to prominence through his work on the Calthorpe Estate, which enabled his practice to develop both architectural and planning strengths.

As explained in two previous articles, Birmingham's redevelopment programme was resulting in population overspill despite the use of high-rise flats to raise densities. Adjoining two of the redevelopment areas was the privately owned Calthorpe Estate. This covered some 1,500 acres (625 ha) about a mile from the city centre and seemed an anomaly, which could be used more effectively if housing densities were increased from the very low level of 10 persons per acre (25 per ha). As part of the *City Development Plan* (Birmingham City Council, 1952), it was agreed that future densities should be raised to 30 persons per acre (75 per ha) and some fringe areas were sold to the City Council to develop at much higher levels. However, over time the attitude of the Council started to change and councillors began to consider compulsory purchase powers to make more use of the area for municipal housing. This pressure made the Estate consider more actively its future form and the way in which redevelopment could take place as leases fell in. As a result, in 1957, the Estate commissioned John Madin to prepare guidance and redevelopment proposals to conform to the Council's minimum density requirements. These proposals also had to retain, as far as possible, the magnificent tree cover and work within the pattern of leaseholds.

The proposals featured three residential density levels, namely 100 persons per acre (250 per ha) in high flats; 60 persons per acre (150 per ha) in walk-up flats or terraced housing; and 15 persons per acre (40 per ha) in individual houses in large plots of about a third of an acre. By proposing varying densities in this form, much of the fine planting could be retained, whereas development at an overall density of 30 persons per acre would have resulted in major destruction.

As well as the residential areas, there was a business area of some 70 acres (28 ha) adjoining Five Ways, some of which had resulted from housing being used to accommodate city centre businesses displaced by bombing. It also conformed to the proposals in Sir Patrick Abercrombie's West Midlands Plan, which recommended expansion of the city centre into Edgbaston. Plans for the business area featured a number of tower blocks along Hagley Road interspersed with three and four storey blocks to give a total floor-space of 3.2 million sq.ft. (300,000m^2). The principle for the redevelopment of the individual sites was based on thirds – one for the building footprint, one for car parking and the other for landscaping. The City Council approved the scheme in 1958 and implementation proceeded piecemeal in accordance with the lease pattern.

Offices in the Calthorpe Estate, Birmingham, which won a Civic Trust award in 1969.

Most of this redevelopment was designed by John Madin and gained a number of awards, both for the housing and commercial buildings. Other commercial projects included the Birmingham Chamber of Commerce and BBC Pebble Mill, all of which added to the firm's growing reputation. Here I should mention the late Michael Holt, an architect/planner who joined Madin's in 1959 and later became a partner with responsibility for the group dealing with major planning commissions, which followed in quick succession in the early 1960s as the next phase of new towns was announced and city centre redevelopment gathered pace.

The first of these was the expansion of Corby New Town to double its size to 80,000 people. This project carried on the principles adopted in the Calthorpe Estate plan, where various elements were tested in detailed studies to underpin the basic thinking and these included the town centre expansion and residential neighbourhoods. Then West Bromwich Corporation commissioned the firm to prepare proposals for the renewal and rehabilitation of their town centre and this was taken through a major public local inquiry to justify the necessary compulsory purchase orders. The detailed implementation of the first two phases, in the form of the covered shopping complexes of King's and Queen's Squares, was carried out for developers, followed by the pedestrianisation of the High Street.

In 1963 the firm was asked by the Ministry of Housing and Local Government to look at the expansion possibilities for Worcester City as part of a wider study with other consultants doing similar tasks for Peterborough and Ipswich. The brief required an examination of the physical, social and cost implications of 50% and 100% population increases over two different time frames of 15 and 25 years. Also in 1963, the contract for preparing a Master Plan for Dawley New Town was awarded to Madin's by the New Town Corporation. This was part of a second phase of new towns promoted by the Government, but following different thinking. The Mark I New Towns of the late 1940s and early 1950s were largely on virgin sites and planned to house ultimate populations of about 50,000 people. The Mark II versions often embraced quite large existing settlements and the last designations foresaw expansions up to 200,000-250,000 people – in fact a new city. As mentioned earlier by Michael Barker, just as a draft Master Plan to accommodate 55,000 overspill at Dawley had been produced for public consultation, the Minister, Richard Crossman, decided to increase this by a further 50,000.

The earlier new towns had proceeded on the basis of predetermined designated areas defined by the Ministry's own technical team, after which consultants were appointed by the development corporations to produce the master plans. Because of this, several years could pass before any significant new housing and industry was completed. In the case of Telford (as Dawley was now known), Madin's were appointed in 1965 to carry out a two-stage study. The first stage, following an appraisal of alternative ways of planning the development, was to propose a designation area and recommend a preferred pattern of expansion. The second stage was to produce a master plan based on the final designation order. By overlapping the two procedures, the Ministry hoped to shorten the whole process by one-and-a-half to two years.

As these proposed towns were now larger, the work involved became more complicated and the consultant team included planners, architects, economists, sociologists, demographers, traffic engineers, landscape architects and, additionally for Telford, mining engineers because of the legacy of past and current mining activity. The period of the 1960s also saw an increase in the use of more complicated mathematical models made possible by the development of computers. This allowed alternative land use arrangements to be explored with their effect on trip generation, peak hour flows and modal splits. This kind of detailed analysis of the effects of alternative locations for industry, commercial centres and housing fell out of favour in the 1970s and 1980s, but it is interesting to see how the pendulum has now swung back as we wrestle with the complexities of sustainable development.

Of major interest was the history of the Telford area and its place in the industrial revolution. Michael Holt and his team spent many hours beyond what was expected in tracing and recording the many buildings and sites of historical and architectural interest, with the result that not only were the statutory lists expanded based on this information, but a separate report, 'A case for an Open Air Museum', was presented to the Development Corporation. This resulted in the Corporation setting up a distinguished working party, which in turn led to the formation of the Ironbridge Gorge Museum.

The study team was also required to give recommendations to the planning authority, then Shropshire County Council, on all planning applications, initially within a defined area of search and then within the confirmed Designated Area. This carried on until the Master Plan was produced and the Development Corporation took over this function.

Madin's planning section was also involved in major housing developments around the country, including renewal and 'enveloping' schemes in Birmingham, industrial zones, leisure projects, marinas, quarry restorations and initial work on many of the commercial and other projects being built by different groups in the firm. With all this major work, the planning section became nationally known and was one of the top half dozen consultancies in the country, the others all being based in London. This provided the platform to expand overseas – in tourism, leisure and major housing projects – but the firm had to contend with the uncertainties of working in less stable political climates, such as in Cyprus and Iraq. However, a notable success was winning, in an international competition, the commission for the detailed urban design for the central area of the new city of Yanbu, sited on the Red Sea in Saudi Arabia.

Circumstances changed after the 1960s, with fewer commissions from local authorities following local government re-organisation in 1974 and then the recession of the 1980s. But the reputation that had been established attracted new clients, such as the Housing Corporation, Bournville Village Trust, the water authorities and the Regional Health Authority. The later work for these bodies was carried out by a joint venture, Bigwood Madins, which is still in being, although the John Madin Design Group ceased to exist in 1994.

In recognising the achievements of the John Madin Design Group, tribute must be paid to Michael Holt who did much to build up the consultancy's reputation at home and overseas. He also taught at the Birmingham School of Planning and did substantial voluntary work on behalf of his two professions, including being chairman of the RTPI, West Midlands Branch and president of the Birmingham Architectural Association.

Chapter 3:

The 1970s – The Changing Agenda

Overview

Bob Stokes

The 1970s were times of change and turmoil nationally, which in turn brought about a changed agenda for planning in the West Midlands. Planners in the region had never before had to adapt so quickly to such a fundamental 'sea-change' with a steep decline in the economic prospects of the region, which led not only to a major restructuring of the economy, but also to a restructuring of its land use and environment. Underlying this change was a current of worker discontent and unemployment allied to outdated processes, under-investment, reduced productivity and escalating national borrowing.

Early in the decade, in 1971, decimal coinage was introduced, Rolls Royce went bankrupt and postal workers went on strike for a 19.5% pay rise. They were to be followed by striking miners and a State of Emergency was declared in 1972 to be repeated again in 1973. Despite the efforts of the Heath Government to resist pay rises, the miners strike was eventually ended in 1974 with a 35% pay increase. However, depleted stocks of coal at power stations and an oil crisis in the Middle East meant that industry was only able to operate at a reduced capacity and unemployment reached the one million mark and was later to rise to 1.25 million. The three-day working week was announced in 1974 to combat what the Government called 'the gravest situation by far since the end of the war'. Public spending was cut, a 50mph speed limit imposed to conserve fuel and television was blacked-out at 10.30pm in a similar bid.

The Wilson Government came to power in 1974 against a background of a worsening balance of payments and rising inflation, which reached 25% in July 1975. The social contract of 1974 failed to curb huge pay rises and 'rough justice' pay limits were introduced. However, this did not prevent further pay strikes by dustmen, lorry drivers and rail workers leading to 1978/9 being dubbed 'the winter of discontent'. Throughout the latter half of the decade there were swingeing cuts in public expenditure and higher interest rates on the back of Government borrowing. The Thatcher Government was elected in May 1979.

Against this background, the West Midlands had no option but to undergo a period of very major restructuring. Restructuring of the economy, the fabric of

Region and Renaissance

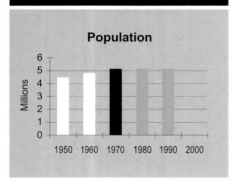

Population

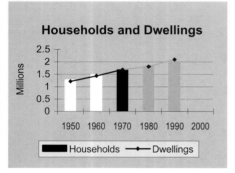

Households and Dwellings

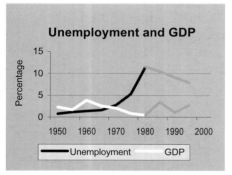

Unemployment and GDP

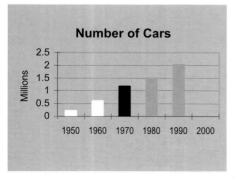

Number of Cars

inner areas and of local government. It was a time for reassessment of planning aims. Plans for the future, formed in the 'boom' years of the 1960s, were by the mid-seventies being redrawn against a background of a national oil crisis and an accelerating decline in the region's under-invested vehicle and metal manufacturing industries. Rising unemployment and concern for the environment of inner city areas led to a movement outwards of those who could relocate and to planners concentrating on acquiring new skills to plan in a period of economic decline in the metropolitan area. The period of rapid construction in the sixties had passed and new techniques had to be learnt to find ways to generate additional investment in order to improve the existing environment and manage traffic with the aim of attracting people and jobs back to the heart of the urban core.

Not only were planners learning how to plan for 'non-growth', they were also learning how to operate in a new system of local government. 1974 saw a reorganisation of local authority boundaries and functions under the Local Government Act 1972. A new tier, the West Midlands County Council (WMCC), was formed with a structural function over-arching the work of the seven districts and boroughs in the metropolitan area. One of these, Solihull grew substantially in size taking in the 'Meriden Gap' from Warwickshire and the Chelmsley Wood area from Birmingham, the latter almost doubling the authority's population bringing it close to the 200,000 figure said at the time to be the smallest size for a metropolitan authority. Coventry was administratively placed within the metropolitan county area. In the shire counties, Hereford and Worcester came together as one county council (only to be separated again in the 1990s). Across the region, a tier of shire district councils was created with local plan making and development control powers.

Initially the creation of two-tiers of planning authorities, counties and districts, resulted in some strained working relationships. The WMCC was particularly unpopular with the seven metropolitan authorities, which had, during the sixties, been responsible for their own development planning. Indeed, the timing can be seen in retrospect as being somewhat ironic. The West Midlands shire and metropolitan authorities had already established a Regional Study team, based in Birmingham, whose purpose was to prepare an urban and rural region-wide framework for their plans. At the same time, in Kenilworth, the Coventry-Solihull-Warwickshire Sub-Regional Study Team was preparing a report for the south and east of the region, which was presented to the three authorities in 1971. Also in the same year, the Town and Country Planning Act 1971 brought into being a new requirement for structure and local plans. The Sub-Regional Study Report formed the basis of the three authorities' structure plans, which blazed a new trail being the first such plans to be prepared and approved in the country. In the articles which follow, Urlan Wannop gives his personal view of this period of regional and sub-regional plan-making.

With this established background of plan making in the metropolitan authorities, and for other political reasons, the country wide logic for an additional metropolitan tier of local government did not endure and the West Midlands County Council was to have a short life of only twelve years. However, for all its short existence, the WMCC was in place at an important time in the development of the West Midlands and can be credited with recognising and promoting the urgent need for restructuring, and for economic redevelopment and environmental improvements in particular.

Overall, it can be seen that the 1970s marked an increase in pressure on planners to perform as never before. The planning agenda had changed and was continuing to change. Planners were now expected not only to allocate land and plan for new developments, but to be visionary and instrumental in schemes for economic regeneration, conservation, urban improvements, land reclamation and countryside recreation, as well as demand management of the motor vehicle and pedestrianisation of town centres.

In the 1970s out-of-centre retailing and 'hypermarkets' arrived, see the article by John Lillywhite. As its contribution to the retailing debate, the West Midlands Branch published *Predicting Shopping Requirements 2* (RTPI West Midlands Branch, 1977). This publication, by the Branch's Research Group, developed the work of an earlier report prepared ten years before and gave a framework for the assessment of major retail proposals.

The planning process, too, was changing – the move from a prescriptive, definitive approach to a permissive, enabling one had begun. There was a realisation that developments, particularly economic developments, were to be encouraged rather than fitted into pre-existing notions. This move took another turn following the publication, in 1969, of the Skeffington Report on public participation in the planning process, so that we began to see the beginnings of a growth in 'bottom-up' community involvement in the plan making and decision processes. Interestingly, at this time the West Midlands Branch decided that it was not urgent to act on a Royal Town Planning Institute (RTPI) paper on

Planning Aid. Later, during the 1990s the Branch became a leader in this service and now has staff specialising in dealing with public concerns on planning matters.

In summary, the challenges of the 1970s were ones to which planners in the West Midlands rose. The location of the region at the centre of the country was highlighted with the opening in 1972 of 'Spaghetti Junction' (M6/A38) and the Midland Links motorway network – Ian Dickins gives his view on transport policy in the 1970s. Following the European Year of Conservation in 1970, conservation of buildings and areas increased apace and Peter Larkham, assisted by Will Scott, amply illustrates this in his article. On the ground, Stoke-on-Trent led the way with land reclamation schemes, the success of which is described by John Cornell and Fiona Colville. The 1970s also saw the establishment of the first country parks, such as Cannock Chase Country Park and Kingsbury Water Park.

In 1975 the National Exhibition Centre (NEC) was constructed on a greenfield site alongside the region's major international airport at Elmdon. The centre is well served by the M42, M6 and A45 roads and has its own mainline railway station linking to Birmingham and London (Euston). As its name implies, the NEC is the largest in the country, initially some 100,000m^2 (1 million sq. ft.) of exhibition halls (and later doubled in size), which gave a much needed 'spin-off' boost to the region's economy and a showcase for its products.

One of the best understood and enduring of planning policies, the West Midlands Green Belt, was confirmed in 1975 and has been instrumental in shaping developments in and beyond the metropolitan area from its inception as a proposal in the 1960s up to the present day.

The contributions which follow have been chosen to illustrate some of the major planning achievements in the West Midlands region in the 1970s.

The former Midland Railway Grain Warehouse, Burton-on-Trent, accommodates a new commercial use whilst retaining the building's heritage.

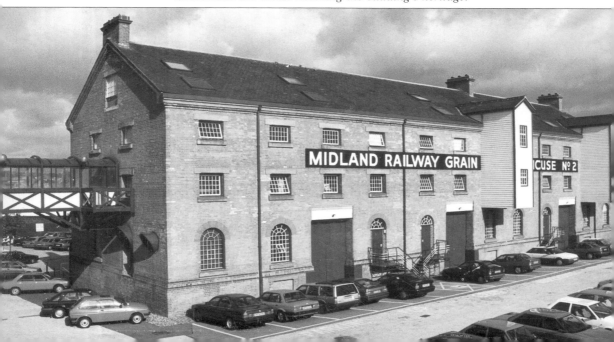

The Time of Regional and Sub-regional Studies

Urlan Wannop OBE

A personal memoir

For three years between 1968 and 1971, colleagues and I worked on the Coventry-Solihull-Warwickshire Sub-Regional Study. No three years of my career were more enjoyable or satisfying than those in the company of the team at Kenilworth. On some evenings it was exhilarating to walk home from the team's office in the old Police Station in Kenilworth, so much was the pleasure of making progress on work and of delighting in – even if not always fully understanding – what outstandingly able and mutually supportive colleagues were developing.

The context

The Sub-Regional Study and the parallel study of the West Midlands were parts of a vigorous revival of regional planning in Britain. The wave of regional studies and plans which finally broke in the mid-1970s originated in the 1960s, when national population growth was projected to rise to levels never subsequently reached. Studies of the potential for massive urban growth were being made throughout Britain, not just in older industrial regions with long established need for overspill and expansion, but also in possible new metropolitan regions such as Severnside, Humberside and Tayside.

In the West Midlands, Government ministers of the 1960s had been particularly frustrated at the lack of co-operation amongst the region's planning authorities. Creating space for the then still vigorous economic growth was a persistent problem. Worcestershire was notably reluctant to re-house 'Brummies' in new council estates and the public inquiry and subsequent rejection of Birmingham's proposal to build a council estate at Wythall, in north Worcestershire, had been a disaster for the City Council.

Although rejecting Wythall, the Government supported Birmingham in developing Chelmsley Wood in Warwickshire, re-launched Redditch as a new town and designated a second new town at Dawley. This was not enough to meet the expected scale of Birmingham's overspill in particular, nor the expected need for Coventry's further expansion. There was no framework for regional planning as had been created for Greater London and Clydeside by Abercrombie's influential plans of 1944 and 1946, respectively.

In south-east England, the innocuousness of the South-east Regional Planning Conference's (SERPLAN's) predecessor regional organisation had led the Government to establish its own regional planning team in 1968, led by its Chief Planner, Wilf Burns, and largely staffed from government departments or by special recruits. Similarly, the Government led in staffing the other major regional studies of the 1970s – in the North West, the North and in West Central Scotland. The West Midlands was the exception. Rather than allowing a government team, the Planning Authorities' Conference, formed in 1966, preferred to run its own study, starting in autumn 1968.

The West Midlands Regional Study

John Stevenson from the Birmingham Planning Department was seconded as Director of the Regional Study, supported by John Moreton as deputy on secondment from Staffordshire County Council. The other planners in the team were a shifting group, coming and going on short-term secondments from their regular council posts. John Stevenson's strongly independent leadership style and the secondment arrangements made it difficult for the regional team to cohere. There were also difficulties in developing good relations between the study, its constituent authorities and planners of the Government's regional office headed by Bill Ogden. A series of joint topic working parties highlighted, rather than eased, the problems of confidence surrounding the study, which was housed above Woolworth's in New Street, Birmingham, adjoining the conurbation Transportation Study.

The regional team employed consultants to evaluate alternative strategies for the region, but outsiders found the technical process of the study sometimes opaque, and the West Midlands Economic Planning Council complained that

West Midlands Regional Study proposals, 1971

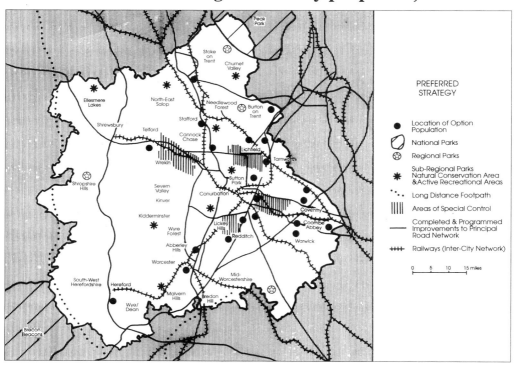

it was being excluded from it. Early in 1970, the Secretary of State, Anthony Crosland, wrote to the Conference chairman to stress his concerns. It was subsequently decided that any resolution must await the Study's conclusions.

When the final report on *A Developing Strategy for the West Midlands* was published (West Midlands Regional Study, 1971), it advocated a principal axis of growth running through Birmingham from beyond Lichfield in the north-east to Redditch and mid Worcestershire in the south-west, together with detached islands of growth on the periphery of the conurbation. The proposals were contentious. They satisfied neither those favouring growth edging the conurbation, nor those seeking to disperse it. The proposals accorded with the completed strategy of the sub-regional team over the scale of growth to occur in the Coventry-Solihull-Warwickshire sub-region, but not as to where it should go. Detaching growth from the conurbation was contrary to the Sub-regional Study and against the advice of the Government's regional officials. Birmingham's view that detachment would threaten the city's economic future was flouted. Beyond the conurbation, however, the new towns and several authorities complained that there was more potential for dispersal than the *Strategy* proposed.

Birmingham's dissatisfaction caused the City Council to withdraw the Director and other seconded staff and to leave the regional Planning Conference for a period. The residual regional team and steering group of officials consulted, debated and negotiated, subsequently reporting that it considered that no objections were sufficient to require the *Strategy* to be rethought overall. So, a year after publication, the Conference commended the *Strategy* as broadly acceptable. This was a sanguine conclusion, ignoring the structure plans already in preparation, which collectively assumed larger migration to the region's periphery than did the *Strategy*.

Conference's bland conclusion was rejected by both the Government's regional office and the Economic Planning Council. The Minister told the Chairman of Conference that the Government would not approve the *Strategy* and that Conference would be obliged to substantially revise its proposals. New and reduced projections of population growth and of jobs and households dispersed from the conurbation were to be adopted, and there was to be total incorporation of the strategy for the Coventry-Solihull-Warwickshire sub-region already adopted by those councils.

When revision of the regional work was completed in 1974, it had taken six years of preparation, negotiation and upsets to give the West Midlands its first formal, regional planning strategy. Yet, it was only irregularly matched by the region's first structure plans, submitted prior to the local government reorganisation of 1974 by all authorities except Shropshire. Some old political attitudes re-emerged in the structure plan drafts. Solihull and Warwickshire had underprovided for households to move from Birmingham; Staffordshire and – rather surprisingly – Worcestershire overprovided. By 1976, the reconstituted Planning Conference saw a need for an earlier review of strategy than could have been expected.

Conference saw that:

1. population growth in the next ten years might be only a fifth of that assumed by the 1971 strategy, and might occur mostly beyond the conurbation's green belt;
2. trends including opportunities to renew housing in the conurbation were much reducing overspill;
3. a loss rather than a growth in jobs now seemed more likely, and fewer might be able to relocate; and
4. the inner conurbation had social and economic problems requiring action not recognised previously.

The new West Midlands County Council (WMCC) was already reviewing the plans inherited from its predecessor councils, but some county councils were loath to share in any regional review which might reduce commitments to overspill schemes distant from the conurbation. However, the regional context was too changed to ignore and a review began in 1977 on a tripartite basis between the Government, the Conference and the Economic Planning Council. Aimed at completion within one year, the review took two and a half, producing one consultation document on proposals for physical planning and one on regional economic development. Government officials would not associate themselves with the economic document, for the implications of Government urban policy conflicted with the economic ambitions of the shire counties. The updating of the region's plan proceeded uneasily. It was possible for the tripartite alliance to agree in mid-1979 to recommend Conference's favoured, but rather imprecise physical strategy, which offered concessions to all parties. But the Government would not agree to the ideas on economic policy with which Conference and the Councils persisted.

The change of Government in 1979 intervened before a ministerial decision on the strategic review, which did not come until 1980. When it came, the decision was confused in the view of local authorities, perhaps matching the ambiguities and unresolved issues of what they had recommended. Some of the imprecision and omissions of the strategy were exposed in 1981 at the examination-in-public of the structure plan of the WMCC. But when earlier that year there was an urgent search up and down the British regions for a site for the rich prize of the Nissan car plant, none of the three sites proposed by the WMCC had been included in its structure plan, let alone anticipated in the regional strategy.

The Coventry-Solihull-Warwickshire Sub-Regional Study

The sub-regional study team for Coventry, Solihull and Warwickshire was fortunate by comparison with the West Midlands team. Sub-regional planners met periodically, but carefully, with counterparts in the regional team. There was a total overlap of interest, but the sub-regional councils had established no formal relationship between the two studies. Terry Gregory of Coventry, Tom Richardson of Solihull and Ron Norris of Warwickshire, the three planning officers, comprised the steering group for the sub- regional study as well as having places on the regional steering group. The regional planning officer at Five Ways House, Bill Ogden, was primarily occupied with the regional study, but kept a keen but kindly eye on sub-regional progress.

Unlike the West Midlands Study, the sub-regional team had a stable basis. Core staff were specially recruited on full-time contracts. I came in from a consultancy post to lead the team, whose two key members, Graham Harrison and Ian Turner, had already excellent access to the sub-regional planning departments. Its purpose-designed basis helped the team to a much easier passage than that experienced by the regional study.

The problems of staffing and relationships afflicting the regional study were a preoccupation for the chief planning officers of the three sub-regional councils to the benefit of the freedom given to their local team. This favourable political context continued throughout the study, notably in the Government's proposals for local government reorganisation published in 1971. On the day after the printer delivered the team's final report, the announcement that Coventry was to be extracted from its sub-region and absorbed into the West Midlands County was totally unexpected – by the team at least. Initially, this surprising development seemed as if it might wreck the chances of the team's recommended strategy. Ultimately, it may have ensured the strategy's acceptance.

The Terms of Reference set for the team obliged it to "generally.....look forward towards the end of the century, although some elements may not be predictable with reasonable certainty for more than twenty years." The study was "to be based on current projections of natural increase....together with best available estimates of migration." This amounted to growth of population in the sub-region from 1 million in 1967 to about 1.4 million by 1991.

The team quickly adopted a highly methodical approach to its process. Later, Peter Hall would describe the study as 'the high water mark of systems planning'. Systems planning was often criticised in the abstract by planning theorists for its supposedly apolitical and therefore unreal and even antisocial basis. Systems planning spread in England from the mid-1960s through Lyn Davies on the Teesside Survey and Plan, Brian McLoughlin on the Leicester-Leicestershire Sub-regional Study and Mike Batty supporting the Notts-Derby Study. Graham Harrison developed the approach in Kenilworth in his method for crystallising alternative strategies, and Ian Turner took over the concluding methodology for evaluating the alternatives. As written up in the team's final report (Coventry, Solihull, Warwickshire Sub-regional Study, 1971), the techniques were widely read and perhaps became too much of a model and were insufficiently criticised by others.

Thirty years later, it is the circumstances in which the team's strategy was adopted by the councils which are more interesting than the team's technical methods. Ultimately, the political implications of the recommended strategy would be paramount to the councils' decisions. If at the outset the three chief planners had been asked to put their own preferred strategy in a sealed envelope, none of their preferences is likely to have coincided with the team's recommended strategy. Coventry regarded itself more as a national city than as one of the West Midlands; Terry Gregory looked to London rather than Birmingham as Coventry's focus and he might have seen the considerable growth which the city expected to be in the form of a linear city stretching to Rugby. Solihull's motto of 'Urbs in Rure' signified its satisfaction with its size and setting; Tom Richardson's council wished only the well-to-do to join the borough from Birmingham, and few enough of them so as not to threaten encroachment on the green belt. Ron Norris, representing Warwickshire, which anticipated capturing Coventry at local government reorganisation, would probably have preferred relatively little further growth in the shire detached from the conurbation and keeping the gap between Coventry and Kenilworth.

What emerged was a strategy varying appreciably from a mere extension of the established trend in the sub-region. It was less dramatic than the solutions of a linear city or of a new town and put relatively large emphasis on growth around Solihull and on balanced growth north and south of Coventry within the corridor from Nuneaton to Stratford-on-Avon.

The Government's reorganisation proposals allowed Coventry to remain a partially independent administration rather than to be absorbed into Warwickshire. Although demoted to be a district within a metropolitan county, Coventry would remain an education authority and the City's Conservative administration could thereby save its historic grammar school. Solihull was also to become a district of the new West Midlands County, which was better than elimination as the borough's relatively small population had previously suggested as possible. Warwickshire was to be the loser in the changes. It was to lose Sutton Coldfield, as expected, but was not to have more than adequate compensation by gaining Coventry. The loss of status shocked the County's politicians. Expecting to represent one of England's larger county councils with a population of around a million, they now represented a minor county of barely half the population. The image pictured by the County's senior politicians was of having been relegated to the lower end of the league table of counties.

Nonetheless, the political scene had turned strongly to the advantage of the Sub-Regional Study. Why? At first, it seemed that the strategy's strong emphasis on axial growth from Nuneaton to Stratford-on-Avon had been dealt a perhaps fatal blow. A senior Coventry planner quickly told me that our newly circulated final report would "be put on the shelf." Superficially, it did seem unfavourable that Coventry's local political axis was to link westwards to Birmingham, rather than to consolidate into Warwickshire. Only after a few of the public meetings at which the team publicised our proposals did I realise the answer to this point. Replying to a councillor of the Coventry Labour group (then in uncommon opposition), I pointed out that the north-south axis of growth through Coventry

Coventry-Solihull-Warwickshire
Sub-regional Study proposals, 1971

THE RECOMMENDED STRATEGY

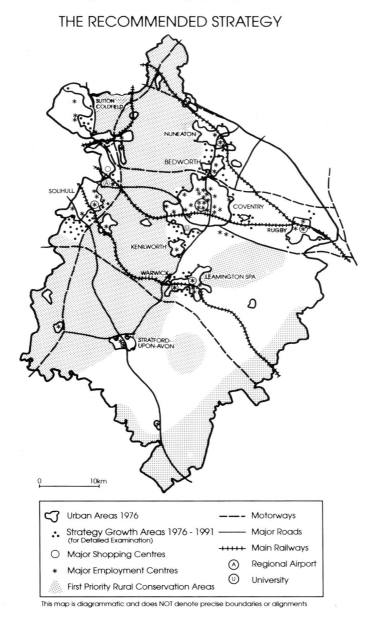

🖤 Urban Areas 1976		— — - Motorways	
⸫ Strategy Growth Areas 1976 - 1991 (for Detailed Examination)		——— Major Roads	
○ Major Shopping Centres		+++++ Main Railways	
✳ Major Employment Centres		Ⓐ Regional Airport	
⠿ First Priority Rural Conservation Areas		Ⓤ University	

This map is diagrammatic and does NOT denote precise boundaries or alignments

had grown without ever the benefit of common administration for the City and Warwickshire. The formation of the West Midlands County Council would scarcely alter the economic and social circumstances in which urbanisation had grown on a north to south axis. However the proposed reorganisation might have disadvantages for the strategy, I added, it did not negate it.

While my stance was perhaps more hopeful than confident, it was borne out by the strategy's speedy adoption. Five strands of political rationale underlay the consensus for approval:

1. All three councils urgently wished to keep the conurbation green belt. Warwickshire wanted to limit the eastward encroachment of Birmingham so as not lose more administrative territory. Coventry had similarly long protected its western buffer of green belt. Solihull wished to keep the larger part of its green belt, to protect its environment and its political stability which more overspill from Birmingham could threaten;

2. Although a unitary county borough for some years, Solihull's relatively small population was near the limit of acceptability for some of the reorganisation solutions recently discussed. Modest expansion could ensure a population safely above the threshold of security. When assured of its status as a metropolitan district, Solihull later tried in its structure plan to scale down the scale of growth inherent in the sub-regional strategy;

3. Although gaining territory to its west in becoming a metropolitan district, Coventry gained no new outlet for the City's growth. Its boundaries remained as tight as before to the north, east and south, and the western green belt was regarded as inviolable. Coventry was as much a prisoner of its boundaries as before;

4. Having been swept from near the top to the lower level of the league table of English counties, Warwickshire was eager to grow sufficiently to climb back towards its former dignity. So the sub-regional strategy offered the County both growth – more than Warwickshire might have desired at the outset of the Study – as well as a means of rapidly legitimising it in a structure plan; and

5. Finally, the sub-regional strategy accorded with the Department of the Environment's principles for growth in the West Midlands and it fitted in a major piece in the revision of the jigsaw of the regional strategy. Ministers could be pleased that political tensions had been eased in part of the West Midlands, at least.

When a letter from the Chief Executive's office sought help in appraising the costs and benefits to Coventry of our recommended strategy, I replied that it offered the only and adequate means by which the City could expand. This paramount benefit overwhelmed any conceivable disadvantages, and was a political truth which seemed to me to leave little purpose in any pedantic appraisal of minutiae of costs and benefits. So, like Solihull and Warwickshire, Coventry adopted the strategy and the three councils were together invited to prepare England's first structure plans and subsequently together went to the first Examination-in-Public.

The Retail Revolution

John Lillywhite

The 1970s were a watershed for the region's town centres. At the start of the decade they were the normal location for new shopping development, by the end of it the out-of-centre revolution was well underway and town centres were becoming the exception rather than the rule as the first choice location for developers and retailers. This article looks at how the planning system in the West Midlands responded; how it sought to maintain 'the vitality and viability' of town centres in the face of the increasing pressures towards decentralisation.

I have begun with a brief survey of changes in shopping over the decade, then focused on two particular events – firstly the public inquiry in 1973-74 into a proposed out-of-town regional shopping centre at Stonebridge, between Birmingham and Coventry, and secondly the formulation between 1976 and 1980 of the shopping policies in the West Midlands County Structure Plan. Through these 'case studies' it is hoped to cast some light on the changes with which planners were grappling and the influence that they had on the emerging pattern of shopping in the region.

A decade of change

During the 1970s the era of post war prosperity and social-democratic political consensus came to an end. We moved into a harsher world of recession and de-industrialisation; of the free market economics and new right politics, which came to full fruition as 'Thatcherism' in the 1980s. These changes, allied with the continued growth of car ownership, encouraged a fundamental change in the nature of shopping development.

Since the war consumer spending had grown rapidly, particularly in the West Midlands where an expanding demand for labour, and a preponderance of large manufacturing plants and strong trade unions, sustained a relatively high wage economy. Local authorities had helped to accommodate the growth in spending by vigorously promoting town centre redevelopment, which in turn expanded their tax base and also gave their town centres an enhanced status in the region. Relatively abundant public sector resources enabled councils to play a pivotal role – acquiring sites, providing infrastructure and often working in partnership with a developer to retain a share in the associated profits.

The property boom, which started in the late fifties, had seen the entry of large development companies into retailing, promoting the construction of what were in effect town centre shopping malls. The concept of the mall had appeared in the USA around 1950 in edge-of-town 'freeway' locations. However, it was imported to Britain in the form of the large scale *town centre* redevelopment and by the early 1970s most towns in the West Midlands had at least one new large town centre mall development providing accommodation for the main supermarkets as well as for the rapidly growing multiples in the fashion goods and other 'high street' retail sectors.

With the economic downturn of the early 1970s the property boom came to an end and local authorities became more limited in their ability to promote town centre redevelopment schemes. As a result retailers, particularly in the food sector, turned to undertaking development themselves. Taking advantage of the accessibility which growing car ownership and motorway and other road construction was providing, they increasingly sought sites away from established town centres. The first food superstore in the West Midlands, albeit in an edge-of-centre location, was Asda at Bloxwich, Walsall, which opened in 1971. By the end of the decade there were more than twenty superstores in the metropolitan county alone. Some of these, such as Sainsbury's in Solihull, had been fitted into established town centres, but others, such as Carrefour (now Asda) at Minworth, adjoined major roads on the edge of the built-up area. Furthermore, by the end of the decade, large foodstores were being joined by other new retailing forms in seeking out-of-centre locations – in particular the retail warehouse and the 'retail warehouse park'.

Stonebridge

A key event in establishing the local authorities' position on out-of-centre shopping in the West Midlands was the submission in 1972 of a planning application for an out-of-town 'regional shopping centre' at Stonebridge, mid-way between Birmingham and Coventry. This was to have over 75,000 m² (800,000 sq. ft.) of shopping floor-space and parking for 7,000 cars and, in retail sales terms, would have been equivalent to the whole of an established centre such as Coventry or Wolverhampton.

The concept of the large *out-of-town* shopping mall had been imported from the USA to Europe in the early sixties – 'Parly 2' on the western outskirts of Paris for example – and had made its appearance in the UK in the middle of the decade with a number of proposals, most notably at Haydock in Lancashire. However, none had received planning permission apart from Brent Cross, which was located within the existing urban area, in north-west London.

The site of the Stonebridge application was within the then boundaries of Warwickshire, close to the (then proposed) National Exhibition Centre. It was between the line of the proposed M42 motorway and the A45/A452 junction and only two miles from the M6/M42 interchange. This was probably the most accessible location in the Midlands as far as car travel was concerned and its choice for such a proposal was hardly a surprise. The specific site for the proposal was determined, as is often the case, by land ownership. It comprised a tenanted farm within the Packington Hall estate of Lord Aylesford, who was by this time a director of Town and City Properties Ltd., the potential developer of the shopping centre.

The application was opposed by Warwickshire County Council, by a consortium formed by Birmingham, Coventry and Solihull councils and by the owners of the nearby Chelmsley Wood shopping centre, Bryant Samuel Properties. The Secretary of State for the Environment called in the application for determination through a public inquiry, which ran from November 1973 to April 1974.

Town and City Properties instructed Frank (later Sir Frank) Layfield QC, probably the leading planning barrister of the era, and marshalled a formidable team of expert witnesses in support of the proposal. The Birmingham-Coventry-Solihull consortium responded by instructing Lionel Read QC, a regular sparring partner of Layfield, and engaged a team of consultants comparable to that fielded by the applicants.

In some respects the inquiry, along with much of the ongoing conflict over out-of-centre retailing, could be interpreted as a battle, fought by proxy, between two conflicting property interests. On the one side landed capital, represented by Lord Aylesford, was allied with the 'new' property development capital in the shape of Town and City Properties. On the other side established town centre property interests were in alliance with the local authorities, which were concerned to protect the vitality and viability of their town centres and the stake of their local communities, including sizeable financial investments therein. Consistent with this interpretation, the urban authorities' consortium appointed as their principal retailing witness Edward Erdman and Co., London based chartered surveyors and property consultants, who had major developer and retailer clients in most of the main West Midlands town centres.

The case presented by Warwickshire County Council emphasised green belt and other physical planning issues, while that put by the consortium concentrated upon the economic implications of permitting the decline of city and town centres. On counsel's advice important social issues, such as the inability of the more disadvantaged groups to gain access to out-of-centre locations, were treated as subsidiary. The tactical wisdom of this course of action was borne out in the inspector's recommendation, and consequent ministerial decision, that the application be refused. As Michael Law has already said, most weight in the decision was placed on green belt considerations, particularly intrusion into the vulnerable 'Meriden Gap' between Birmingham and Coventry. Issues of retail impact were also cited, in particular the impact on Solihull town centre, where there had been recent investment in the Mell Square development, and on Chelmsley Wood. Had the Stonebridge application been approved, it is unlikely that it would in practice have been implemented. By the time the decision was announced in 1975, the downturn in the economic climate was such that funding for the full project would almost certainly not have been forthcoming. The Stonebridge decision very much influenced the climate in which the structure plan for the new county of West Midlands was prepared.

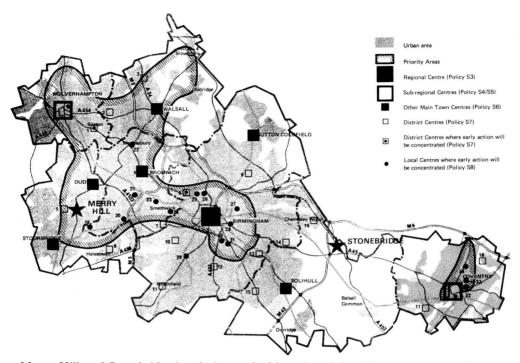

Merry Hill and Stonebridge in relation to the hierarchy of shopping centres proposed in the West Midlands County Structure Plan.

The Metropolitan County Structure Plan

The West Midlands County came into existence on 1st April 1974. Its population of around 2.75 million (some 54% of the region's total) made it the largest of the six new metropolitan counties nationally. The crucial stage in the preparation of a structure plan for the new county extended from the issuing of a preliminary statement in August 1976 to the publication of the final plan in October 1980. The policies for shopping and town centres accorded well with the key theme of 'urban regeneration', which underpinned the plan. The potential threat to town centres from out-of-town shopping was acknowledged and the policy formula adopted was one which focused on reinforcing the role of the established centres in such a way that out-of-centre shopping simply was not needed. These policies were infused with a strong element of 'market realism' as a result of the County Council using consultants Edward Erdman and Co., together with their associated planning advisors John Trott and Son, who had acted for the urban consortium over Stonebridge. Discussions with the Department of the Environment had established that the use of such consultants would help in legitimising policies in this highly sensitive area. Their appointment was endorsed by both main political parties within the County Council – at a time of change in political control – it being seen as crucial to 'saving the town centres from the perceived threat of the superstore revolution'.

The essence of Erdman's approach was to provide opportunities for in-centre development and to create the conditions for this investment by removing what they saw as a surplus of outmoded shopping in the county. Local councils were seen as playing a key role in this process: "The fundamental problem facing the county....is a surplus of shops, many of which occupy outmoded premises in twilight locations. These marginally profitable shops, which are individually weak but collectively account for a significant proportion of turnover, have a debilitating effect upon the centres in which they are located and discourage improvement therein....The consultants therefore consider that the primary aim of future shopping policy should be to reduce substantially the amount of fringe shopping throughout the county and to encourage qualitative improvement by selective redevelopment, particularly in district centres."

One might perhaps have questioned whether a majority of shoppers, particularly the poorer and less mobile, would have identified 'the fundamental problem' as too many shops – a lot of which should be swept away to support 'selective redevelopment'. Clearly, without implying any cynicism on the part of the consultants, this was an approach which accorded with the interests of their established clients, the multiple retailers and development companies. However, it was also potentially appealing to the planners, who were concerned about the environmental effects of rundown and vacant shops strung out along radial roads in inner city areas and who were also anxious to see development taking place.

The consultants recommended that superstores should be strictly limited in number and size, steered towards district centres where rents were high enough to justify other retail development and generally resisted in freestanding locations. However in the cause of legitimacy – recognising that the Department of the Environment would wish to see some kind of balance between retail interests – they also recommended that two out-of-centre hypermarkets should be permitted, one 'in the Greater Coventry area' and the other in the 'southern part of the Birmingham conurbation' – *i.e.* in Solihull. These were omitted from the final structure plan following representations from Coventry and Solihull councils. Otherwise, the policies included in the draft structure plan followed closely the consultants' recommendations. Other policies in the plan, including those on the location of office development and the provision of transport infrastructure, were consistent with their defined hierarchy of regional, sub-regional, main town and district centres (see illustration).

Looking Forward

How effective was the planning framework for shopping and town centres established during the 1970s – through the rejection of the Stonebridge proposal and in the policies of the new county structure plan – in dealing with the pressures to which it was exposed? To answer this question we need to look forward briefly into the 1980s.

The overriding emphasis was on retaining and promoting shopping investment in town centres. Conversely, other than in very narrowly defined circumstances, out-of-centre pressures were to be resisted. The structure plan sought to guide the demand for food superstores into centres, particularly district centres, where they would be widely accessible and where the heavy 'footfall' which they encourage would act as a catalyst for further investment. Control policies, combined with some direct action by the district councils in providing sites, yielded considerable success for this approach. A review in 1986 found that, of 31 large foodstores opened in the metropolitan county since 1977 (when the policies had begun to bite), 21 had been located in centres, including 10 in district centres. This was certainly a much higher proportion than would have been the case had things been left entirely to the 'market'. Furthermore, several of the developments which had taken place out-of-centre – the Minworth hyper-market for instance – had been approved before the policies were in place.

The first out-of-town 'hypermarket', approved at Minworth near Sutton Coldfield in 1975, catered primarily for the once-a-week shopping trip by car.

A similar, although perhaps less dramatic, impact was achieved on the location of 'retail warehouses'. The plan recognised that in certain exceptional circumstances stores selling bulky builders merchants and DIY goods or self-assembly furniture might be located out-of-centre. However, in general, retail warehouses would be confined to in-centre locations, with a particular emphasis on locations adjoining declining local centres where the new stores could contribute to regeneration. It is evident that in the early years of the policy a considerable number of retail warehouses were located in or on the edge of centres.

The policies which the county council's consultants had envisaged as supporting investment in centres – *i.e.* the removal of 'fringe shopping' – were never really effective partly due to a lack of resources, powers and 'political will' on the part of the local authorities. More importantly, an entirely different policy approach, with its source outside the planning system, came to be pursued. Under the Urban Programme, public sector resources were increasingly directed at upgrading and improving the viability of just the kind of shops which it had been envisaged would be 'removed'.

Over the 1980s as a whole, structure plan policies came to have diminishing effectiveness in steering the location of retail development. This was due to fundamental changes in the national policy climate within which the local policies were being applied. Three main aspects of these changes can be identified.

Firstly, the capacity to apply strategic policies at a sub-regional level was systematically eroded. The Local Government and Planning Act of 1980 removed the direct development control powers of the metropolitan county councils. Henceforth, they could no longer determine applications of strategic significance themselves and could only 'recommend' a decision to the district council concerned. Whilst the district councils shared a desire to protect town centres, they tended to take a more opportunistic view of out-of-centre development. The abolition of the metropolitan county in 1986 further reduced the capacity to apply a strategic view across the conurbation and provided additional opportunities for inter-district competition.

Secondly, a number of special planning regimes were established where local authorities' planning powers were reduced or removed, most notably enterprise zones and urban development corporations, both of which had an impact in the West Midlands. As Colin Wood describes later, the Dudley Enterprise Zone, established in two stages in 1981 and 1984, paved the way for what was the biggest departure from planning policies of all, the establishment of the Merry Hill out-of-town shopping centre. Incrementally by 1990, this produced on the west side of Birmingham a development of similar scale to that which had been rejected to the east, at Stonebridge, fifteen years earlier. Whatever the merits or otherwise of Merry Hill, it is undeniable that a major centre, with a retail turnover second only to that of Birmingham, emerged in a location where it was not 'planned' and where the implications for other town centres and supporting infrastructure, particularly access by public transport, were not taken into account.

The establishment of urban development corporations had similar, if less dramatic, effects. The Black Country Development Corporation, established in 1987, had a simple brief to secure regeneration with only limited regard for local development plan policies. As a result, there was clearly a temptation to secure short-term results and to achieve development at any price, in particular through facilitating a high-value end use such as retail in what were generally out-of-centre locations.

Thirdly, where local authorities did retain planning control, Government guidance pushed them towards a greater willingness to accept out-of-centre development. The parliamentary statement issued by the Secretary of State in 1985, subsequently enshrined in *Planning Policy Guidance Note 6* (DoE, 1988), established that out-of-centre retail development was acceptable unless it was demonstrated that it would be damaging to the vitality and viability of a particular town centre *'as a whole'*. This was a notoriously difficult test to meet, particularly in the context of the cumulative effects of a number of small developments.

Notwithstanding these major reverses, the policies established in the West Midlands in the 1970s did, when confronted with the full flowering of the superstore revolution, retail parks and out-of-town shopping centres, achieve a good deal in securing at least a balance between town centre and out-of-centre development. Furthermore, the 1990s have seen the re-emergence of the principles on which the policies were based. A new national agenda of 'sustainable development' and combating 'social exclusion' has emerged. This has led to the establishment in national and regional guidance of the 'sequential approach', under which town centres are treated as the normal location for major retail development and for other uses such as major leisure schemes, which attract a large number of trips. Only when there is an established need which cannot be met in or on the edge of a centre should out-of-centre locations be considered. In short, the kind of policies in respect of town centres which were developed and applied in the region in the 1970s are now very much back in favour.

Transport in the West Midlands

Ian Dickins

In the beginning...

The West Midlands established itself as the home of the British motor industry well before the Second World War and a commitment to the motor vehicle became a well-known part of the regional psyche. As a result, the traffic problems of the area are of long-standing. By the early 1930s the centre of Birmingham was experiencing serious traffic congestion and only the onset of war and petrol rationing prevented the central area from developing a severe case of gridlock. Other towns around the region were beginning to experience their own problems, particularly if they were fortunate (or unfortunate) enough to lie along one the major roads, such as the A5, A38, A45 or A34, which bisect the region.

The post-war Government was mainly concerned to improve national road communications and in the late 1940s drew up a plan for a network of 'motor roads' based on American practice. The Special Roads Act, passed in 1949, allowed roads to be built with no frontage access and with certain classes of vehicle excluded. The West Midlands figured prominently in this scheme, with the Birmingham conurbation at the centre of the network.

Work commenced during the 1950s and the first section of the M1/M45 (London to Coventry) motorway was opened in 1959. At the same time the region's local authorities began to draw up and implement their own schemes. Birmingham's were especially ambitious: the Inner Ring Road would relieve congestion in the city centre and would be linked to M6 via the Aston Expressway. In addition, a number of other radials were to be widened (many of these proposals actually dated back as far as 1918!). Birmingham was determined that its position as the motor capital of Britain would be maintained.

The core of the national motorway network was firmly established during the 1960s: after the M1 came the M5 and M6, the main sections of which were opened in the mid-1960s, and plans were well in hand to close the gaps between these two roads and the M1. The Birmingham Evening Mail of June 1st. 1965 proudly announced a "Spectacular £100m Project for the Midlands." The paper reported that "a spectacular 80ft high, eight level motorway junction is to be built at Gravelly Hill (which will be) a key feature of plans announced today for 64 miles of Midland motorways, estimated to cost more than £100,000,000". Christened the Midlands Links Motorways, the final sections were opened in 1972.

'Spaghetti Junction' at Gravelly Hill, Birmingham – an eight level motorway junction on M6/A38 at the heart of the Midlands Links motorway system completed in 1972.

Within the region's towns a new transport system was also evolving. Birmingham's trams ceased to run in 1953 and trolley-buses followed a decade later. The region's extensive network of canals ceased to be used for freight and were on their way to becoming an invaluable recreational resource. Birmingham's Inner Ring Road and other highway improvements were well in hand. For example, the Birchfield underpass, opened in 1962, was the first two-level urban junction outside London. In 1964 the conurbation local authorities commissioned consulting engineers Freeman Fox to carry out the West Midlands Transportation Study, which made large-scale proposals for future road building to cope with the expected increases in traffic. This was in response to a worsening traffic situation: for example by the end of the 1960s, traffic speeds in Wolverhampton town centre varied from 7.5mph to 13mph (Wolverhampton Structure Plan Report of Survey, 1973, p4-3). This was at a time when the total number of motor vehicles in Britain was 13 million, or about half what it is today.

Birmingham's Inner Ring Road tightly constrained the city centre – the design stems from the 'predict and provide' approach to car usage in the 1950s and 1960s.

During the 1960s also, the climate of professional opinion turned towards regarding transport as an integrated activity, rather than as a series of disconnected functions – buses, trains, roads etc. The report *Traffic in Towns* (Buchanan Report, 1963), commissioned by the Government, set the scene. Throughout the rest of the decade the Government leant on local authorities to study and deal with their transport and traffic problems and set out to reform the national context within which they operated. A series of white papers in the mid-1960s led to the Transport Act 1968, whose main impact in the West Midlands was to set up the West Midlands Passenger Transport Authority (PTA). This brought together under one ownership all the various conurbation bus fleets, thus allowing co-ordinated public transport planning at conurbation level. However, the PTA had no responsibility outside the conurbation and no responsibility for highway planning, which remained with the local authorities.

Thus, by 1970, the various elements of transport policy were in place and the scene was set for tackling the ever-worsening traffic position through the modernisation of policy.

The Political Climate

Right up until the late 1960s, the transport problem had been seen in very simple terms. If there were too many vehicles chasing too little road space, then the amount of road space must be increased. This later became expressed in the term 'predict and provide'. All the plans of the 1950s and 1960s from the Birmingham Inner

It quickly became apparent that no amount of road space would solve the problems of congestion.

Ring Road to the Freeman Fox report were based on this approach. However, as the numbers of cars grew and the consequences of catering for them became more and more apparent, the climate of opinion began to change, firstly among some politicians and sections of the public and later among professionals. The 'predict and provide' approach was seen as too biased towards car users and the cause of excessive environmental damage. Highways schemes became the centre of controversy. Whereas the public inquiries into the M1, M5 and M6 had lasted a matter of days, the 1970s proposals to build the M42 through Worcestershire and the M40 through Oxfordshire and Warwickshire were fiercely resisted. The section of the M42 from the M5 at Bromsgrove to the A34 at Shirley was held up throughout the decade by protracted litigation as protesters sought unsuccessfully to have the road cancelled through the courts. The battle over the M40 was even longer, lasting 20 years from 1973. The highway disputes of the 1970s were the progenitors of Twyford Down, Newbury By-Pass and the Birmingham Northern Relief Road. While 'Swampy' and his friends were still in nappies, their forebears were opposing new motorways by disrupting public inquiries and obtaining court injunctions. Not all communities regarded motorways with such hostility, however. Telford campaigned for several years for the M54, as a connection to the national motorway network was felt to be essential to the new town's economic future.

When it came to urban transport, too, the climate of opinion was also changing. The idea that in the long term it would be impossible to cater for ultimate levels of car use, first put forward in *Traffic in Towns* in 1963, was revived. The first sign of this nationally was the publication of the House of Commons Expenditure Committee Report on Urban Transport Planning in 1972 whose main objective was that "national policy should be directed towards promoting public transport and discouraging the use of cars for the journey to work in city areas". This philosophy became known as the 'Balanced Approach' to transport planning – balanced between the needs of the car user and public transport passengers. Nowadays, we would call such an approach 'sustainable'.

Changes in Policy, 1970 to 1974

Some local authorities in the West Midlands, especially urban ones, began to take up these ideas and translate them into policy. The years 1972 and 1973 saw the first structure plans appear in the region and some reflected the balanced approach. The *Coventry Structure Plan* (Coventry City Council, 1973, p44) stated that it was "not acceptable on either financial or environmental grounds to make full provision for the unrestricted use of the private car in the peak period". It was proposed to cater for only 70% of desired peak period trips; parking restraint and public transport improvements would be necessary to avoid congestion. The *City of Birmingham Structure Plan* (1973) proposed increasing the density of development around railway stations, a policy worthy of 1990s PPG 13. One objective of the *Walsall Structure Plan* was "to reduce the effect of traffic on the non-travelling public and the environment" (Walsall CBC, 1973, p61).

Not all authorities were quite so enlightened: while nearly all expressed concern over the environmental impact of traffic, few went so far as to propose restrictions on the private car. Solihull, for example, proposed that "... the Council will seek to provide new roads and road improvements as appropriate to serve the needs of the anticipated population" (Solihull CBC, 1972, p47). However, the second edition of the West Midlands Transportation Study, published in 1972, recommended the establishment of an "integrated transportation system... (to) ...make available the best balance of public and private transport" (taken from Solihull Structure Plan, 1972, p46). The study also concluded that "it will not be practicable on economic grounds, nor indeed desirable upon environmental grounds, to construct a highway network within the conurbation capable of coping with all (car) trips" (taken from Solihull Structure Plan, 1972, p46).

On the whole, the urban local authorities paid at least lip service to the need to limit car use, while not actually introducing effective policies to achieve it. The general feeling was that the need for limitation was still some way off in the future. One area where some action *was* taken was the introduction of what is now known as Traffic Calming, but was then called Environmental Traffic Management. Government advice then was that action should be taken to deter traffic in General Improvement Areas (GIAs), *i.e.* inner city areas where environmental and housing improvements were proposed. Birmingham introduced some minor works in its earlier GIAs (*e.g.* Broadway GIA in Birchfield), but such ideas were still viewed with scepticism by professionals and were not taken very far. The concept was eventually put on ice for over a decade, to be revived again in the 1990s.

Overall, on the roads of the region, especially the urban ones, there was a continuing philosophy of 'keeping the traffic moving'. Any initiative that might have the effect of interfering with the free flow of traffic, such as traffic calming or bus lanes, was viewed with suspicion. The climate of professional opinion was still very pro-car, even if the climate of political opinion, at least in some quarters, was more open-minded. Transport was becoming politicised between the pro-public transport and the pro-car lobbies and the West Midlands was no exception to this.

In public transport policy too, the climate was changing. The WMPTA had responsibility for planning local rail services and ideas were floated to improve rail lines. As early as 1967 the West Midlands Transport Study team was considering upgrading the line between Wolverhampton and Knowle/Dorridge to rapid transit standards. In 1969 the Wolverhampton Engineering and Planning Department produced a memorandum entitled *A Telford and Black Country Transit System,* which was "concerned with the possibility of establishing a rapid transit system on existing British Rail lines between Shrewsbury and Birmingham (Snow Hill) and of such a facility becoming a major factor in the planning of both the conurbation and overspill locations" (Wolverhampton CBC, 1969). Thirty years later much of this route was finally opened as Midland Metro Line One.

Light rail proposals for the West Midlands were slow to come to fruition. Line 1 of the Midland Metro eventually opened between Birmingham, the Black Country and Wolverhampton in 1999 – 46 years after Birmingham's trams ceased to run.

In Birmingham, a 1971 study commissioned by the City Council and the Department of Environment proposed a major improvement to the rail route between Redditch and Sutton Coldfield, which paralleled a congested road corridor (A38). After looking at several road corridors, it concluded that the A38 showed most promise and recommended a modernisation to heavy rapid transit standards, including a tunnel under the city centre between Aston and Edgbaston Five Ways (Modern Railways, September 1971, pp 112-115). In the event, lack of funds reduced the scheme to a modest improvement in suburban diesel services on existing tracks; and as the Cross City Line this was finally implemented in 1976. The 1970s were punctuated with grandiose public transport infrastructure schemes, for example the Pic-Vic tunnel under Manchester city centre, for which funding was never realistically available. The only major survivor was the Tyne and Wear Metro. Many of the others, like the Cross City Line, were subsequently implemented in simpler forms, with the Pic-Vic Tunnel eventually becoming Manchester Metrolink.

Local Government Re-organisation 1974

As described previously, the Local Government Act 1972 comprehensively redrew the administrative map of England and Wales and ushered in a two-tier system of county and district councils. In the West Midlands conurbation, the

County Council took over not only the WMPTA, but also responsibility for highways. For the first time a single local authority was legally responsible for all transport matters and the new County Council was given powers and responsibilities under Section 203 to "develop... policies to promote a co-ordination of (public transport) operations" (Circular 5/73, para 3: DoE, 1973). In parallel with these new responsibilities, the Government also re-organised the funding of local transport by introducing the Transport Supplementary Grant, a block grant which covered most types of transport expenditure. To administer this, councils would prepare and submit to Central Government an annual document called the *Transport Policies and Programme*. These new TPPs were to be compatible with structure and local plans and "transport policies must have regard to the wider planning, environmental and social objectives that are the concern of structure and local plans" (Circular 104/73, para 13: DoE, 1973a).

Changes in Policy, 1975 to 1979

This new system led in the short term to two important developments, the publication of the first TPP and Structure Plan for the new West Midlands County in 1974 and 1975 respectively. The Structure Plan was essentially a reprint of the plans of the various constituent districts from the early 1970s, but the TPP was 'new policy' and included some quite radical ideas. Perhaps the most adventurous (and ill-fated) was the decision to maintain public transport fares at 1972 levels. The TPP stated that this "helped to arrest the previous trend of annual decline in bus patronage" (TPP, para 6.1: WMCC, 1975). The TPP also appeared to favour public transport in its proposal to "give priority in the allocation of uncommitted resources to the development of the public transport system" (para 4(b)). However, the overall bias was still in favour of road spending, with £70m to be spent on road maintenance and £60m on road building over the five-year plan period compared with only £20m on public transport development and a further £60m on bus and rail subsidies.

In the event, the steeply rising national trend in bus and rail subsidies produced inflation rates in excess of 20% and caused the Government to exert pressure on local authorities to rein in their proposals. In 1977 the West Midlands County Council gave in and abandoned its 'constant fares' policy, causing bus and rail fares to rise steeply overnight. The decline in patronage was resumed.

As referred to earlier, by the later 1970s the County Council was engaged in reviewing its Structure Plan and a draft was published in 1979. Following an Examination in Public the final plan was published in October 1980 (WMCC, 1980). This document marked the culmination of transport policy developments in the 1970s and contains some surprisingly modern-sounding, sustainable policies. The Government White Paper on *Transport Policy* (1977a) had given a lead by arguing that "Our policies for transport and energy must be linked also with our planning policies.... Transport must fit in with ... the patterns of where people live and work..." (para 33) and that "we should aim to decrease... the length and number of some of our journeys" (para 35). Structure Plan Policy Tp2 stated that "an effective public transport service will be provided giving reasonable access to jobs, shops, schools and recreation", while Tp6 proposed that "the design and layout of re-development or new development will ensure the maximum accessibility of homes, workplaces and shopping to public transport routes".

The Structure Plan also made proposals for the development of Birmingham Airport. During the 1970s the area around the airport had seen a significant improvement in its accessibility, with the opening first of the M6 and then the M42. The old airport terminal was adjacent to the A45, but the Structure Plan proposed to "develop a new passenger terminal and aircraft apron ... together with associated facilities" (Policy Tp13). The opening of the terminal in 1984, together with Birmingham International Station and the MAGLEV (magnetic levitation) link between them began the beginning of the major expansion of the airport which has marked the last 15 years. The new accessibility of this area, based on rail, road and air modes, has led to the creation of a growth pole to the east of the conurbation, with the National Exhibition Centre, Elmdon and Bickenhill Trading Estates and Birmingham Business Park all contributing.

Afterwards ...

Towards the end of the 1970s the climate of opinion on transport began to change again, away from comprehensive transport planning and towards the concept of making transport more responsive to the demands of the market. The heavy cost of bus and rail subsidies, together with an ever-rising level of car ownership and use and still-declining public transport patronage, led to the 'Balanced Approach' becoming discredited. The Conservative Party, in opposition, made much of the inefficiencies of subsidies and the need to concentrate on capital investment schemes which were deemed to provide greater value for money. After the 1979 General Election, it was given the opportunity to put its ideas into practice and national transport policy was set on a radically different direction for the next decade. In the region, the development of pro-public transport, traffic calming and demand management policies was put on hold during the 1980s. Transport Planning was even declared to be dead (by Secretary of State for Transport Paul Channon in 1987)!

And finally ...

The 1970s perfectly demonstrate the old saying *"plus ça change, plus c'est la même chose"*. In the 1970s we had the 'Balanced Approach', today we have the 'Package Approach'; then there was the West Midlands Transportation Study, re-created in the late 1980s as the Integrated Transport Studies for Birmingham, the Black Country, Solihull and Coventry; then we had environmental traffic management, today we have traffic calming; then we had policies to make land uses accessible to public transport, now we have PPG13 (DoE, 1994) and sustainable transport. It is the 1980s that can be seen as somewhat of a detour in transport policy terms.

The main difference between the situations then and now is that in the 1970s most public transport, road or rail, was operated by the public sector, whereas today it is virtually all privately owned. This makes the task of the policy-maker more complex and challenging – there are more players in the game. In addition, we have lost the overall responsibility provided by the West Midlands County Council (abolished in 1986). Since then, regional direction has been provided by the West Midlands Forum of Local Authorities, an informal grouping, and from the regional Government Office. It remains to be seen how the role of the new Regional Development Agencies develops: the next decade promises to be just as eventful as any since the 1950s.

Conserving our Built Heritage

Peter J Larkham with a contribution by Will Scott

The beginning

Urban conservation became a significant feature of town planning from 1967 with the passing of the Civic Amenities Act. This, for the first time, allowed protection to be given to whole urban areas. Conservation boomed during the 1970s as – with Government advice and persuasion – this new legislative provision was adopted and its powers increased. Throughout the 1980s and 1990s conservation remained high on the professional and public planning agendas, despite the stance of the Conservative Government (1979-1997), which was not wholly supportive.

The origins of conservation lie in the late nineteenth century, with Sir John Lubbock's series of Private Member's Bills seeking to extend protection to ancient monuments. Eventually, with the 1882 Act, some very limited protection was given to a very small number of monuments listed in a schedule – hence 'scheduled ancient monuments'. These were largely prehistoric, although as the legislation became amended, some key mediaeval castles and similar monuments were added. The range of concern for this form of conservation is locally shown by the listings of moated sites and similar monuments in the *Victoria County History* volumes for each county.

Nationally, in the inter-war period, a very small number of Acts for key places such as Bath established the principle of detailed development control to retain the character and appearance of historic areas; while the provisions for ancient monuments gradually expanded. Wartime damage prompted the listing of historically and architecturally important individual buildings and this became a statutory duty in the 1947 Act. But the tremendous period of post-war comprehensive clearance and rebuilding, even in little-damaged towns (for example, see Tony Aldous' critical commentary in *Goodbye Britain?*, 1975) led to the rise of a pro-conservation movement. "During the sixties conservation became a powerful lobby as more and more people began to realise the need to retain a balance between old and new buildings in our cities, towns and villages" (P. Burley, *Architecture West Midlands* issue 26, 1976). Duncan Sandys MP founded the Civic Trust in 1957 and also promoted the Civic Amenities Bill, which became law in 1967. His final definition of a 'conservation area' was "an area of special architectural or historic interest, the character or appearance of which it is desirable to preserve or enhance." This definition persists today. A national re-survey of listed buildings was undertaken in the 1980s and English Heritage is now investigating specific building types, particularly of post-war buildings.

"It is more than a question of aesthetics, conservation touches our basic values. Ever since the war, Britain has been going through a difficult period of readjustment. To some we seem to have lost our sense of purpose, our sense of mission. There never was a time when we more needed to strengthen our faith in ourselves. Pride in the past is the surest foundation for confidence in the future. We must jealously guard our roots in history. We must call a halt to the steady, day by day erosion of the features which give Britain her distinctive quality".
Duncan Sandys, Civic Trust Conference, 1971.

The West Midlands

West Midlands local authorities were quick to jump upon the conservation area bandwagon. By 1974 there were 254 designated areas in the region (of 3,165 in Britain). Worcestershire had 32 areas by 1971 and had appointed four architects to survey existing historic towns "and had increased its planning staff to deal with the many problems that occur in such an operation." In fact, this extended the County Council's surveys of seven historic towns undertaken in 1966, which facilitated early designations and led to a range of related projects – planting, paving, painting, road sign reduction, removal of overhead wires and so on (G. Gooderham *Architecture West Midlands* issue 5, 1971). This was very representative of the national conservation concerns at the time, and influenced by the Civic Trust scheme in Magdalen Street, Norwich. In the West Midlands County, 14 designations were made in 1969 alone. For the seven constituent boroughs there was then another peak in 1972, following the 1971 Act, then a gap while desks were cleared before the 1974 local government reorganisation. Another peak in 1975-6 followed the 1974 Town and Country Amenities Act, which extended control over demolition to *any* building within a conservation area. Indeed, in Birmingham alone 15 designations were made between 1969 and 1979 and by 1983 there were 77 designations in the seven metropolitan authorities. Designation across the region has continued since, although, as the 'obvious' designations of the mediaeval and Georgian town centres had already been made, the character of designations has changed.

The most common type of conservation area nationally is the rural village and there are plenty of these in the region. In particular, virtually every village in the large district of Stratford-on-Avon is designated, giving some 70 villages plus the mediaeval town core. In the Midlands, industrial conservation was quickly recognised as important too. Key designations included Mushroom Green (Dudley) and the watchmakers' housing at Chapelfields, Coventry. Canals were also often designated, as were individual features such as Coventry's London Road cemetery. But the most frequent designation in the 1990s is the suburb. Wolverhampton had made some early suburban designations, for example in Tettenhall, but these were principally the large Victorian and Edwardian villa suburbs. Birmingham led the way with what was probably the country's first designation of a speculative inter-war semi-detached estate, at School Road, Hall Green in 1988. This led to some critical comment and a feature in *The Times*. The Council commented that this particular area was 'of special interest' as it had, unusually, remained so untouched by later alterations and extensions and its original character was worthy of retention. This was at a time when there was high-pressure selling of uPVC double-glazing, about which both English Heritage and the English Historic Towns Forum campaigned. In fact, this type of designation is now quite common nationally, and the London Borough of Brent has about eight such areas. Interestingly, Birmingham innovated a decade later with its designation of the Austin village at Longbridge, the estate of pre-fabricated cedar bungalows imported from North America during the First World War for Austin workers.

There have been similar changes in emphasis with the listing of buildings. Nationally, there was a clear shift in emphasis from mediaeval and Georgian towards an acceptance of Victorian, typified by the listing of a range of Victorian office buildings (for example Lichfield Street, Wolverhampton, and the old post office, Victoria Square, Birmingham). In the mid to late 1980s there was some acceptance of early twentieth century listings and, eventually, of a small number of key post-war buildings. Birmingham has finally succeeded in listing the last coherent original group of 1940s 'pre-fab' bungalows – while, in contrast, small estates of these were completely rebuilt in Wolverhampton. Both Wolverhampton and Birmingham have come to terms with their industrial past in seeking to identify and protect examples of early factories, including those serving the former's car industry and the latter's gun and jewellery industries.

Enhancement Schemes

Not only were designations important, but so was the quality of design for enhancement schemes, individual properties and new redevelopments. An early scheme for shop refurbishment, including an element of mixed use, in Shrewsbury was described by the Planning Officer, H Berry, as "excellent examples of what can be done with listed buildings, internally and externally, with sympathetic treatment to retain and enhance the character of buildings, the street and the historic core generally ... a high standard of shop-front has been created, which has set a standard in the town above the present desire for national uniformity" (*Architecture West Midlands* issue 26, 1976). In Evesham, a replacement for a listed ruinous inn received an RIBA Award in 1976: it was said to be "desirable to design the building in the local vernacular manner and to preserve as far as possible the scale and feeling of the building which it replaced" (*Architecture West Midlands* issue 27, 1976). The continuing pressure for intensive city-centre use, particularly in the 1980s, led to schemes proposing the demolition of all but the facades of (sometimes even listed) buildings, with new structures behind them. This 'facadism' may have little visual impact on the street scene, although some examples, such as at Colmore Row, Birmingham, can be overpowering and inappropriate, but it can be detrimental to the architectural design and historic qualities of the individual building and current guidance advises against it.

The restoration of Malt Mill Lane, Alcester, Warwickshire received a Civic Trust Heritage Year Award in 1975.

European Architectural Heritage Year 1975 (EAHY) was a high-profile event both for the profession and the public. Two Midlands projects received Civic Trust Heritage Year Awards and were also included in the 16 schemes felt to be 'of exceptional merit'. These were Chesterton Windmill and Malt Mill Lane, Alcester, both in Warwickshire (*Architecture West Midlands* issue 23, 1976).

Sadly, however, there have been failures. A high profile one was the derelict, but listed, Union Mill in Wolverhampton's newly-designated Industrial Conservation Area, which caught fire and was badly damaged in the early 1980s. The then planning authority for the area, the Black Country Development Corporation, immediately proceeded to demolished the remnants, despite protests from the Civic Society and prominent coverage in *The Guardian*. This was contrary to standard procedures and is indicative of a contemporary pro-development stance, supported at the highest levels in Government, which did not always benefit conservation aims. Wolverhampton still has problem derelict listed buildings, including the Molineux Hotel (Grade II* Listed) and Low Level Station, where lie *in situ* the last few feet of Brunel's broad gauge line. Other authorities have more rural concerns, with changes in agricultural subsidy and production leading to the problem of redundant buildings, or insensitive proposals for their conversion to housing or other revenue-generating uses. There have also been cases of inertia, as Remo Granelli argued was true of Birmingham in the early 1970s (*Architecture West Midlands* issue 15, 1973). However, as conservation has risen ever higher in the professional and public awareness, it has become impossible simply to do nothing: instead, some very positive and constructive approaches have arisen.

In times of local authority cutback – of which there have been several in this half-century – it does seem that conservation activities and funding are the first to be cut. There are several cases of budget allocations dropping to zero; and of experienced conservation staff leaving and not being replaced. However, this has in some cases led to considerable ingenuity in using other budgets for conservation-related activity, including highways budgets for street furniture and pavement replacement and co-operating with the British Waterways Board for canalside works. Grant schemes, such as Town Schemes and, most recently, Conservation Area Partnerships (CAPs), have been successfully developed. Worcester has had one of the longest-running Town Schemes, lasting for some 25 years, and Leamington Spa was a leader in preparing CAPs proposals in the mid-1990s.

The Development of Conservation Policies

As part of this involvement, and the rising profile of conservation, authorities have been developing more explicit and innovative policy responses to conservation. Following publication of Ministry of Housing and Local Government (MHLG) Circular 61/68 in 1968, both Birmingham (1970) and Worcester (1972) were quick to set up Conservation Area Advisory Committees (CAAC). However, many early area designations were arguably crude and hasty – one county council, for example, apparently using "the office junior, a map and a pencil" to identify designations in the very early 1970s! Designation reports were brief, perhaps only a few lines in a planning committee minute book, and character assessments were rarely done. At the time this was acceptable – even pioneering – work, and responded positively to repeated Government pressures to identify areas and make designations. In the past decade, however, such character assessments have become routine and pre-designation surveys and consultations more detailed. This has been to the benefit of specific policy development, often as supplementary planning guidance to the development plan-led system promoted in the 1990s. More authorities have developed site-specific conservation planning briefs for problem sites and topic-specific design guidance, with shop-fronts, advertisements and house extensions in conservation areas being popular topics. Most notably two authorities, Hereford and Warwick (in Leamington Spa) worked closely with English Heritage and the consultants Rock Townsend in developing an innovative and detailed approach to conservation context, planning policy and design, in two documents published in 1990.

Outside the conurbation, the region's smaller market towns have drawn benefits from conservation, often with a range of enhancement schemes for commercial centres which frequently involved pedestrianisation and repaving, *e.g.* High Street, Worcester and High Street, Hereford (1972-74). Cleaning and painting schemes, as pioneered by the Civic Trust in Magdalen Street, Norwich, were also promoted. Perhaps this had something to do with the arrival at the West Midlands County Council of Alfie Wood, who had been instrumental in the Norwich schemes and who became influential as advisor to a range of conservation bodies including English Heritage. However, smaller market towns, such as Ludlow, have also suffered a range of problems. Pressures have included, firstly, the need to cater for the growing tourist trade. This involved creating more surface car-parks within very easy walking distance of the historic cores and converting properties to tourist-related income-generating uses, such as town houses becoming antiques retailing shops. Secondly, there are problems of rural retailing and the successive 'waves' of retail innovations: small local and specialist shops have closed, and there has been pressure for much larger units, often unsympathetic in size, position and style to the area's character. Thirdly, the problem of providing affordable housing, particularly in rural low-employment areas, has led to the building of some visually unsuitable and extremely small units on 'backland' sites within historic cores. Responses to these broader planning issues have, of necessity, led to changes in the 'character and appearance' of these smaller and vulnerable historic towns.

Among the region's successes have been some high-profile and award-winning refurbishments, including Birmingham's Curzon Street Station, Warndon Court Farmhouse, Worcester (RTPI West Midlands Branch Commendation, 1993), and the EAHY awards already mentioned. Birmingham's contribution to EAHY was to refurbish houses in Ryland Road and Lee Crescent, Edgbaston,

High Street, Worcester, in 1966.

High Street, Worcester, in 1980 after refurbishment to create a pleasant environment for pedestrians.

which were the first of many 'envelope' schemes in the city. These were schemes whereby the local authorities improved homes externally, leaving residents to make internal decorative improvements. As Graham Shaylor later explains, Birmingham pioneered such schemes. The role of open air museums must also be recognised. The West Midlands is fortunate in having four which have been invaluable in rescuing threatened rural and industrial buildings, rebuilding them and displaying them with a wide range of public and interpretative events. These are the Avoncroft Museum of Buildings (Bromsgrove), the Black Country Museum (Dudley) and Blist's Hill and the Ironbridge Gorge at Telford, the latter being one of the UK's few World Heritage Sites.

A relatively recent conservation concern has been archaeology. This was brought under planning control by the 1979 Ancient Monuments and Archaeological Areas Act and, although only five Archaeological Areas have been designated, authorities and developers are now much more aware of the importance of pre-development investigation and excavation. High profile cases, such as the Rose Theatre (London), and programmes, such as *Time Team*, have helped! Thus some excavations have been laid out for public display, as with a site in Corve Street, Ludlow, while a major dig in advance of the Crowngate Centre, Worcester, has considerably aided knowledge of how the mediaeval town developed.

The Future of Conservation

Sustainability has become the most significant current concern in planning. It remains to be seen how this will impact upon conservation, although concepts such as the 'compact city' and proposed policies for significantly higher development densities may have fundamental consequences for the growing number of low- and medium-density suburban conservation areas! Birmingham's third-generation conservation strategy discussion document (Birmingham City Council, 1998) does usefully and explicitly bring together issues such as regeneration and sustainability, discussing how conservation can play an integral part. English Heritage has introduced a new funding scheme, the Heritage Economic Regeneration Scheme, which targets areas experiencing multiple deprivation, and is "directly relevant to the Government's priorities by demonstrating the vital role that conservation-led change has to play in contributing to the social and economic regeneration of cities and the creation of safe and sustainable communities."

The history of conservation in the region has examples of notable successes and, sadly, some problems and failures. We should use these constructively, to learn lessons for the future. A key lesson, building upon the sustainability issue, is the major contribution that sensitive conservation can make to establishing character, identity and a 'people-friendly' aspect in the necessary processes of urban regeneration. A fully informed basis for progress and redevelopment is not only possible, but essential, if our urban areas are not to decline and our rural districts to stagnate. The challenge for the Urban Task Force, and for all of us, is to build upon tradition without destroying it.

The Jewellery Quarter, Birmingham, is an example of conservation being a catalyst for the economic revival of an area and its buildings.

Land Reclamation in Stoke-on-Trent – Making a Difference

John Cornell and Fiona Colville

Synopsis

By the 1970s the West Midlands was at the forefront of pioneering the reclamation of derelict and degraded land. In the Black Country heart of the metropolitan area the county and district councils were endeavouring to find means and techniques to restore mined, quarried and contaminated sites. Often these were a legacy from Victorian times and new uses were sought, whether for housing, employment, retailing or leisure. However, nowhere in the region are reclamation activities better exemplified than in the experience and achievements accomplished in Stoke-on-Trent.

Land reclamation in Stoke-on-Trent has underpinned the transformation of the local economy and landscape for the last thirty years. The process began in earnest in the late 1960s, brought into sharp focus by the disaster at Aberfan, and still forms a crucial element of the continued regeneration of the city. Nationally it was one of the first Councils in the country to rise to the complex challenge of land reclamation and it has achieved tremendous results. The changes in the funding regime for land reclamation over the past 30 years have brought their own challenges, but the City Council has risen to the occasion and is now in the final stages of reclaiming one of the biggest areas of open space in the West Midlands at Berryhill Fields.

Stoke-on-Trent was built on coal mining and pottery manufacture and, by reclaiming the negative legacy of these industries, the city has regenerated itself. In 1968 the city possessed more derelict land than any other local authority in the country, with 10% of its total area affected. Between 1945 and 1961 over 300 hectares (750 acres) were reclaimed, but it was in the late 1960s that the programme of reclamation really began to achieve dramatic results.

Attracting new resources is a key activity, and this is of particular importance for land reclamation. The City Council has never viewed land reclamation in isolation, but rather as integral to the regeneration process. In the 1970s it was the former Derelict Land Grant which provided the funding for the reclamation of the many former colliery sites. Through the 1980s and 1990s matching Government and European funding, in partnership with resources from the private sector, was and still is the key to the successful regeneration schemes.

Background

In 1970 the city was declared a Derelict Land Clearance Area, due in part to its determination to tackle some of its most severe areas of underground dereliction together with its rapidly growing expertise. Some 3,000 pit shafts were known to exist in 1958. By taking a long-term strategic approach to reclaiming land, by having stated and publicly supported objectives, the City Council has subsequently managed the reclamation of over 1,600 hectares (4,000 acres). In the first five years of the programme the public open space provision in the city was doubled, but of equal and now greater importance has been the reclamation of land for jobs and houses. Interspersed throughout the land reclamation programme were many smaller, but equally important, schemes in the heart of local communities. These projects were the backbone of the programme.

Looking back, it is sometimes hard for newcomers to the city to realise and appreciate how degraded the landscape of Stoke-on-Trent actually was in the 1960s. But to those people who had grown up with that landscape and who had worked in the 'pits and pots', the landscape was a familiar friend. When the reclamation began there was many a dissenting local voice. Now the whole city is reaping the benefits of the foresight of the planners, engineers, landscape architects and politicians who looked into the future and saw how reclamation could transform, revive and revitalise Stoke-on-Trent.

Historically, the first major scheme was undertaken in the 1890s with the reclamation of Hanley Park. Some 20 hectares (50 acres) were reclaimed from land damaged by pit shafts, spoil heaps and pottery waste. The scheme gained great public support and remains a popular local resource. The aim of the scheme was to increase access to open space for the people living in the densely populated and polluted Victorian city. This objective is still mirrored in the objectives of today's land reclamation programme.

At the same time as the reclamation programme was being developed, the city embarked on a programme of urban renewal and clearance. The two processes worked together to improve the image of Stoke-on-Trent, not only for potential investors, but equally importantly for the local residents. The effect of the Clean Air Acts on the environment of Stoke-on-Trent was probably greater than on any other city in the country. The juxtaposition of industry and housing meant that reclamation had a direct and substantial impact on every resident in the city.

The challenge was for the city to move on from being 'Smokey Stoke' and to be within reach of, and remain at, the vanguard of regeneration in the West Midlands. This was achieved in the mid-1980s with the reclamation and subsequent development of the National Garden Festival site. The closure of part of the Shelton Steelworks left a landscape ravaged by industry in the heart of the city centre and it provided a once in a lifetime opportunity to prove exactly what could be achieved through master planning, vision and dedication. At the time it was the largest reclamation scheme in the West Midlands, attracting over £10m in Government grant. It was the success of this project which proved that the City could be successful on the national stage and it was a turning point not only for the reclamation programme, but also for the whole regeneration process. Whilst 2,000 jobs were lost at the Shelton Steel Works in the early 1980s, 3,000 have been created on the most successful post Garden Festival site in the country.

The first programme of reclamation

The fabric of the city was, and still is, interspersed with areas of heavy industry sitting directly alongside terraced housing; literally in the very heart of local communities. This meant that when these industries closed down vast areas of derelict land made a very direct impact on the lives of the local population.

The Local Government Act of 1966 provided grant aid towards derelict land reclamation costs and the City Council embarked upon a crash programme of reclamation to tackle some of the very worst problems it was facing. This was helped by new procedures, which enabled speedy reclamation. The sheer scale of derelict land in the 1960s and the high levels of community support meant that the programme could make an instant impact. Today Stoke has more reclaimed derelict land per head of the population than any other city in Britain. The outward flow of population migration that was reaching a peak in the late 1960s was a major cause for concern at a time when the existing economic base was contracting. The land reclamation programme was recognised as being one of the key mechanisms in stemming this flow, by making substantial improvements to the environment and the quality of life and aiding inward investment. Some of the first land reclamation schemes included:

Central Forest Park, Hanley, before …

… … and after reclamation.

Central Forest Park

Hanley Deep Pit was a prime example of the juxtaposition of heavy industry and terraced housing. Coal mining on the site ceased in 1961, leaving over 50 hectares (125 acres) of derelict land comprising conical black colliery spoil heaps, gaping marl holes, redundant colliery buildings and machinery, rubble and mine shafts. Hanley Deep Pit was chosen as a priority area for reclamation because it is strategically located in the heart of the city; the site had a negative impact on the surrounding area due to the sheer scale of the colliery spoil tips; it offered the potential for an immediate visual improvement; the owner was willing to co-operate and release land for the project, which is always a key consideration; and a high impact, low cost scheme could make a huge impression.

The forest park concept was inspired by the topography of the site, maximising the potential offered by the massive spoil heaps which towered over surrounding communities, and stabilising the site through planting. The original idea was to establish a semi-natural landscape of wooded slopes, grassed areas and wild-flower meadows. There were many technical difficulties to be overcome, namely how to establish vegetation on inert material, create a sustainable but low cost scheme to meet grant funding requirements and develop a varied and interesting landscape.

The reclamation scheme tackled a wide variety of problems, none of which was unique within the city. There were unstable slopes, pit shafts to locate and cap, coal washings to excavate and treat, toxic substances to neutralise and landforms to reshape. Some 45,000 trees were planted and interspersed with wildflowers and a variety of indigenous grasses. The scheme won first prize in the national Conservation Awards Scheme in 1971. Local folklore includes the tale that on the day the Queen came to officially open the site all the water drained from the lake shortly after she left. The water had drained back into the mine workings under the site. Local people are now fiercely defensive of the site, setting up action committees every time someone suggests building on their greenspace.

Westport Lake

Reclamation began in 1970 and, because of a lack of water-based facilities in the city, this rapidly became one of the most popular of the land reclamation schemes. The aim was to carry out effective, but simple, reclamation treatment, reinforcing existing uses of the site and protecting and enhancing the nature conservation value of the wetland and marshy areas surrounding the lake. The technical difficulties encountered included; water-logging, which made the site impossible to walk on, let alone use heavy machinery; a tar pit which would not drain and therefore had to be treated *in situ* and compacted with pottery waste; and toxic waste which was capped with marsh dredgings and stabilised with planting. Managing the pollution was one of the major problems and bathing, a popular summer pastime in every pond, pool and canal, was banned. In spite of this the scheme remains a popular resource today, especially with its strategic canal side location. It won a Civic Trust award in 1972 and is now a cornerstone of the latest canal regeneration project, which has attracted resources from Europe, Advantage West Midlands and the private sector.

The Loopline Greenway

One of the most notable schemes in the 1970s was the Loopline Greenway. This project was the reclamation of the many mineral railway lines – the Potteries loop line – which linked the areas of heavy industry; the mines, the steel works and the pottery factories with the residential areas. These redundant railway lines provided an ideal opportunity to create walkways, stretching the length and breadth of the city, which were free of cars. Work began in the late 1960s and was the most important single factor in binding the City's reclamation programme into a cohesive whole, by providing local access into the major reclamation schemes. The problems faced were enormous; decaying buildings, bridges, tunnels and embankments to stabilise and extensive areas of rubbish. Maintaining and emphasising the identity of the Loopline was of paramount importance. This was achieved by using railway artefacts as landmark features which may be regarded by some as *passé* in the 1990s, but are a timely reminder of the importance of this railway to the growth and development of the city. The greenways are now a popular cycle network as they provide a safe system of cycleways and are part of the national Sustrans network.

The Whitfield Valley

This scheme covers 92 hectares (227 acres) and links the former Chatterley Whitfield colliery, now a scheduled ancient monument, to Ford Green Hall, a Grade 2 timber framed listed building. The reclamation scheme on the colliery spoil mound required the removal of two million tonnes of material, reducing the cone in height by more than 70 metres (230 ft.). Chatterley Whitfield was the first colliery in the country to produce one million tonnes of coal in a year and the waste from this high level of production was tipped on the mound. The spoil heap remains impressive today, dominating the landscape of the north of the city and affording excellent views of the city and the north Staffordshire countryside. The site is considered to be the finest surviving example of a 19th Century colliery complex in the country and its regeneration is a top priority for English Heritage.

Berryhill Colliery and Berryhill Fields

The reclamation of land at Berryhill colliery in the early 1970s provided a rare opportunity to fill a marl hole with material from an adjacent colliery shale tip on site and create land for development. This was more than simply pushing the heap into the hole! The tip was 60 metres (200 ft.) high and the hole had a capacity of 1.7 million m³ (2.25 million cubic yards). The technical problems encountered included managing and controlling the dust, a major health and safety issue, and compacting the loosely deposited colliery shale as it went into the marl hole to provide suitable land for development. Another technical problem was that the colliery mound was on fire, which meant that the tyres on the earth-moving equipment would catch fire unless they moved quickly!

Berryhill Fields is almost 60 hectares (150 acres) in size, yet represents less than half of the overall site. In 1996 resources were attracted from English Partnerships and the Millennium Commission's 'Changing Places' programme. Groundwork Stoke-on-Trent, a rapidly evolving organisation adding value to the City Council's environmental initiatives, is playing a key role in the project development and implementation. The project involves enhancing access to the site by creating a hierarchy of footpaths reflecting and protecting the ecology of the site. An innovative approach to landscape interpretation has been taken, with land reclamation programme funds being used to create a community amphitheatre and to make landscape features of the 'gateways', drainage ditches and culverts. The community has been actively involved with the development of the project and will be key players in its long-term management. The reclamation is very much a partnership, with each partner feeding into different aspects of a community agreed master plan to maximise the use of resources and skills. It is due for completion in 2000.

The 1980s – a turning point – the National Garden Festival

The success of the large schemes in the 1960s and 1970s proved to central government what the City Council could achieve using a single source of grant, in spite of the fact that this only met 50-75% of the reclamation cost. A high profile central government urban regeneration initiative during the 1980s was the promotion of Garden Festivals. These were inspired by the German "device for regenerating post-war bomb sites by imaginative reclamation, attracting visitors and commercial sponsorship and stimulating permanent developments on profoundly unpromising sites" (Ward, 1994). The awarding of the National Garden Festival in 1984 to Stoke-on-Trent meant that almost 70 hectares (170 acres) of severely degraded land, then the largest area of dereliction in the West Midlands, had to be reclaimed, restored and developed in two years to host the Festival in 1986. This deadline had a catalytic effect, not only on the decision-making process, but also on the master planning and reclamation processes. The reclamation of the site required the removal of 1.4 million m³ (1.8 million cubic yards) of material, the treatment of pit shafts, removal of substantial areas of reinforced concrete, excavation of slurry and tar lagoons and the removal of asbestos. The most contaminated material was formed into a central ridged

The National Garden Festival, Stoke-on-Trent, 1986 – the reclamation of land for the festival proved to be the catalyst for the subsequent regeneration of the Festival Park and adjoining land for shopping, offices and leisure uses.

area, running the length of the site, and stabilised with a one metre clay cap and then planted. The immense success of Festival Park, where a public/private funding ratio of 1:14 was achieved, has led to the direct regeneration of adjacent land for retail, leisure and office space. Known as Etruria Valley, this is a linchpin in the City's regeneration strategy.

As a direct consequence of the success of Festival Park, a partnership was formed in 1993 between the City Council and developers St Modwen to tackle those derelict sites which otherwise would remain undeveloped for years to come. The exercise is proving a success with, for example, Festival Heights – an area the size of Festival Park – having already been reclaimed and redeveloped.

The 1990s – a new direction

Many of the complex problems of the 1960s and 1970s have almost been eradicated and the city is now one of the greener in the country. The sheer scale of these reclamation schemes is matched today by the large regeneration and job creation schemes. Trentham Lakes (formerly Hem Heath Colliery) is now being transformed into a high quality environment and flagship employment site to attract inward investment and create over 6,000 new jobs. The project hopes to attract over £200m of private sector investment and is the single most significant brownfield development site in North Staffordshire.

It is crucial to the continued regeneration of Stoke-on-Trent to work with the private sector and the community to develop brownfield sites to create land for development and new jobs. Working in partnership is the key to delivering successful projects, but it can slow the process down. Gone are the days of the 'quick in quick out' approach to land reclamation. Not only are the challenges more problematical, but meeting the varied agendas of stakeholders and grant agencies can be both time consuming yet very rewarding.

The early reclamation schemes are now becoming vital local assets and are adding value to new brownfield development opportunities for housing and industry, creating a much improved environment in which to live, work and play. Reclamation schemes currently being designed, implemented and managed include: a major programme of work alongside the Trent and Mersey canal with Groundwork and British Waterways; projects in the Stoke Approach Single Regeneration Budget (SRB) area matching land reclamation resources with SRB funds to upgrade the environment of older industrial areas; ongoing treatment of pit shafts; and small scale high impact community based projects.

We know we still have a long way to go, but reclaiming land scarred by our industrial past has been the key to Stoke-on-Trent's future.

The award winning Sandwell Park Farm has been restored as a countryside interpretation centre and working farm museum.

Chapter 4:

The 1980s – Fighting back from recession

Overview

David Chapman

T he dominant concern of the early 1980s for both planning and economic
development was the need to address the massive problem of unemployment. Unemployment rates were high across Britain as a whole, but
the West Midlands had extensive areas suffering extremely high levels. Parts of
inner Birmingham, Sparkbrook for instance, were experiencing levels of around
40% unemployment. The need for economic restructuring was then vitally
important for the whole region. While the 1970s had been a slide from 'boom'
into recession, the 1980s were characterised by a fight back from politicians,
local communities and planners. Although central government seemed to be
determined to dismantle the supposedly inhibiting bureaucracy of the public
sector, people on the ground were fighting depression and inequality. Taking
their name from an unemployment benefit form, the reggae group UB40
represented a popular example. Today "with worldwide sales topping 30 million
albums during their career, the UB40 story demonstrates just how far people
can go by staying true to their roots". Their first national media appearance
was in January 1980 on the John Peel show and their music became an icon
of the 1980s. With recording studios in Digbeth, they remain in the heart of a
major regeneration area of Birmingham. Sir Simon Rattle, who became the
Principal Conductor of the City of Birmingham Symphony Orchestra in 1979,
took the orchestra from provincial to international status during the same
decade.

It was quickly recognised that West Midlands' manufacturing industry, as the
bedrock of the economy, was severely weakened and, though still vital, the
search for viable economic alternatives began. In Birmingham, it had been
noticed that convention business was taking off in the USA and that Chicago
and Cleveland (Ohio), the self-styled 'come back city', seemed to be models
for regeneration. People were also beginning to ask whether tourism could be
promoted across the region and whether employment in the finance and service
sectors could be stimulated. Graham Shaylor recalls below how Birmingham
and its planners responded.

Signs of the Times

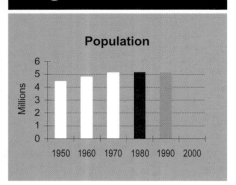

Population

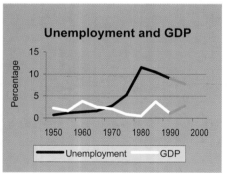

Households and Dwellings

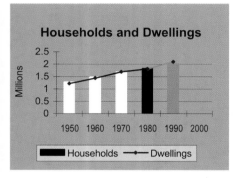

Unemployment and GDP

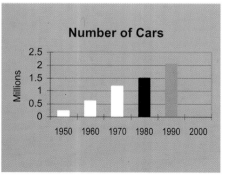

Number of Cars

The West Midlands County Council (WMCC) played a role, not just in the provision of strategic planning guidance, but also co-ordination of environmental and economic initiatives across the whole conurbation. An influential study of the early 1980s explored four possible scenarios for the region; 'the spiral of decline', 'traditional growth', 'economic and social regeneration' and 'individual and community enterprise' (Thew *et al*, 1982). This work, led by Bill Ogden, John Holliday and Peter Roberts and facilitated by David Thew, guided much of the subsequent thinking. Alan Cave reflects upon the achievements of the WMCC. After its abolition in 1986, there was inter-district competition for inward investment, particularly in the competition that grew up to capture major regional out-of-town shopping facilities. The Merry Hill and Sandwell Mall proposals were recognised by Birmingham as threats to the city's place as the regional centre for retailing. In typical 'Brummie' style, the City Council immediately promoted the redevelopment of the 1960s Bull Ring Shopping Centre as an 'out-of-town' shopping centre, in town!

Ironically, the recession reduced development pressure upon historic buildings and the countryside, giving time for the conservation initiatives which were growing in the 1970s to be consolidated. These were supported by the National Heritage Act of 1983, which gave greater powers to the newly formed English Heritage. The growing conservation activity was manifested in many innovative projects. During this period there was greater attention paid to environmental improvement, including schemes for 'greening', especially along key routes through the older industrial areas. The industrial heritage was also increasingly recognised as an asset and the canal network provided the focus for many regeneration schemes. Environmental education became an important activity of the RTPI West Midlands Branch during this period and Peter Wright relates how it influenced national policy.

It was a time during which the many ethnic minority communities were supported in meeting their social, cultural and religious needs. The establishment of temples, mosques and gurdwara had begun slowly in the 1960s and 1970s, with the conversion of houses and redundant buildings, but during the 1980s the construction of fine new buildings began. The Handsworth riots of September 1985 were an exceptional example of racial tension. Exacerbated by the economic disadvantage, an exceptionally hot summer and a few activists, the violence and destruction shocked the nation. The response that followed included a major programme of urban renewal and community economic development. There has not been the slightest hint of anything like those riots since then in the region.

The Central Mosque in Birmingham is a symbol of the contribution and cultural diversity which the successful establishment of various ethnic minority communities has brought to the West Midlands.

Throughout the decade there was an increasing recognition that planners had a role in supporting the process of regeneration, economic development and participation. Promotion of the image of the region and its distinctive parts became vital in the new style of proactive and entrepreneurial planning. The quality of design, development, infrastructure and environment were increasingly being valued. Coventry was one of the six participants in the Department of the Environment's 'Time for Design' initiative launched in 1985. Significant innovations included design awards, design guides and most significantly more effective approaches to development briefing.

During the decade planning education came under close scrutiny from central government, which, as *Tripwire* (1987) explained, sought to "rationalise the pattern of course provision into a smaller number of larger centres to cater for an annual graduate output of between 300 and 400." Coventry Polytechnic's planning course (now re-established) was closed in 1987.

The abandonment of planning?

During the early 1980s, official attitudes towards planning were at best negative and at worst hostile, although the pendulum was swinging back by the end of decade, when business and industry recognised the uncertainties which deregulation had brought. The election of the Thatcher Government in 1979 had a dramatic impact upon planning nationally. Thornley (1991) highlights several significant changes in planning legislation, institutions and status, while Reade (1997) claims that the Conservative Government was "dogmatic, doctrinaire, market-obsessed, and pervaded by a naïve conviction that economic outcomes have single and simple causes..."

The Government's plans for deregulation, or 'lifting the burden,' were intended to free the private sector from bureaucratic controls, but also represented a challenge to local democracy. One of the clearest indicators of the new attitude to planning was the introduction of Circular 22/80, which instructed local planning authorities not to interfere with the detailed design of development. The introduction of 'special status' for certain areas was more profound. There was a belief that if the involvement of local government or existing statutory requirements was lifted, then action would be speeded and enterprise freed. Enterprise Zones (EZs) were introduced in the Local Government, Planning and Land Act 1980 and the concept of Simplified Planning Zones (SPZs) was subsequently introduced in the Housing and Planning Act of 1986 as an evolution of the idea (Ward, 1994). The introduction of Urban Development Corporations (UDCs) was perhaps the most significant innovation and Colin Wood describes the West Midlands experience.

Central government also had a profound effect upon the structure of local government in the metropolitan area. The West Midlands County Council had been established in 1974 and, despite some early resentment from the metropolitan districts, it had played a major role in promoting regional planning, economic development and environmental conservation. An interesting example of collaboration between County and District was the response to Birmingham's Jewellery Quarter, where a dual approach to regeneration and conservation was adopted. In January 1980 a County/City designation of a combined Industrial Improvement Area (IIA) *and* Conservation Area (CA) was approved. Grant aid and direct action supported local businesses and made the area attractive to visitors from home and abroad.

The Stoke Garden Festival took place in 1986 following the first UK festival, held in Liverpool in 1984, and received the Branch Award for planning achievement. As the culmination of years of planning, it had significant benefits for local regeneration, an immediate impact on image and the long term benefit of attracting new businesses.

For some people the 1980s seemed a period of marking time. The conventional processes of plan making and development control were being challenged and the scale of economic decline rendered these reactive planning methods relatively ineffective. In the earlier periods of boom and growth, the importance of directing and shaping development was vital and generally effective, but when development pressure vanished a more proactive and entrepreneurial style was needed. Economic development strategies to promote long term economic restructuring and inward investment and programmes of job creation and training were urgently needed. Enabling and facilitating became the guiding words of planners throughout the region. How could development proposals be attracted? How could obstacles be removed? What incentives could be created?

Many agencies and partnerships were mobilised. Examples include the Anglican Church, which stimulated debate with *Faith in the City* (1985), *Faith in the City of Birmingham* (1988) and *Faith in the Countryside* (1990). The Manpower Services Commission (MSC), which had been created in 1974, provided resources for job creation, which became of great importance at local level during the 1980s. The county and district councils established large-scale conservation and landscape teams under MSC programmes and, together with several voluntary sector agencies, carried out a wide range of community training projects. The 'Greenstreet' project in Hanley, Stoke-on-Trent, won the Branch Award for planning achievement in 1987 and the following year Sandwell Park Farm, restored as a countryside interpretation centre and 19th century working farm museum, won the Royal Institution of Chartered Surveyors/The Times Conservation Awards 1988.

Throughout the region, planners worked vigorously with local people, politicians, commerce and industry to overcome real difficulties. Initiatives like Operation Green-up, derelict land reclamation programmes and the redevelopment of brownfield sites improved environments and land supply. A new style of planning developed, based upon vision, place-making and marketing, and enabling. An important aspect of this was getting to grips with European Union (EU) membership, in particular the structural funds that were available when the West Midlands became an Assisted Area in 1984.

The Planners Response to Recession

Graham Shaylor OBE

Recalling what happened twenty years ago is not easy – to get it anything like accurate is even more difficult. It is important to record the contributions made by city councillors and members of staff to the efforts of Birmingham during this period. There were disagreements and squabbles, but the goal of improving the lot of Birmingham people was always in everyone's minds. There were debates about how to do things, but not about what to do. Many times a Secretary of State has looked across the table at members of the City Council's opposing parties and said: "It must be Birmingham, you're the only lot who come united in a common endeavour." But outside the confines of the Council there were also many individuals and institutions with the same common purpose. The Chamber of Industry and Commerce was particularly active, but so too were the builders and developers. Many small firms were keen to help and everyone knew that there was serious competition from outside the region and that the loss of jobs was really hurting. Survival was the name of the game. To maintain morale and provide a vision is a key job for a public authority, particularly in times of deep recession.

This article is limited to my experiences in Birmingham and it is to some extent anecdotal. I make no apologies as I can only write about what I know and believe to have been the key points of the eighties. As outlined in the overview, the West Midlands was hit by the effects of a major international recession during the late seventies and early eighties. In some months Birmingham's jobless alone would increase by more than 10,000. The Government's efforts to encourage small businesses seemed to me to be well out of scale with the needs. The real attack on the problems of recession came in two new ways. Firstly, in 1978 Peter Shore, the then Secretary of State for the Environment, seized the Urban Programme run by the Home Office and produced a White Paper proposing the establishment of Partnership Committees in major cities. Birmingham was one such body and the Inner City Partnership Programme had its first year of operation starting in April 1979. £10 million was made available and, because it was new money, there was an opportunity to try out new initiatives. The second major opportunity was provided through the Manpower Services Commission's (MSC) temporary employment programmes. Under these the local government and voluntary bodies provided jobs for over 7,500 people working on environmental improvements and the restoration of listed buildings. The historic Curzon Street Station, for example, lying derelict and owned by British Rail, was bought for £1 and The Prince's Trust employment initiative restored the building to use for employment and training purposes. The use of the Local Government Act provision for discretionary local income-raising produced about £2 million per annum and was important in funding the cost of

*Curzon Street Station, built 1838-42, was the original terminus of the London –
Birmingham railway. Now a Grade 1 listed building, it was saved from dereliction by
Birmingham City Council and The Prince's Trust.*

many local MSC projects' materials. These initiatives were developed at a time
when local government had little experience of dealing with employment and
economic initiatives, but the low level of knowledge was counter-balanced by a
lot of enthusiasm.

The very word regeneration has an emotive ring to it and is in my view an
ideal way of describing the all-embracing united effort required to respond to
the challenges of urban decline. Partnership is another word, but this now tends
to be seen in a formal, institutionalised way rather than in the informal way
many partnerships in the 1980s started. In my view the role played by the
Chamber of Industry and Commerce was unique. In 1980 it started Birmingham
Venture, which still runs today and was a serious attempt to get big firms to help
small firms. About thirty major firms contributed to the funding of staff, who
worked with small firms, offering advice, contacts and training. It recognised
that the bedrock of the city's wealth was about saving and restoring small firms.
Later in the decade the role played by the Birmingham Chamber was again
critical when, with four major firms (Douglas, Tarmac, Bryant and Wimpey), it
encouraged the City to go into partnership in East Birmingham to form the

Birmingham Heartlands Development Agency. The City Council was anxious not to have a development corporation exercising separate planning powers within its boundaries and it steered the Secretary of State at the time to opt for a development corporation in the Black Country rather than in the city. This choice was clearly right, as the subsequent achievements have been significant and would not have been achieved by four local authorities acting separately. Eventually, though, the City ran out of resources and succumbed to the Heartlands Development Agency becoming a Development Corporation. By the time that happened, however, the Heartlands Board had been operating for five years and had scored a number of notable successes, including regenerating the Bloomsbury Estate and developing Bordesley Urban Village.

Apart from organisations there were many individuals who worked hard over a wide variety of tasks. Among them were many who were unemployed and they often found strength from local authority staff and members who were actually working to support change both social and physical. Planners are particularly good at helping to bring about change especially once they realise that it is 'peoples' plans that get real commitment. Sometimes this involved learning new skills – writing the articles of association for a development agency from scratch was a real challenge. New ways of doing things were tested and lateral thinking was encouraged. It was always made clear to everyone that they should not be ashamed to admit they did not know the answer to any particular problem. It was not a disgrace to ask for help. You were only considered a fool if you made the same mistake twice. Everyone tried to avoid that.

Employment requires a separate note because it was the critical problem in the early eighties. Very early on we realised that full employment did not necessarily equal wealth creation. For many years the city had been home to firms who used mass production techniques requiring large volumes of shift workers, whose levels of skill were often limited to one part of the mass production process. However, when unemployment came, it was not just these people who were out of work, but also highly skilled workers. Some areas of the city – not used to economic recession - suddenly discovered they were not immune from change, and it was a nasty shock. Some wards in the city had over 40% unemployment rates. Everyone was looking at each other and wondering what should be done and we decided to seize the opportunity to try some new projects. One of the early experiments was to start a workshop where people with skills could start their own businesses. They were helped by having cheap accommodation, common workshop machinery they could use, advice from secondees from the private sector, who would help write business plans, and industrialists who would take an interest in offering business contacts and help - some even gave contracts.

Birmingham New Enterprise Workshop I (BNEW) opened in Clifton Road Balsall Heath in 1980, followed in 1981 by BNEW II at Hockley Port and later BNEW III and IV. Between them, they provided for more than five hundred firms and several thousand jobs. The concept of shared workspace was also pursued by taking over multi-storey 'flatted' factory buildings and converting them into enterprise space. The idea behind both was simply that people who wanted to start their own business should be able to invest in their business and not on property rentals, for units that were too big for them, and machinery, which was under utilised for much of the time. After all, many new businesses start in a room at home or in a shed at the bottom of the garden – usually without planning consent!

In addition to trying to help the traditional skills in the city, there was also a need to look for new industries. The interaction between academic research, new products, creating new businesses and new markets is very dear to the Midlands. The United States experience on Route 129, Stanford University and Massachusetts Institute of Technology was inspirational. In 1981 the new Vice Chancellor of Aston University joined forces with the City Council and Lloyds Bank to create the Aston Science Park, which has successfully nurtured new industries that are creating a new business stream in the city. Aston was the first Inner City Science Park in the country and has continued to prosper over the years on the former site of the Pilkington Glass Works, next to the University.

Aston Science Park was a major innovation jointly developed in phases from the early 1980s by Birmingham City Council, Aston University and Lloyds Bank.

Also on the subject of wealth creation, I must mention here the development of the International Convention Centre (ICC), which followed on from the development in the early 1970s of the National Exhibition Centre. These facilities, by the mid nineties, were generating £486 million, a wealth equivalent to 16,800 jobs according to studies undertaken by KPMG (1993). These figures are disputed by some, but it is evident that something has happened in the city. An alternative source of wealth for the city has been created in a relatively short space of time and, to support this, skill change and training have been encouraged, for without the workforce able and willing to support new businesses the whole enterprise fails.

Traditionally, Birmingham has been entrepreneurial, some would say too much so, but it is the nature of the people, and planners are foolish if they do not understand the nature of the place where they work. It had been in 1980 that the City Planning Committee considered the draft City Centre Plan, which included the provision of a conference hall on the site of Bingley Hall. This was an historical proposal based on grandiose, pre-war City Council proposals, which included a massive City Hall of which Baskerville House was part of one wing. These plans had resulted in major land acquisitions by the Council to provide for a wide boulevard along Broad Street and the linking of Five Ways with the city centre. The 1980 draft plan received a mixed reception, including the comment that conference halls were 'old hat' and what was now needed was a convention centre. None of us knew what a convention centre was, so we took steps to find out. The Chief Executive of Indianapolis Convention Centre, who was also the 1982 President of the American Federation of Convention Centres, was invited over to Birmingham to give us advice. As a result a feasibility study was undertaken in 1983. This showed that the centre should be in the central business district and not at the NEC, as some people advocated, and that a five star hotel would be needed close to the convention centre. The hotel needed to be run by an operator of international standing and Hyatt Hotels were quickly invited to talks with the City. Whilst this was going on there had been an Anglo American Colloquium organised by Aston University. One of the important outcomes was the perception that the city should concentrate on its 'downtown business district' and promote the business and financial centre. It was hoped this would avoid the worst experiences of American cities, which had had similar problems to Birmingham some twenty years earlier.

In 1985 it was necessary to visit Chicago to negotiate with Hyatt. On the first morning's inevitable breakfast meeting we were applauded by the other diners and, when we asked why, we were told Birmingham had won the nomination to become the UK city competing for the 1992 Olympics. The Americans considered this a marvellous publicity stunt in bringing the city to the attention of the world. We asked about the comparison between Olympic and Convention Centre business and were told that Chicago's Convention Centre supported six Hyatt Hotels but that, to the man or woman in the street, the Olympics were still better known than the convention business. Our stay in Chicago was short lived as we failed to agree on that occasion, although subsequently agreement was reached as testified by Hyatt's presence in Birmingham today. We went on to Baltimore and saw the regeneration of a large harbour area with tourist attractions and refurbished housing that was drawing half-a-million American holiday-makers a year. The Rouse Corporation had been the developer of Harbor Place, following its successful festival market place concept in Boston in 1975. This expedition to Baltimore subsequently helped us establish the concept of Brindleyplace, where the sale of land helped finance the construction of the National Indoor Arena.

The International Convention Centre is the centrepiece of Birmingham's Broad Street development and led the transformation of the West Midlands from an industrial to an international region.

As the designs for the International Convention Centre (ICC) emerged it became clear that new money would be required from Europe. The setting for the ICC including the canal system and Centenary Square area were included in the bid and the task of getting appropriate funding took some two years to achieve. In 1986 work started on the Convention Centre and other investment poured into the city following the lead of this major initiative. It was hoped that the whole project would be completed in 1989 to celebrate the centenary of the city's Royal Charter, but the negotiations in Brussels, although ultimately successful, meant that the complex was not opened until 1991.

The *City Centre Local Plan*, which was finally approved in 1986 (Birmingham City Council, 1986), was considerably modified and followed, rather than led, events. The city centre was seen as everything inside the Middle Ring Road, so that the opportunity for expanding downtown business functions could be promoted across the Inner Ring Road, which was acknowledged to be a 'concrete collar' inhibiting city centre development. Steps were initiated to complete the Middle Ring Road, to allow the progressive breaking of the collar to downgrade the Inner Ring Road to a distributor road servicing the business district.

In the 1980s the business community formed City 2000 as a meeting point and forum where ideas, projects and views could be debated. Vision and image were words bandied around with little coherent expression. The Highbury Initiative, a symposium sponsored jointly by the City Council and the Government's City

Action Team, was held in March 1988 and changed all that. Sixty leading figures in urban renewal and regeneration from around the world were brought to Birmingham to try to offer tangible advice on what the city could do. Two major pieces of work emerged, which influenced the shape of things to come. One set out a hierarchy of streets and spaces and how they should be treated, while the other gave urban design guidance on the form of buildings and their relationships to public space. Much of the advice was subsequently acted upon and used as guidance for developers, producing the city centre we see now. As described later by Martin Eade, other studies of integrated transport, marketing and promotion led the way in Government policy and provided models for many other places.

It is important in describing the 1980s to say something about what was happening on the housing front. The city had over 100,000 houses that were 100 years old or more and, as the Government reduced the local authority housing programme, there was a real problem emerging. Many houses were found to be in a dangerous state as a result of poor construction and established inter-war estates such as Pype Hayes were thrown into turmoil by needing complete rebuilding. The leadership and commitment of the staff in the Housing and Architects Departments was outstanding in helping tenants and owners cope with the problem. As far as the older houses were concerned a unique programme of integrated rehabilitation of groups of properties including houses and shops, funded by the Urban Programme and led by the Urban Renewal Section of the Environmental Services Department, was started. The concept of 'enveloping', developed with the aid of Inner City Partnership funding under the Inner Areas Act of 1978, was so widely praised that the approach was incorporated into the main Housing Investment Programme, without any additional financial provision; a real victim of its own success!

With the benefit of hindsight, it is fairly easy to justify what was done in Birmingham in the 1980s in terms of strategic thinking, policy formulation and efficient implementation. In truth, the major contributions were made by grasping opportunities, acting with clarity and persuading others that their plans, hopes and ambitions were a real part of the effort of regenerating the city and its people. Throughout, planners worked closely with local residents to discuss how they would improve the area in which they lived. This local involvement has now become regular good practice, but in the 1980s it was treading fresh ground. The result of all this work produced better living conditions for hundreds of residents, the prospect of jobs emerging from the black hole of recession and a flagship city centre which matched the region's ambitions in Europe and the world.

The Rise and Fall of
The Metropolitan County Council

Alan Cave

Thirteen years on, older and wiser, I write to reflect on the role and success of the metropolitan counties, particularly having had the tremendous opportunity to act as Deputy County Planner and thence County Planner for the West Midlands in the period 1982-1986.

1974 was a milestone in the development of the United Kingdom planning system. Establishment of the metropolitan counties and Greater London Council (GLC), not as an experiment but as a primary level of local government, confirmed for the first time the importance of strategic metropolitan planning. Such confirmation related not only to town and country planning, but to the strategic significance of selected community services within which land use and transportation planning play a major part. This establishment posed a challenge for effective two tier local government relations. Equally, it provided an opportunity for planners, and others, to develop their careers in a new and challenging environment.

Having regard to the West Midlands experience I will seek to address the following questions. How long did the settling in period take to ensure orderly and effective two tier political and professional relationships and strategic service delivery, and what was the basis of the continuing tensions and emerging consensus? What were the lasting benefits of metropolitan county operation and what were the consequences of abolition?

Settling in and the Tensions

Establishing a strategic authority to undertake both new functions and those transferred from the previous county boroughs created inevitable tensions – both creative and destructive. These tensions were the focus of attention in the early months, arguably years, post 1974 and, having worked in a metropolitan borough after the establishment of West Midlands County Council (WMCC), I could observe some of the tensions from 'district' level.

There was little argument on the statutory functions for the Metropolitan County, namely:

- preparation and review of a structure plan;
- preparation of a development plan scheme and certification arrangements for local plans;
- minerals and waste planning;
- transportation planning;
- development of the Airport; and
- parallel responsibility with 'district' councils for derelict land reclamation and urban regeneration.

In addition, the principle of strategic planning in its wider sense, to co-ordinate county level services met with general accord.

Tensions, however, focused on 'negotiation of the middle ground' and the operational aspects of the county role in practice. The establishment of a 200 strong interdisciplinary professional team, with salary levels and grades way beyond those many had ever dreamed of, attracted high calibre individuals from metropolitan boroughs, imposing resource losses on some authorities.

The early Structure Plan (1980) identified growth areas for housing and employment on and around the urban fringe and large scale greenfield, often green belt, development was seen as the major opportunity to meet projections. Consequently the growth potential focused upon certain areas, namely Solihull, Birmingham and Walsall. Other boroughs, which were either land-locked (Sandwell) or possessed major internal land resources (Wolverhampton – Bilston Steel Works and Dudley – Milking Bank), were able to contain the outward expansion of the conurbation. Coventry had a reasonable balance between both internal resources and some opportunity for peripheral expansion.

The Development Plan Scheme and the degree of County Council intervention in borough-led local plans created tension in some metropolitan boroughs, which had limited staff resources for local plan preparation in stark contrast to the newly established team at the County. More tensions arose when Alfie Wood, the charismatic County Planner, vigorously promoted his philosophy that conservation and some other associated issues were of strategic significance. This was highlighted in the County's attempt to influence the details of a number of local plans prepared by the 'district' authorities.

There was also local resistance to strategic decision making on mineral extraction, land filling and waste disposal, where, despite extensive protective conditions, some local communities continued to resist extractive industry and waste disposal, perceiving detrimental environmental effects. Many would argue that the tensions on the planning side, however, were small scale compared with negotiations on highway agency arrangements and winter gritting! As a generality, though, the creative tension led in due course to earlier, rather than later, resolution of outstanding matters, in contrast to the experience in some of the other metropolitan county areas, where tensions were longer lasting.

Coming of Age

The period from around 1977 to 1984, after which Government proposals for abolition became more certain, represented a maturing of county and district relationships and the establishment of strong interpersonal relationships between staff in the two tiers. A desire for added value from the County's contribution enabled a concentration of resources and consensus, as opposed to confrontation. This in my view provided the foundation for the lasting benefits to be derived from county operations.

The notable areas of consensus were centred on strategic plan making, regional data analysis, conservation and environmental improvement.

Examples of consensus included:

- the early production of a countywide Structure Plan from the seven previous borough-wide plans that had not together achieved consistency in all policy areas;
- strengthening the interface between the Metropolitan County and the shire counties;
- formulation of a regional plan, with some reduction in the tensions with regard to the urban fringe;
- recognition that areas such as minerals and waste disposal required a strategic approach, with effective protective conditions, that may require the overriding of purely local considerations; and
- the establishment of private sector partnerships in the formulation of the Structure Plan and a county-wide land development programme.

Success was also achieved in determining equitable proportions of Metropolitan County overspill into the surrounding shire counties. Indeed the later stages of regional plan formulation acknowledged the opportunities for regional corridors of growth along public transport routes. A proposition slightly ahead of its time!

The West Midlands is at the heart of Britain's canal network and this is a focus for recreation, tourism, conservation and regeneration.

There was a growing recognition of the value of the County Council's Joint Data Team in the development of databases and analyses to support strategic policy development. The establishment of a Joint Land Use/Transportation Planning team also helped to prioritise highway investment projects in the Transport Policies and Programme (TPP) through servicing strategic land use development requirements. Conservation also achieved recognition as having a strategic dimension and this was subsequently endorsed in the 1990s as a central component of major regeneration schemes in many other urban areas. The considerable influence of Alfie Wood led to the recognition that canals had a strong strategic dimension as communication routes, as linear recreation routes and as a focus for land restoration and improvement. Early inter-authority ratification of a canal towpath agreement and strong liaison with British Waterways Board (BWB) stimulated a focus for future canal based reclamation strategies and improved public access.

The County Council added value as a key participant in determining policy priorities and translating them into action programmes for regeneration. Firstly, a £2 million per annum land reclamation programme was initially based on success by quantity of land reclaimed. This early approach, 'if its derelict, reclaim it', developed into a more complex and more focused process, and the market testing of land for housing and industry was groundbreaking. Secondly, true partnership in the development and operation of the Birmingham Inner City Partnership and Programme (BICPP) and Urban Programme involved the County

Birmingham Business Park provides a high quality environment for firms and employees, but its reliance on car access is a challenge for sustainability.

contributing on economic development, reclamation, environmental improvement, police expenditure and transport improvements. Despite differences of political persuasion between national and local authorities, Ministers regularly contributed to the BICPP with considerable support for local action initiatives. Thirdly, the opportunity was taken to channel County generated resources into priority action areas where, in the case of Sandwell for example, such areas became a key metropolitan focus for regeneration, including land reclamation.

A rapidly emerging consensus developed between county and district with regard to the required focus that was needed in the early 1980s towards the regeneration of inner city and other older areas. The County provided an important contribution to obtaining European Regional Development Fund (ERDF) funds from Brussels. Identifying and demonstrating the strategic relationships between economic development and supportive infrastructure fell on receptive ears in Brussels and a £20 million per annum allocation of ERDF was not uncommon. The County established a strong Economic Development Unit. This reflected the increasing emphasis in national regeneration programmes towards revenue support to combat social disadvantage and support training, as well as personal and community development. The establishment of a 700 strong Manpower Services Commission (MSC) Programme, with training centres established across the county, enabled young and old to benefit from new construction and environmental training. A major contribution was made to environmental improvements while recognising that such improvements play a fundamental role not only in the physical but also in the social and economic aspects of regeneration. In all these respects the County was able to rely on a strong measure of Government Office support in policy development and regeneration initiatives.

It was deeply regrettable that, once the Government's determination to abolish metropolitan government became irreversible, some of the tensions of the early years re-emerged, but happily at a more limited level and with little impact on the impetus of the Structure Plan Review, staff commitment and motivation, and regeneration programmes.

The Legacy of the County

It is ironic, following the demise of the metropolitan counties, that little was heard from the Government on the cost savings that were to have accrued to the public purse as a consequence of abolition. I suspect, in reality, that the assumed savings simply failed to materialise. This is, of course, all history, but what of the Metropolitan County's achievement? Was there a legacy about which we can say – yes it was a worthwhile investment, short lived though it may have been?

There were a number of important areas of achievement in both professional and technical terms. From the perspective of the ambitious staff who joined the County Council by choice not compulsion, there was a real opportunity to participate in both policy development and implementation in parallel. Internal barriers between strategic planners and action people never existed. With a £25 million per annum capital programme, or expressed another way £100,000 per working day, for the planning department alone, staff were clearly motivated to ensure programmes were met. It is often easier to obtain the external resources than actually spend it effectively! The open plan office encouraged interface between planners, economists, researchers, quantity surveyors, reclamation engineers, architects, graphics staff, conservation architects and landscape designers, together with strong corporate links to economic development specialists, transportation planners and others, which allowed the cross fertilisation of ideas and a strong commitment to corporate working.

Establishment of the land use transportation team and an economic development unit gave planners opportunities to explore new challenges and new areas of professional activity. Regular liaison with the other metropolitan county planning departments assisted in the development of innovative thinking and the transmission of experience based on best practice. In technical terms the Structure Plan Review (WMCC, 1986) endorsed the first exceptional peripheral high-tech business park for the region, confirming the imperative of diversifying the regional economy into new areas of leading edge technology. Birmingham Airport expansion, designed in the planning department and ratified through a public inquiry, was opened prior to abolition as the foundation for a truly

Since the expansion of Birmingham International Airport in the 1980s (as seen here), the dramatic growth of air traffic has been matched by increased capacity and improved facilities.

international gateway for West Midlands enterprise as well as the overseas holiday industry. Staff who subsequently transferred to the Airport Company have been party to the continuing rapid expansion of this economic focus of the West Midlands, with passenger throughput fast exceeding original expectations.

Over 1,000 hectares (2,500 acres) of derelict land were reclaimed by the County Council between 1974-1986, testifying to the capabilities of specialist teams, with a County Council and Government Office consensus on the way forward. With County Council support, the canal network emerged as a key focus for regeneration and environmental improvement, particularly in the absence of a significant West Midlands river system. Establishment of the land use/transportation planning joint working team was arguably ahead of its time in view of the only relatively recent political emphasis on sustainability, and the need for integrated land use and transport planning.

The additionality of County involvement and resources in regeneration provided impetus to priority area renewal. Over 3,000 unemployed people were enabled through MSC schemes to participate in training and enhance their prospects for future employment as well as contribute to environmental and physical regeneration. The County role as spokesman for inter-metropolitan authority working with the shire counties at regional level helped form a basis for subsequent co-operative dialogue in local authority-led regional planning. The economic development initiatives, and measures to combat social exclusion, provided substantial achievement in parallel to physical regeneration. The County became a seedbed for innovation in waste recycling, guided buses and the gestation of the Midland Metro. The inclusion of the private sector in partnership arrangements within strategic planning was also a forerunner of subsequent public/private partnerships across a wide range of planning and regeneration programmes.

Abolition and the Future?

Are the regions any worse off for the demise of the metropolitan counties and are there prospects for the re-emergence of metropolitan government? It is ironic that the GLC, as the target of abolition, is likely to re-emerge in some form, while the development of Regional Chambers and Development Agencies makes it unlikely that there will be a return to metropolitan county level political operation elsewhere. It is equally ironic that the Government of the time encouraged the metropolitan boroughs to accept abolition. Yet having done so, they imposed a major Development Corporation outside of local government control in key regeneration areas of the Black Country, leading once again to tensions as to the respective decision making powers. Birmingham Heartlands, though a political compromise, achieved a greater level of local authority participation in decision-making within its area. I feel sure, however, that the establishment of development corporations was an appropriate response, and a basis for maintaining regeneration and focusing public and private sector resources.

The one benefit of the County was the ability to take a roving brief over a wide metropolitan area. This enabled a focus to be given to certain areas or projects at a point in time, with the ability to move on without excessive boundary restriction. This roving brief is now the approach by which the Regional Development Agency (RDA) will establish its enabling role, although the establishment of Regeneration Zones will provide a short to medium term approach to focusing investment.

A key question, as yet unanswered, is whether the principle of development corporations and the RDAs reflects a real inability of local government to provide the *framework* within which economic development and regeneration can be achieved at a large scale. Despite the model provided by the Birmingham Inner City Partnership Programme, there is yet no positive answer to the question, which for many is a sad reflection on the image of local government to implement large-scale programmes of regeneration.

I suspect that future biographies will show that amongst the Ministers involved in the abolition process were some who saw the real value of retaining key specialist county council teams, for example on land reclamation, in order to maintain post abolition momentum. Alas, that option failed to emerge, but it was at least continued in terms of momentum by the emerging urban development corporations (UDCs). Many will argue the metropolitan county councils achieved adolescence and early middle age. Would the development corporations have come about had the county councils been retained? The answer is most probably no. Were the UDCs a replication of the metropolitan counties, but with a more tightly defined brief? Insofar as a focus on regeneration policy and action programmes is concerned, the answer is most probably yes. A more fundamental question also arises. Would all that the metropolitan counties achieved have happened in any event? I believe the focused approach to reclamation, regeneration, strategic policy formulation, airport development and European funding amongst other initiatives would suggest the answer is decidedly no.

My observation of events after 1986 is that numerous initiatives with which the County Council was heavily involved have now developed in a way which suggests that, at the very least, it laid the foundations for subsequent initiatives on a larger scale. I believe without question the county councils, by the example of West Midlands County Council, provided additionality in the areas with which they were centrally involved. For this, in addition to strategically minded elected members, we thank those professional staff who have subsequently progressed their careers since 1986, those who are now retired from practice and those who have sadly left us, including Alfie Wood, John Stevenson, Ron Joyner, Fred Parker and Mike Fox. Each of these contributed to what were new experiences; new ways of thinking; and an exciting opportunity in career progression that perhaps will never be replicated. Or will it?

The Growth of Environmental Education

Peter Wright

A Priority Agenda

One of the most popular issues to catch the public's imagination in recent years has been the environment and the future. Hardly a person can have failed to have heard of global warming, acid rain or genetically modified crops. With the Sunday broadsheets leading debates on house building in the green belt and green warriors actively campaigning to reverse the road building programme, the environment has never had a higher profile. It is surprising then to reflect that this has all happened in a short period of time, at best no more than 20 years! A period that coincides with the growth of the Royal Town Planning Institute's (RTPI) own highly praised Environmental Education (EE) work.

Early Beginnings

The early beginnings of the Institute's interest in EE are not wholly clear, although they owed much to The Skeffington Report (Skeffington 1969) and the early attempts to involve people in plan preparation. The recommendation that "People should be encouraged to participate in the preparation of plans by helping with surveys and other activities as well as by making comments" broke new ground and opened up the profession to public involvement. Whether or not planners now agree, their efforts were far from satisfactory, being too partial and directed, and there was a huge learning curve ahead. For the public, things were frustrating, as few people understood how the planning process or the development market operated. Successful involvement would therefore require education.

Adams and Ingham (1998) observed that "The publication of the Skeffington Report in 1969 heralded an explosion of initiatives in the 1970s to develop an education based on social justice principles, to create a more active and involved citizenry." Organisations such as the Town and Country Planning Association, The Civic Trust and the Royal Institute of British Architects developed specific education initiatives, there was a growth of urban and rural studies centres and authorities employed specific community development or environmental education officers. The RTPI was behind the field when, in 1978, the Public Relations Board recommended the establishment of an EE working group. A workshop to explore the Institute's role in EE was held in October 1978 in Bristol and the seeds of branch-based activity were sown. The first major achievement of the national group was the preparation and publication of a handbook, *The Role of the Planner in Environmental Education* (RTPI, 1979). This was complemented by a major feature published in *The Planner* (1979) entitled, 'Growing up with the Environment'. The latter reflected a growing number of 'A' Level GCE syllabi, which were beginning to address environmental issues. From the outset, children and young people were seen as a main target for EE work. The group recognised the key role the branches should play in promoting EE and identifying examples of good practice, reflecting the fact that local authorities were already doing a considerable amount of work. The West Midlands County Council (WMCC), under its Operation Green Up programme (Inner City Partnership Programme), and Coventry City Council's EE Project, (funded by the Manpower Services Commission), were early players producing excellent results.

The West Midlands had two enthusiast experts who became representatives on the National Panel, Ian Parkin (WMCC) and Malcolm Crocker (Bridgnorth DC), and by 1981 the Branch had published *Environmental Education – Resources available from Planning Authorities in the West Midlands Region* (RTPI West Midlands Branch, 1981). It was clear that much of the early efforts of the group went into raising EE awareness, with the foundation being a series of planner and teacher workshops. Inviting the education profession onto the Branch EE group through curriculum advisors became one of its strengths. From the outset, planners were keen to acknowledge they did not possess sufficient knowledge and skills of the teaching world but, if the group was going to encourage pupils to study planning and environmental issues, it should ensure the work the Branch did was informed, targeted and needed by teachers.

Resource Registers

In 1985, by now under the chairmanship of George Wilkie, an MSC grant had been secured for the Group to produce a major set of *EE Resource Registers* that were to put the West Midlands Branch firmly to the forefront of the EE work. The aim of the project was to publish summarised lists of all planning department publications that could be used as a resource by teachers and schools. This covered all five counties within the region and referred to documents as diverse as structure and local plans, canal trails and guides on the conservation and reuse of historic buildings. Illustrated by Coventry Polytechnic's second year art students, the five volumes of registers were finally published in November 1986. Over the next few months there followed a series of seventeen planner/teacher events – most fitting as 1987 was European Year of the Environment. With additional financial support coming from the Countryside Commission and the eleven local education authorities, giving a total budget of £14,000, the registers were also circulated free of charge to 3,000 primary and secondary schools.

The registers received widespread praise from both the planning and educational world, with *The Times Educational Supplement* (1987) describing them as "Files of facts for budding planners." In May 1987 George Wilkie, who had been the driving force behind the project, suddenly died of a heart attack and, in gratitude for all that he had contributed, the Group organised a memorial lecture for sixth form pupils. At the same time school interest in the environment was

Young people getting involved with planning.

growing. 1986 had seen the introduction of the General Certificate of Secondary Education (GCSE) and EE was becoming a required part of the curriculum. When the George Wilkie Memorial lecture was advertised in September 1987, under the heading "Is there a future for the inner cities?", the response from schools was overwhelming. Over 450 pupils and 50 staff registered to attend, resulting in hurried rearrangements to find a venue large enough! The lecture, held on 25th November 1987, was given by John Dean, City Planning Officer for Leicester and also President of the RTPI that year. A second successful lecture was held the following year, given by the architect Jake Brown.

The growing interest in EE stimulated discussions with the Women's Institute (WI). With over 61 units in the region and a structure that included an Environment and Public Affairs Committee, the WI was working actively on a variety of environmental concerns (internationally with the World Conservation Strategy, nationally on the Keep Britain Tidy campaign and locally on issues such as the Warwickshire coalfield). Several meetings explored how planners could link in with the WI's local environmental campaigns.

The National Panel – Good ideas, No resources

During the second half of the eighties the national panel produced a poster promoting the role of the planner in EE based on a mock school report for 'a Town Planner'. Aimed primarily at planners, it gave an indication of the potential involvement of planners in various areas within the school curriculum. In June 1985 a presentation was made to the RTPI Council on the work of the group, following which a policy statement on EE was adopted. Other work included the production of a slide tape presentation, *How Planning Works* and a planner/teacher handbook *Plan back to the Future* to celebrate the Institute's 75th anniversary. Production of these resources was handicapped by a lack of funds, giving the appearance that the Institute still saw EE as a Cinderella activity.

Questions were being raised amongst the West Midlands Branch EE members. What was the Institute hoping to achieve by its partial and very limited support of the national initiatives? Without help resource materials would have little impact in schools, nor would many planners get to see them. The problems seemed to lie in the structure of the Institute. The EE Group had no place in the Institute's governmental structure and any request for help or resources had to be made through the Public Relations Board to other, higher Committees. Lack of clear lines of responsibility and access to resources were major problems.

The West Midlands takes a National Lead

During the late 1980s, and now under the leadership of Shirley Trafford, the West Midlands Group continued to promote EE within the region, and by now several local authorities were active and a considerable amount of good practice was in evidence. In 1988 Birmingham City Council won the Branch's 'Special Branch Award for Planning with the Community' with the production of its *Planning a New Road* pack. This was a school resource pack, produced jointly with teachers, which specifically targeted the GCSE syllabi. Elsewhere, Walsall Borough Council had appointed an EE Officer to initiate environmental schemes and work with school and community groups. Sandwell MB was producing various eye-catching information sheets and case studies, such as *Planning – the inside story* and *West Bromwich – Open Fields to Town Centre,* whilst Dudley MB had a dedicated EE team producing planning games and role-play exercises. In places as far afield as Malvern, Staffordshire Moorlands, Stoke-on-Trent and Lichfield there were many good initiatives with schools and community groups.

As the new national curriculum emerged in 1990, it became clear that the guidance on EE not only required schools to study local planning issues in their work, but actively encouraged them to make direct contact with their local planning authority! The mood of the initiative was summed up in the phrase, *education about the environment, in the environment and for the environment.* But it became clear to teachers that EE, identified as a cross curricula theme, had very few, if any, tailor made resources available. The education advisors on the Group, confident that issues such as the out-of-town superstores, industrial location and green belt housing were sure to be popular topics, urged us to help teachers as much as we could. Two initiatives emerged. The first was the publication of an occasional education bulletin *Places and Spaces,* which appeared in September

1988. It was a networking bulletin in which planners tried to inform teachers of examples of good practice, resources and planning help within the region. Produced on a shoestring budget, and using the then magical technology of desktop publishing, the bulletin was to be produced six times over the next three years. Distribution to schools was never straightforward, and whether the publication ever reached the right teachers was never known. Despite this, posting an RTPI publication into every school in the region was no mean feat! The second initiative was a *Handbook* outlining in detail how to use planning issues to deliver the national curriculum. Though requiring monumental efforts, the publication proved a crowning glory.

The increase in demand for our services revealed new challenges. Many teachers knew little of how planning worked and most planners didn't know a *key stage* from an *attainment target*. It became clear something had to be done and the result was the decision to produce a training guide to help both planners and teachers. For the teacher there would be an explanation of the planning process, examples of planning issues suitable for study, guidance on how to structure a classroom project and what information to ask for, and from whom. For the planner, the guide would demystify the new education agenda and give practical tips on how best to help. The *Handbook* was produced by a team of planners and representatives from education authorities and also guided by Brian Milton, Chair of the National Association for Environmental Education (NAEE) and Advisor to the National Curriculum Council (NCC).

A project such as this was worthy of national, not just regional, coverage and, although the National Panel contributed some funding, the first edition was published in 1992 to praiseworthy reviews, with just a print run of 300 copies. Given the work that had gone into the manual, this was a disappointing end result, as was the title, *The Local Environment in the School Curriculum – Using Planning Issues – A Guide for Teachers and Planners*. The Group never lost faith in its handbook and, through the combined efforts of Brian Milton and Mike Grace, sponsorship for the handbook was eventually secured with a grant from Sainsbury's. A glossy version of the manual was re-launched in 1995 (RTPI West Midlands Branch, 1995) with the NAEE as joint author to give it credibility for the education world. The result was a copy of the manual being circulated to every secondary school in the country free of charge, an achievement of which the Institute can be proud. In recognition of its groundbreaking work, the Group received the Branch Award for outstanding achievement and had the distinction of being short-listed in the national finals.

What is happening today?

Environmental Education has had a chequered history, but is now on a high. Having completed the planner/teacher handbook, the group membership had fallen away, but a publicity campaign led to an influx of new members.

The group has now concentrated its efforts on three fronts:

- working with planners through Continuing Professional Development (CPD) and networking events;
- working with schools through activities with teachers and pupils; and
- working with the wider community.

Leaflet explaining how planners can help teachers to use planning issues in the National Curriculum.

Successes have included hosting schools conferences in collaboration with the Geographical Association (GA), with up to 200 sixth form pupils attending; producing a leaflet *Planners, Teachers and Environmental Education* circulated to every member of the GA; and commissioning a planning student to explore best practice amongst planning authorities in working with the local community. Networking Environmental Education CPD seminars have been held and relationships forged with 'A' level examiners, including advising on the planning content of an emerging 'A/AS' level Geography syllabus.

In late 1999 the first edition of a new quarterly networking newsletter *Keeping in Touch* was produced to support the many EE enthusiasts who work in relative isolation. With the 1998 Branch Award going to Cannock Chase District Council for its innovative EE board game, *Chase the Future,* there continues to be recognition for EE work and, with new volunteers coming forward, the future for the Group into the new millennium looks secure.

At national panel level the future also looks to be on the up. For many years a drawback of the national panel was its limited membership, this being by invitation only. For most Branch volunteers there was no contact or rapport with it, or its work. Its aim of disseminating best practice or focussing branch activity had, by default, been largely ignored. Requests for additional resources were rejected and in 1993 a paper was presented to the Institute which recommended that the panel should be disbanded and all future EE done solely by the branches! Despite this, and the Branch's concerns about the previous operation of the panel, we saw the consultation as an opportunity to enhance EE by fighting vigorously for the National Panel. The Branch argued that the proposal to disband the panel was illogical, particularly as the environmental agenda had never been higher. We argued that the strength of the panel would be that it should provide the very thing its previous membership had lacked – real representation from all the branches. By being reformed in this way it could not only remain as the Institute's vehicle for commenting on national and strategic EE issues, but also help co-ordinate branch activity so that we could benefit from each other and not re-invent the wheel! Against the Institute's initial wishes, this proposal was accepted. Our initial fear that EE was still seen as a fringe activity was reinforced in 1998 when a recommendation came out that EE should be viewed not as a core activity, but as a discretionary branch activity. Again the West Midlands Branch saw red and, following further protestations, EE was upgraded to that of a core activity.

Since then, and in the words of its retiring Chairman, Tony Duc, "the Institute has never had such a strong or enthusiastic national panel." It has rewritten and updated the Institute's EE Policy, undertaken a comprehensive national survey of all EE activity and is currently about to embark upon two major publications. One will be a guide for planners on best practice in delivering EE and the other a guide for teachers using locally focused examples of planning issues to help deliver the curriculum.

In the recently completed national survey, the West Midlands comes out as the Branch that has perhaps achieved most in the EE field by way of activities, initiatives and tangible resources. Through our publications we have shown the Institute we can secure sponsorship partners and raise a national profile for the profession. As such, the Branch has been held in high regard for many years and looks set to continue this position for many years to come. Our thanks should be warmly expressed to all those volunteers over the last 20 years who have contributed so richly to what is a most enjoyable and rewarding area of the profession's work.

Urban Regeneration: Enterprise Zones and Urban Development 'Corporations'

Colin Wood

The 1980s heralded different approaches to the problems of older industrial towns and cities. In the early post-war years the emphasis had been on providing new homes to replace those lost or damaged during the Second World War. Attention next turned to the issue of housing quality, as new towns were built and whole areas of housing deemed to be 'unfit for human habitation' were replaced by new municipal housing. This was the period of comprehensive slum clearance and redevelopment that saw the reconstruction of Nechells and Newtown in Birmingham and the building of Chelmsley Wood in Solihull.

By the late 1960s the concern had shifted towards social issues. There was a growing realisation that the worst physical effects of post war reconstruction and slum clearance (decentralisation and the break-up of working class communities) were also accompanied by many people on incomes too low to enjoy a decent standard of living, despite the best efforts of the welfare state. Wholesale slum clearance gave way to 'gradual renewal' and the rehabilitation of areas of older housing, and the Urban Programme (UP) was established to provide educational and welfare support to help residents of older areas escape from what was described at the time as a 'culture of poverty'. The UP was one of the first of a series of national urban experiments targeted at the inner areas of older towns and cities which sought initially to tackle perceived social ills and, subsequently, the increasing problems of job losses and unemployment with the 'de-industrialisation' of the older conurbations. Amongst the more radical of these in the West Midlands were the Community Development Projects in Saltley (Birmingham) and Hillfields (Coventry). These challenged the prevailing notion that the causes of, and the solutions to, the problems of the inner city could be dealt with through social welfare initiatives targeting individuals and families in small geographically defined locations. They argued that the problems of these areas were merely symptoms of wider economic change and they couldn't, and shouldn't, be treated in isolation (CDP, 1977).

The Inner Area Study of Birmingham in the 1970s explored the relationships between industrial decline, job losses, a degraded environment and poor housing, and argued that a comprehensive approach was needed (Llewellyn-Davies and Associates, 1977). This would involve both local government and central government coming together with voluntary organisations, the private sector and local communities, so that all were 'singing from the same hymn sheet'. The report also stressed that a more equitable distribution of national resources would be needed if the problems of the inner cities were to be properly addressed. This set the scene for the 'partnership' and 'programme' areas introduced by the Inner Urban Areas Act of 1978, legislation which also signalled the end of the new towns programme and a re-directing of effort and resources on older declining areas. The emphasis now was on maintaining existing and creating new jobs, with the local authorities having a key role in identifying *and tackling* the problems in their areas.

1979 saw the return to power of a Conservative Government and the perspectives on the nature of inner cities' difficulties, and the ways of tackling them, shifted significantly. Local authorities, especially large, Labour controlled ones, were now seen to be part of the problem rather than the solution. Urban regeneration and job creation were still high on the Government's agenda, but the emphasis was on encouraging the private sector to invest in inner cities, speeding up the planning system, reducing the level of local state bureaucracy and creating new agencies to lead the attack on urban decline. The Urban Development Corporations (UDCs) and Enterprise Zones (EZs) were the first, and amongst the most important, of a series of initiatives introduced during the 1980s aimed at stemming economic decline. This article describes the history of the Dudley Enterprise Zone and the Merry Hill shopping mall; the work of the Black Country Development Corporation; and the Birmingham Heartlands initiative. There were many other projects up and down the West Midlands.

The Dudley Enterprise Zone

Enterprise Zones were initially conceived as an experiment to bring the free market processes of places like Hong Kong and Singapore to the inner parts of British towns and cities. They were intended to be models where entrepreneurialism and private enterprise could thrive, unfettered by the dead hand of state bureaucracy (Howe, 1979). Once designated by the Secretary of State, they would last for ten years and a series of incentives was put in place in order to attract business investment. These included exemption from local taxes; 100% allowances for corporation and income tax purposes for capital expenditure on industrial and commercial buildings; a simplified planning regime to speed up development; and fewer requirements for employers to provide statistical returns to government.

The Dudley Enterprise Zone was one of the first to be approved. Successive local planning authority development plans had earmarked land in the Brierley Hill part of the borough for industrial uses, but the downturn in the regional economy had meant very little interest from prospective developers. Over 200 mineshafts, toxic tips, derelict land and shallow coal workings punctuated the area. The designation of an Enterprise Zone usually followed an invitation from the Secretary of State, but in order to encourage development and investment in this run-down part of the borough, Dudley Metropolitan Borough Council had submitted a bid uninvited. It was pleasantly surprised when it was accepted. Late in 1982 the Round Oak Steelworks site came under the control of the British Steel Corporation and was subsequently closed with the loss of some 1,300 jobs. The

44 hectare (109 acre) site was acquired by Richardson Developments and added to the Enterprise Zone. In 1984 a start was made on what was to become the Merry Hill shopping mall, with the construction of nearly 15,000 m² (160,000 sq. ft.) of retail floor-space.

The Merry Hill Shopping Centre began under the simplified planning regime of an Enterprise Zone. It is now being promoted by the Borough Council as the Town Centre for Dudley.

The planning scheme prepared in advance of EZ designation had tried to limit food and drink retail units, but had not anticipated the cumulative impact of other forms of retail development. Concerned about the effects of the Merry Hill project on adjoining shopping centres, the local authority made a formal submission to the Secretary of State in 1985 requesting that the EZ planning scheme be amended to give the Council more control over the scale of retail development. Meanwhile just under 50,000 m² (550,000 sq. ft.) of retail floor-space were under construction, with further proposals for over 100,000 m² (1.1m sq. ft.) of retail and leisure use in the pipeline. The Borough Council again referred the matter to the Secretary of State, indicating that the scale of retailing ran counter to the strategic planning framework for the West Midlands as set out in the County Structure Plan. However, the Secretary of State decided not to intervene and the Council had a change of heart, possibly influenced by the potential for compensation claims if the planning scheme were to be amended. Despite objections from the opposition Labour group, the scheme got the go-ahead from the full Council in May 1986, just before the local elections saw a change in Council control. By the end of the 1980s the Merry Hill Centre was comparable in size to Wolverhampton town centre, with over 160,000 m² (1.7m sq. ft.) of retail floor-space and over 170,000 m² (1.8m sq. ft.) of industrial/warehouse development either completed, under construction, or committed.

The Merry Hill Centre provokes strong reactions to this day. Its supporters argue that it has physically transformed an abandoned and neglected site; attracted new activity to a depressed part of the region; helped to create confidence in the future for the area; and created new jobs. Its detractors argue that it has taken trade from surrounding centres, including Dudley town centre and Stourbridge; that it benefits car users rather than those dependent on public transport; and that the number and types of jobs created do not help those laid off with the collapse in manufacturing (Tym *et al*, 1993). Despite the serious reservations about the original decision, it is interesting to note that the local authority, Dudley MBC, is now promoting Merry Hill as *the* Town Centre for the borough.

The Black Country Development Corporation

Urban Development Corporations were introduced by the Local Government, Planning and Land Act of 1980. They were single purpose, largely autonomous agencies charged with regenerating the areas for which they were responsible. They were to bring land and buildings into effective use; encourage the development of existing and new industry and commerce; create an attractive environment; and ensure that housing and social facilities were available to encourage people to live and work in the area. They were given extensive powers to acquire, manage, reclaim and dispose of land and property; seek to provide basic infrastructure; and 'generally do anything necessary or expedient' to achieve their objectives. They would be run by up to 13 members appointed by the Secretary of State for their local knowledge or business contacts. The first ones were announced in 1981 in London Docklands and Merseyside. The Black Country Development Corporation (BCDC) was set up in 1987 along with those for Trafford Park (Greater Manchester), Teesside, Tyne and Wear and Cardiff Bay.

The Black Country had problems of a degraded environment, poor internal communications, contaminated and underused land and fragmented land ownership, compounded by low pay and high unemployment. There were over 400 hectares (1,000 acres) of derelict land in Sandwell alone. The Secretary of State initially designated some 2,300 hectares (5,700 acres) of land in Sandwell and Walsall as a development area, against some resistance from Labour group members on both councils. A further 250 hectares (600 acres) were added in Wolverhampton in 1988, but this was largely at the behest of the Conservative Council, which had petitioned for this extension. A development strategy was prepared by Ecotec, which sought to improve the general environment, diversify the local economy, secure inward investment and upgrade the area's infrastructure

(Ecotec, 1987). The BCDC's 1989 corporate plan anticipated that £167m of public money would be needed to tackle the problems and this would 'lever in' a further £845m of private funds (BCDC, 1989). Altogether, it was expected that 28,000 jobs would be created.

In the early years much of the Corporation's energies were devoted to land acquisition and reclamation, but the value of the land acquired represented less than 60% of the purchase costs owing to the fall in land and property prices in the wake of the late 1980s/early 1990s recession. The Development Corporation also gave emphasis to a housing-led regeneration strategy, which planned for up to 5,000 new homes, mostly for owner-occupation and mainly in the south and west of the development area. This represented up to 2,000 more dwellings than allowed for by the Sandwell Unitary Development Plan and involved the reclassification of land allocated for industrial purposes in the statutory development plan. This led to some concern that the private housing emphasis ignored the problems of poor housing conditions and marginal home ownership in much of the borough, and the danger of increasing social polarisation (Nevin, 1993). Whether the same sort of arguments, which had been levelled against the London Docklands Development Corporation, were really as relevant to a depressed part of the West Midlands is a moot point. By the late 1990s, the re-use of redundant industrial land for housing purposes was to form part of the Government's advice to local planning authorities on sustainable housing development (DETR, 1999).

The BCDC strategy envisaged opening up the area by improving road links to the M5 and M6 motorways. The main schemes were the Black Country New Road (Spine Road) and the Black Country Route and their construction was seen as essential to releasing the development potential of a number of hitherto land-locked sites. In the event, delays occurred in the implementation of both schemes, mainly to do with land acquisition (there were negotiations with 1,500 land owners on the New Road project) and problems over Government funding. The BCDC also had ambitious ideas to redevelop the former Patent Shaft Steelworks, some 50 hectares (125 acres) of heavily contaminated land on the northern boundary of Sandwell. The plans here were for a major retail and leisure complex, attracting £450m of private investment and creating 8,000 jobs. The effects of the recession, delays in the provision of highway infrastructure and competition from the now flourishing Merry Hill scheme led to the project being abandoned and the BCDC was obliged to revise downwards its earlier overall investment targets.

Doubts have been expressed about the BCDC's housing and retail schemes, the concentration of resources in the urban development area at the expense of other parts of the Black Country, an over-optimistic assessment of the level of private sector interest and the Government's reluctance to provide sufficient funds to enable major infrastructure projects to be built on schedule (Nevin, 1993). Moreover, it would take much longer than the life of the BCDC to tackle the economic and environmental problems of large parts of Sandwell, Walsall

The construction of the Black Country New Road was essential to unlock the development potential of a number of sites.

and Wolverhampton. However, few would deny that the Development Corporation has made a positive contribution to assisting in the physical regeneration of the area. By March 1995, the BCDC claimed to have generated over 650,000 m^2 (7m sq. ft.) of industrial and commercial floor-space, just under 2,500 homes and 19.5 miles (31 km.) of new roads; to have reclaimed nearly 350 hectares (800 acres) of land; and to have attracted £690 million of private sector investment (BCDC, 1995).

Birmingham 'Heartlands'

As Graham Shaylor has already described, there was much speculation that the Government might be considering setting up a UDC with responsibility for an inner district of Birmingham. The Bordesley-Duddeston-Nechells-Bromford area to the east of the city centre was home to some 13,000 people, most of them renting from the local authority. Birmingham 'Heartlands', as it was to become, had experienced 5,900 redundancies in the first half of the 1980s and over half of all jobs in the area were lost during this decade. Unemployment was double the city average, 70% of children in some schools were from one-parent families and the Nechells ward was in the lowest 10% of all wards in the country on various indices of deprivation. There had been very little inward investment, and although there were nearly 300 hectares (750 acres) of vacant land, development opportunities were limited by a lack of major sites, contamination from previous industrial users and poor communications within the area. The City Council, mindful of the criticisms directed against UDCs elsewhere (and the London Docklands DC in particular) and proud of the history of co-operation between the local authority and the private sector, entered into discussions with the then Secretary of State, Nicholas Ridley, about the possibility of an alternative agency.

In July 1987 Mr Ridley gave his support to a partnership arrangement between the private sector and the City Council, and the Heartlands Urban Development Agency was established in March 1988. The board comprised nine directors chaired by Sir Reginald Eyre, five representatives from major development companies and three city councillors. The shareholding was split 65:35 between the private companies and the City Council, with the Chamber of Commerce holding one share, which entitled it to voting rights. The UDA operated as an 'enabling' agency, providing the broad framework within which development was expected to take place; making the case for the area to the Government; 'trouble-shooting'; liaising between the City Council and the local community; establishing priorities; and trying to ensure that all the public, private and voluntary agencies in Heartlands were aware of its aims and encouraged to work towards their implementation (Wood, 1994). Unlike a UDC, the agency received no direct funding from the Government and had no 'end-date.' It had a small core staff and its effectiveness depended on a limited number of key personnel, who had worked in the area over many years. Local democratic accountability was safeguarded to the extent that the City Council remained the only planning authority for the area.

The Waterlinks at Aston is a key development in Birmingham Heartlands, providing high quality offices and premises in a regenerated canal-side setting.

A leading firm of consultants prepared a development strategy the main elements of which focused on the following seven areas:

- 'Waterlinks', which aims to exploit the opportunities along the canals;
- the 'Star Project' site on the former Nechells Power Station, which is intended to be a 'flagship scheme' to give the area a national name;
- recommendations and proposals for improving and developing existing industrial areas;
- the major improvements proposed for the local authority housing estates of Nechells and Bloomsbury;
- the new urban village planned at Bordesley;
- major improvements to the highway system to overcome the poor links within Heartlands; and
- 'greening and screening' schemes to improve the visual features of the area.

(Tym *et al*, 1988).

The strategy envisaged the development of some 200 hectares (500 acres) over ten years – 40% for housing, 40% for industry and the remainder for flexible business space. Approximately 7,400 jobs were to be created in industry, 5,300 in business and a number of others in the 'Star' project, services and the construction industry (Birmingham City Council, 1988).

By the early 1990s considerable progress had been made. Waterlinks had benefited from a £26m investment (including over £6m in city grant) for the provision of business space and retail uses at Aston Cross. A £10m package of measures had been secured in Nechells to improve the existing housing stock, involving housing associations and private developers in the provision of new homes for sale and rent, and to set up one of the first estate management boards in the country. Phase 1 of the new Bordesley Village had been completed with the construction of 118 homes for sale, most of which had gone to purchasers living within a three mile radius, and £100m of Transport Supplementary Grant (TSG) had been committed to a new spine road linking the area to the M6 at junction 5 (Bishop, 1992). A master plan had been drawn up for retail uses, hotels, restaurants and leisure and recreation facilities on the 'Star' site. However, due to site acquisition issues, difficult ground conditions, concerns about the consistency of proposals with the Unitary Development Plan (especially on retailing) and a downturn in the economy, this project was not on site until late in the 1990s.

Bordesley Urban Village made a major contribution towards regenerating Birmingham Heartlands, with most of the homes for sale going to local people.

Concern about the lack of direct Government funding led the partners in Birmingham Heartlands to review their position over UDC status and, in January 1992, the Secretary of State announced his intention to set up an UDC. Five additional City Council members were to be nominated to the new board and five others nominated by the Secretary of State. More than £50m of additional financial resources from the Government were anticipated initially, though this sum was subsequently reduced as a result of the Chancellor's autumn statement in 1992. This successor UDC, though now time-expired, has been portrayed as a recommended model for urban regeneration, with partners, clients and the community expressing general satisfaction with its aims and achievements (Cook, 1999).

Conclusion

The 1980s represented a new approach to urban regeneration. The emphasis now was very much on private sector initiative, 'flagship schemes', physical transformation, a belief in 'trickle-down' and re-imaging older urban areas. Local authorities were seen as facilitators to the private property market, packaging and selling off land for development and administering the various grant regimes to encourage private sector investment in run down areas. With reduced financial resources and greater control exercised from the centre, the municipalities had to devise new ways to promote their areas (Birmingham's 'prestige projects') or tackle depressed localities by forging new partnerships (Birmingham Heartlands). A range of incentives was offered to industrial and commercial interests to develop derelict land and create jobs (the Dudley Enterprise Zone), although the jobs created and investment generated were sometimes at the expense of adjoining areas. New agencies with a single-minded approach to regeneration were created by the Government, which sought to improve the general environment of older, poorer areas through land reclamation, infrastructure provision and new homes and jobs (Black Country Urban Development Corporation). One could also mention in this context the Housing Action Trusts (HATs) set up to improve areas of poorer council housing and diversify housing tenure, such as Castle Vale HAT in Birmingham.

Much was done during the decade to improve the physical environment of older towns in the West Midlands through land reclamation and new construction. The overall economy of the region was rather healthier towards the end of the 1980s than it had been at the beginning. However, all the evidence at the national level suggests that, despite all initiatives, the gap between the 'haves' and the 'have nots' and between the more affluent suburbs and the poorer inner areas and peripheral council estates had widened rather than narrowed (Robson *et al*, 1994; Social Exclusion Unit, 1998). There is no reason to believe that this was not the case, also, in the West Midlands. Increasingly conscious of the criticisms that the 1980s' approach had neglected the interests of local communities, undermined local democratic accountability and benefited developers and investors rather than producers and consumers, the Government revised its urban regeneration policies in the 1990s. This became the period of competitive bidding, with a renewed and more pro-active role for local government and a greater involvement by local communities. City Challenge and the Single Regeneration Budget were the initiatives now.

Chapter 5:

The 1990s – The Renaissance Years

Overview

Clive Harridge

Aspirations were high at the start of the 1990s as the economic and development boom of the mid-late 1980s continued into the early years of the decade. The decade began with a change in political style when John Major took over as prime minister in 1990 – the days of Thatcherism were now over. There was a strengthening of European influences – the signing of the Maastrict Treaty in 1992 was a milestone. Memorable events on the international scene at the beginning of the 1990s included the release of Nelson Mandela in 1990, the beginning of 'Desert Storm' in 1991 and the start of the troubles in Yugoslavia in 1991, when Croatia and Slovenia declared independence.

Back in the UK, the early boom did not last and the middle years of the decade were marked by a sharp decline in overall development activity. Increasing concerns about the environment led to high profile campaigns, such as the protracted protests by 'Swampy' and others against the proposed Newbury bypass in 1996. The election in 1997 of a Labour Government, led by Tony Blair, provided a major impetus for change and an opportunity to modernise and review the 'old ways of doing things'. The economy strengthened and as the millennium approached there was a strong mood of optimism.

The 1990s were a period of major change in land use planning and planning for the environment. Legislation was put in place giving enhanced status to development plans and the role of planning. International, European and national initiatives for improving the environment and achieving more sustainable forms of development began to have significant influence (*e.g.* Brundtland Commission, 1987).

In the West Midlands the 1990s were the renaissance years – a renaissance that is continuing into the third millennium. During the decade, the region strengthened its identity, urban regeneration initiatives transformed parts of the Black Country and other inner city areas and, as Martin Eade describes, Birmingham city centre was rejuvenated.

From my perspective, I observed three themes of change which strongly influenced planning and development in the region.

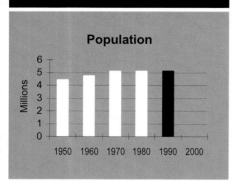

Signs of the Times

Population

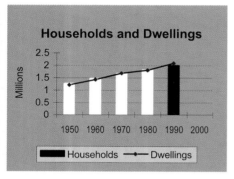

Households and Dwellings

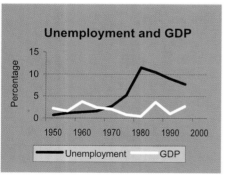

Unemployment and GDP

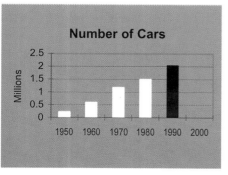

Number of Cars

1. The Plan-Led System

The Town and Country Planning Act, 1990 and the Planning and Compensation Act, 1991 were landmark pieces of legislation which put in place the 'plan-led' system. These were the 'green light' for the preparation of development plans. From then on local authorities were primed with the statutory responsibilities to prepare development plans for the whole of their areas and for planning decisions to be made in accordance with the development plan "unless material considerations indicate otherwise" (Town and Country Planning Act 1990 (Amended)). The aims were to make planning more effective and to inspire more public confidence in the system.

Gone were the days of the 1980s, when Government initiatives had seemingly sought to 'clip the wings' of planners. The significance of the changes were highlighted by Michael Welbank, the then President of the Royal Town Planning Institute (RTPI), who said at the annual conference of the RTPI which was being held in Birmingham in 1992: "We stand at the commencement of a new era in planning. This Government has committed itself wholeheartedly to the concept of the plan-led system to provide the framework for the future development of this country. It is a mark of the greatest confidence in planning itself, in the planning system of this country and the planning profession. We are grateful to this because at certain times during the 1980s planning was seen by many – and even in Government – as a brake on progress rather than – as I would strongly argue – the vehicle for progress."

Local authorities throughout the region began preparing development plans in the early 1990s, but the Government's target of achieving complete coverage of local plans by 1996 was not met and indeed, even at the time of writing in early 2000, some local authorities still do not have an adopted local plan under the new system. In short, the new system proved to be extremely time consuming, particularly the public local inquiry stage, with inquiries commonly lasting many months and the inspectors' reports often taking a long time to be prepared. These problems with the plan-led system led the new Labour Government to introduce measures to speed up the whole process (DETR, 1999b) – measures which are now being put in place as local authorities in the region roll forward their plans.

2. Urban Regeneration

The 1990s saw the implementation of urban regeneration initiatives which had commenced in the 1980s, when the emphasis had been on physical projects. As projects moved from the planning phase to implementation in the 1990s, several parts of the region experienced major construction activity as former derelict and contaminated sites were redeveloped and new infrastructure was put in place. For example, major developments initiated by the Black Country Development Corporation (BCDC) were completed during the decade – the most significant of these was the Black Country New Road, which was opened in 1995 by the then Deputy Prime Minister, Michael Heseltine MP. It was the focus of an urban regeneration corridor extending from Junction 2 of the M5 in the south to Junction 10 of the M6 in the north. The New Road substantially improved mobility in and around the area and opened up some 120 hectares (300 acres) of previously derelict and mostly contaminated land. Alongside the New Road, and elsewhere in the Corporation's area, major industrial and commercial developments took place throughout the 1990s.

A very different approach to urban regeneration took place under the City Challenge Programme, which was launched in 1991. As Clive Dutton's article describes, projects funded under City Challenge brought major benefits to parts of Walsall, Wolverhampton, Birmingham and Sandwell.

At the end of the 1990s, the vehicle for delivering urban regeneration initiatives had changed – the Development Corporation and City Challenge initiatives had been wound up and responsibility for urban regeneration transferred to English Partnerships and subsequently to Advantage West Midlands, the economic development agency for the West Midlands.

3. The Environment and Sustainable Development

During the 1990s increased weight was given to environmental and sustainability considerations in the planning and development of the region. Policy development at international and national levels led the way for regional and local initiatives; the Government's environmental strategy *This Common Inheritance* published in 1990 (DoE, 1990), the UN Conference on Environment and Development (the Earth Summit) in Rio de Janeiro in 1992, and *Sustainable Development – the UK Strategy* published in 1994 (UK Parliament, 1994) were all highly influential. Throughout the West Midlands, local authorities and community groups began developing their own policies and programmes for implementing sustainable development initiatives under Local Agenda 21.

The Government placed greater emphasis on protecting and enhancing the natural environment through a number of measures, including for example, guidance in *PPG12: Development Plans* (DoE, 1992). This required local authorities to take nature conservation and other environmental aspects into account in the preparation of their development plans.

Another key development in the 1990s was the creation of the Environment Agency in 1996. This merged the expertise of the National Rivers Authority, Her Majesty's Inspectorate of Pollution, the Waste Regulation Authorities and several smaller units from the Department of the Environment and sought to protect and enhance the environment in an integrated way.

Graham Harrison's article identifies the diversity and richness of the region's natural environment both within urban areas and the countryside. The natural environment is under enormous pressure as demands for new development continue and as the countryside becomes increasingly important for leisure, recreation and tourism. During the 1990s in the West Midlands, as elsewhere in the UK, there was increasing concern about the environment and the possible adverse impacts of development.

In the West Midlands, growing awareness of environmental issues within the business community led to the formation in 1991 of the Midlands Environmental Business Club. This is a network of businesses, organisations and individuals with the aim to "promote the pursuit of environmentally sound management in industry and commerce with a view to protecting and improving the environment."

With increased importance being given to nature conservation issues, local authorities began to look at new ways of addressing these matters in their development plans. Of particular note were the *Warwickshire Landscapes Guidelines* (Warwickshire County Council, 1993), which were an innovative and pioneering approach to assessing the Warwickshire landscape. They served as a basis for developing detailed management plans and directly informed the preparation of the Warwickshire Structure Plan.

Many successful environmental improvement projects were carried out in the West Midlands during the 1990s, which again reflected the enhanced importance being given to the environment over this period. An environmental scheme which achieved national acclaim was the Sheepwash Urban Park in Sandwell. This project involved the reclamation of 37 hectares (91 acres) of polluted, despoiled and derelict land to form an urban wildlife park, and was a test bed for new ideas in reclamation practice, natural landscape design and nature conservation. The scheme won the 1995 RTPI Silver Jubilee Cup for Planning Achievement.

Conclusions

The themes of change I identified in the 1990s were the plan-led system; urban regeneration; and the environment and sustainable development. The high aspirations for the plan-led system heralded at the beginning of the decade have not been fully realised however – development plans have been far more complex

The award winning Sheepwash Urban Park has turned a previously derelict and despoiled area into a superb wildlife habitat.

and time consuming to prepare than originally envisaged. The themes of urban regeneration, and the environment and sustainable development have resulted in considerable improvements and benefits throughout the region, most noticeably in the inner city areas of the West Midlands conurbation.

During the 1990s the West Midlands was noted for two areas of practice at opposite ends of the planning spectrum – regional planning and planning aid. John Finney's article on regional planning traces the background to the pioneering approaches adopted in the West Midlands, while Sheena Terrace describes how, during the decade, the West Midlands Planning Aid Service grew to be one of the most successful in the country.

At the end of the 1990s planning is again under the spotlight and again centre stage. In the words of John Prescott the Deputy Prime Minister: "..... I believe planning for the future of our communities is one of the most important issues facing us all. And why it is too vital to be left to chance or the old ways of doing things" (DETR, 1998). The Government's national target of 60% of new housing to be built on previously used land focused debate on where new development should take place and what the balance should be between greenfield and brownfield development. The Government's Urban Task Force, under the chairmanship of Lord Rogers of Riverside, reported in 1999 and sought practical solutions to bring people back into cities, towns and urban neighbourhoods to help achieve an 'urban renaissance' (DETR, 1999c).

Much has been learnt from many examples of successful planning and development in the West Midlands during the decade. The 1990s renaissance years were only a beginning. How to achieve an urban renaissance is the major challenge facing town planners and others in the early years of the third Millennium.

Birmingham, the International City: Vision to Reality

Martin Eade

A Vision for the 1990s

Planning, at its best, has always incorporated a visionary aspect, a willingness to think the unthinkable, and to imagine a future that is radically different from the present. In the 1980s, as Birmingham struggled to come to terms with the effects of an economic recession which had devastated its manufacturing base, a sense of vision was certainly required to conceive a recovery in the 1990s inspired by tourism, conventions and modern business services, rather than the traditional motor and metal-bashing industries which had been the mainstay of the city's prosperity for a generation.

At that time, the suggestion that Birmingham might become one of the most visited cities in the UK would have been treated with incredulity. True, the National Exhibition Centre already existed and was already a success – but for most outsiders the over-riding impression of Birmingham City Centre was of a classic car-dominated concrete jungle, an impression reinforced by images of Spaghetti Junction and the Bull Ring and which, it has to be acknowledged, was by no means wholly inaccurate. Fifteen years on, Birmingham has hosted a string of major events, notably the Lions' Convention, the G8 Summit, the Davis Cup and, of course, the Eurovision Song Contest. Those of us who work in the city are still sensitive to the occasional comment, usually in the London-based media, which harks back to the Birmingham of the 1970s – but now we are able to counter such observations by pointing to a string of successful recent developments and by listing the architectural and environmental awards which the city has won, not least being the RTPI Jubilee Cup for Planning Achievement, awarded in 1991 for the creation of Centenary Square. The vision of the early 1980s is now well on the way to becoming reality: Birmingham is an international city.

Very many people, and very many organisations, have contributed to this achievement, not least the people of Birmingham who have, for the most part, welcomed the changes taking place in their city centre with enthusiasm. In an article of this length, it is obviously not possible to do justice to all of these individual contributions and so the following pages concentrate on the key milestones in the planning of the city centre and attempt to show how these have created a framework for positive change.

The City Centre Strategy

As Graham Shaylor has described, development decisions concerning the city centre in the mid-1980s were taken within the context of the statutory *City*

Centre Local Plan (1986). Like most plans, this was a child of its time, and it adopted what could be broadly described as a 'zoning' approach, defining areas for particular activities, such as retail and offices. The plan was an effective tool for managing the status quo, but was not well suited to promoting the kind of radical change that was now felt to be required. The first step along the road was therefore the preparation of a new *City Centre Strategy*, which would articulate the new vision for the city centre. Produced in 1987 as a non-statutory document, it was quite brief, but also in many ways a seminal document. It set out for the first time a series of themes which have now become established wisdom in the planning of the city centre and which have been major factors in guiding and promoting change.

The most important themes were:

- a positive and promotional approach – a basic philosophy of welcoming and promoting activity and new development;
- a commitment to high quality standards and a high quality environment, in the belief that this would itself attract more activity;
- the promotion of mixed uses, and especially of lively, active uses on ground floor frontages – a 24 hour City;
- a 'Quarters' philosophy – the identification and promotion of distinctive quarters within the wider city centre and the encouragement of better links, especially for pedestrians, between these quarters;
- a commitment to 'break the concrete collar' of the Inner Ring Road, now known as the Queensway, and to improve conditions for pedestrians, especially in the city core; and
- a continued understanding of the need for the city centre to be accessible by all forms of transport.

The *City Centre Strategy* was the focus of much debate in the years which immediately followed its preparation. In particular, it provided much of the agenda for what became known as 'The Highbury Initiative' – two international symposia held at the former home of Joseph Chamberlain, Highbury in 1987 and 1988. As Graham Shaylor explained earlier, these brought together local politicians, council officers, the business community and national and international consultants, to examine the strategy and discuss ways forward. These events were important because they engaged widespread support. They also identified the need for a lot more work to develop and put flesh on the bones of the Strategy.

As a result of 'Highbury', the City Council commissioned the series of studies described by Graham Shaylor. The *Pedestrian Movement and Open Space Study* (LDR/HLN Consultancy, 1988), otherwise known as the 'Hilderbrandt Report' after its main author, was one of the most influential of these. It recommended a flexible approach, which would promote better physical integration between the various parts of the centre. Specifically, the report supported the creation of tree-lined urban boulevards in place of the Inner Ring Road and the removal of traffic from key streets within the core area. It is the 'streets and squares' approach to improving the pedestrian environment of the city centre that has been so successfully pursued during the 1990s. This was followed by the *City Centre Design Strategy* (Tibbalds, Colbourne, Karski, Williams, 1990), which provided a coherent urban design approach for the whole of the central area. Again, it placed emphasis on the creation of a 'people friendly' environment, with barriers to pedestrian movement removed, local topography emphasised and the individual character of particular quarters encouraged to develop.

The City Centre Design Strategy recommended a new
'people friendly' environment such as the 'café culture' of Brindleyplace.

One issue which emerged strongly from these studies, and from the Highbury discussions, was the need for effective ways of managing traffic in the central area, while at the same time ensuring that overall levels of accessibility were maintained and, if possible, improved. These issues were addressed in two studies, the strategic *Birmingham Integrated Transportation Study* (MVA, 1989) and the more focused *City Centre Traffic Studies* (Ove Arup, 1988 &1989). The recommendations for the city centre which emerged from this work highlighted the need to complete the Middle Ring Road, as the main route for through traffic, to enable the Inner Ring Road to be 'downgraded' in highway terms. The improvement of rail access, both heavy and light, was also supported, as was the extension of pedestrianisation as a contribution to the urban quality of the city centre. The final study looked at the prospects for further growth in the office sector and was carried out by Ecotec (1998). Its overall conclusion was that growth prospects were good, that there was a need for a 'balanced portfolio' of development opportunities and that this would require the expansion of office uses beyond the existing core office area. The last of these points led back to the need to 'break the concrete collar' of the Inner Ring Road to enable this expansion to happen.

One area not covered by these studies was the future of the city's retail sector. However, at the same time as this consultancy work was taking place, the initial proposals for the redevelopment of the Bull Ring Shopping Centre were being considered by the City Council. It was already recognised that Birmingham's retail facilities needed to be dramatically improved if the city was to re-establish itself as a genuine regional shopping centre and so the principle of redeveloping the Bull Ring was rapidly accepted. However, the detailed challenge of producing a scheme that would be both commercially viable and satisfactory in urban design terms has proved to be an exacting one and, at the time of writing, the 'old' Bull Ring remains in place, although a start on its redevelopment has now been made.

As Graham Shaylor explained, the start of work on the International Convention Centre (ICC) in 1988 was the first major indication that a process of change was truly underway. The arrival of tower cranes on the ICC site also underlined the importance of ensuring that the city had the right policies in place to capitalise on the investment and the ability to deliver the much needed improvements to the public. To this end, the Council established a substantial City Centre Investment Programme which, together with grants from Europe, provided a firm basis for funding a series of major environmental enhancements, notably Centenary and Victoria Squares. The Council's commitment to positively promoting change was also reflected in its use of compulsory purchase powers, where necessary, in order to enable redevelopment sites to be assembled.

The Birmingham Unitary Development Plan

By the beginning of the 1990s, the *City Centre Strategy*, 'Highbury' and the consultants' studies that followed had produced a broadly based consensus within the city on the right way forward. However, the statutory basis for development decisions continued to be the increasingly outdated *City Centre Local Plan* (Birmingham City Council, 1986). This situation changed with the adoption of the city's *Unitary Development Plan* (UDP) (Birmingham City Council, 1993), which took a radically different approach from that of the earlier Local Plan. The emphasis was on key principles, rather than detail, and on flexibility and mixed uses, rather than zoning. It is a tribute to the degree of consensus, which had been built over previous years, that the city centre policies of the UDP attracted very few objections during the consultation and deposit stages of the process. In taking this approach to its UDP, the City Council explicitly recognised that there would be a need for more detailed policies for particular areas, especially those where significant change was envisaged. This is true of most of the city centre and this local planning work has taken the form of 'Quarter Plans', produced in association with local people, local businesses and other interested parties, and then adopted formally as supplementary planning guidance. One of the features of these plans is that they have a strong urban design theme. The fact that they are non-statutory has enabled a flexible approach to be taken to their preparation, tailored to the needs and opportunities of particular areas. So, in the case of the Jewellery Quarter for example, the recently adopted framework, which has as its centrepiece the promotion of a new urban village, derives from a consultant's study, while in the case of the Digbeth Millennium Quarter Plan the work was entirely 'in-house'.

Although the Quarter Plans provide a fuller planning framework than does the UDP, even they are unable to provide detailed, specific guidance for particular sites. This level of advice is supplied through 'master' plans and development briefs, again incorporating a strong urban design element. The City Council has found this approach to providing policy guidance to be particularly effective in the city centre context. It has enabled a clear sense of direction to be established in the UDP and for that sense of direction to be afforded the full statutory weight that comes with incorporation in the development plan. However, it has also enabled the Council to retain the flexibility to respond to changes in circumstances and to develop new opportunities as they arise, without discovering that its hands are tied by over-detailed policies in the statutory plan. Importantly, given that resources are always limited, it has the additional advantage of enabling it to focus its local planning efforts on areas where the need is greatest. The potential value of this approach has been reflected in some of the recent changes to national advice. Examples include the references to supplementary planning guidance in PPG1 (DETR, 1997) and the revision of PPG12 (DETR, 1999b) – although the City Council would wish to see these changes made still more explicit.

The Results

The best way to judge any planning process is by the results on the ground. Against this measure, it has to be concluded that the combination of certainty at the strategic level and flexibility at the more detailed, local level, which has been the hallmark of the City Council's approach within the city centre, has been a success. Rather than seeking to list the various schemes and initiatives that have been implemented over the last ten years, it may be more useful briefly to review the progress that has been made against the key themes of the *City Centre Strategy*, which were identified earlier.

The first of these themes was to welcome and promote activity. The development of the ICC and National Indoor Arena (NIA), together with a string of new hotels and office schemes, as well as leisure uses, bars, restaurants and increasingly new housing, is a clear testament to success. In the Broad Street area, the scale of new activity has been so great that there are now calls for limits to be put on certain types of use, notably pubs and bars. New schemes under construction, for example Broadway Plaza, the Mailbox and Millennium Point, together with others in the pipeline, in particular the major retail redevelopments at the Bull Ring and Martineau Galleries, and Arena Central all indicate that this process is set to continue. Arena Central has recently received outline planning approval, with conditions, from the Secretary of State and includes what might become the tallest building in Britain!

Visitor reaction to the redesigned Victoria Square is almost universally positive.

The second theme was to place an emphasis on quality. This is inevitably a more subjective area, but the reaction of visitors to new developments like Brindleyplace and Victoria and Centenary Squares is almost universally positive, suggesting that the design awards which these schemes have won reflect something more fundamental than just academic or professional approval. The arrival of public art in the city centre has sometimes been more controversial – for example the 'iron man' at the top of New Street – but it has certainly generated interest and debate. Overall, no one would deny that the city centre still has too much that is poor in quality, the Bull Ring being the most obvious example, but more recent developments have set a new and higher quality standard for future redevelopment schemes to follow.

The third theme was mixed uses. This is an idea whose time seems now to have come, with just about every new piece of planning advice or commentary seeming to advocate a mixed use approach. Brindleyplace, now nearing completion, is undoubtedly Birmingham's best example of what a mixed use scheme can mean in practice and its success has paved the way for many other schemes to follow, to the extent that mixed use development is now almost the norm in the city centre. A particularly interesting example is the Mailbox scheme, which involves the conversion of the former Royal Mail Sorting Office, Birmingham's largest single building, into a mixed use development. This will include hotels, high class shops, offices, restaurants, bars and residential development, all arranged around a new pedestrian street created through the centre of the building and extending to the canal at the rear.

The fourth theme was the 'Quarters' approach, which has already been described. Progress on the ground has inevitably been more rapid in some areas than in others. The City Centre Core and the Convention Centre areas have been transformed; the Jewellery Quarter has flourished and an urban village proposal is underway. On the 'Eastside', schemes provide many examples of things beginning to come forward in the Curzon Street and Digbeth quarters. The key catalyst here is the Millennium Point project being led by a partnership initiative between Birmingham City Council, the University of Central England and partners from industry. It has been supported as the major regional project by the National Lottery through the Millennium Commission and will provide a discovery centre, technology innovation centre and 'university of the first age' for young people. As well as educational and technological innovation facilities which look forward, there will be major historical exhibits of science and industry, together with shops, places to relax and an IMAX cinema (Millennium Point Trust, 2000).

The first step towards achieving the objectives of the fifth theme – 'breaking the concrete collar' of the Inner Ring Road – was taken with the remodelling of Paradise Circus. This involved lowering the road, removing the underpasses and creating a wide pedestrian bridge as part of an important pedestrian route from New Street Station and the retail areas to the ICC, Brindleyplace and Broad Street. Further progress has subsequently been made in other locations, including Smallbrook Queensway and Old Square. The next major steps await the implementation of the Bull Ring, Martineau Galleries and Masshouse redevelopments, all of which will enable the re-establishment of links that were cut off by the construction of the Inner Ring Road.

The last theme, accessibility, has often been the most controversial, mainly because it has tended to degenerate, especially in the media, into a car versus public transport debate. In fact, the *City Centre Strategy* is quite clear that the aim should be to maintain accessibility by all forms of transport and this is the basis on which policy has been developed. Progress has certainly been slower than most would have liked, but there have been more achievements than are often recognised. The Middle Ring Road, for example, has been completed; Broad Street has been remodelled; and new, more secure and more attractive car parks have been provided in several locations. Heavy rail services have also been improved, with the electrification of the cross-city line (linking Lichfield to Redditch through Birmingham); and the first Midland Metro light rail line is now in operation.

The Next Ten Years

After this brief review of progress to date, it may be appropriate to end with a few thoughts on what further challenges – and changes – we can expect in the first ten years of the new Millennium. Undoubtedly the key themes of the last ten years will continue to be relevant. In particular, the preoccupation with quality, promoting activity, developing a pedestrian friendly environment and accessibility will certainly remain. But within this framework, there are likely to be some shifts in emphasis. The 'Eastside' developments of Millennium Point, Masshouse, the Bull Ring and Martineau Galleries and a new City Centre Park should create a second pole of activity to balance that already created around Broad Street. These developments should also ensure that Birmingham is able to achieve its full potential as the regional shopping centre, this being a sector that has lagged behind others in the past ten years. This should be matched by continued diversification of the city's leisure and entertainment venues.

A major priority will be housing, both new housing provision which will bring more people to live in the central area, for example in the new Jewellery Quarter Urban Village, and improvements to the existing housing stock, a prime example being the regeneration of municipal housing estates in the Lee Bank area, within the Great Convention Centre Quarter. The removal of the 'concrete collar' will continue. So will the effort to maintain and improve accessibility, with the provision of a new coach station, extension of the Metro system, more secure car parking and perhaps even the formulation of serious proposals for the provision of a high quality, inter-city railway station worthy of the twenty-first century. By any standards, this is an ambitious agenda, but it is an agenda which is firmly rooted both in the vision for the city centre, which was formulated in the 1980s, and in the practical progress of delivering that vision which has already taken place in the 1990s.

City Challenge

Clive Dutton OBE

The City Challenge Programme was launched in 1991 with the aim of transforming specific rundown inner city areas and improving significantly the quality of life of local residents. Some of the country's most deprived communities are represented in the West Midlands and therefore the programme offered great potential by targeting action to be of benefit to some of these areas. Within the conurbation, City Challenge status was awarded to regeneration programmes for Tipton (in Sandwell), Newtown South Aston (in Birmingham), Whitmore Reans (in Wolverhampton) and Pleck/Town Centre (in Walsall).

The aims of the City Challenge Programme were:

- to support strategies for a defined area that would assist it to attract outside investment that would stimulate wealth creation and widen social provision;

- to create a climate of environmental quality and enterprise culture likely to attract people to live and work there;

- to support the development and implementation of locally devised and time limited plans for the regeneration of disadvantaged areas within our cities which would significantly benefit the residents of those areas and provide added value to current public and private initiatives in the area;

- to promote effective mechanisms for delivery of these plans including effective co-ordination of the resources available to the area;

- to promote successful partnerships for the delivery and development of the plans between local authorities and all those that have a stake in the area, including public, private and voluntary bodies and local communities; and

- to develop the capacity within the areas selected for self-sustaining regeneration and self help which would continue after the period of the funding.

Urban Programme local authorities, in partnership with private, public and voluntary sector organisations and the local communities, were invited to develop a comprehensive strategy for the sustainable regeneration of key areas of deprivation and to compete for resources to implement the strategy. The strategies were to be based upon the definition of a clear vision for the area.

Two City Challenge competitions were held and 31 bids were accepted. Eleven "Pacemaker Partnerships" started in April 1992 and were wound up in March 1997: Wolverhampton was one of these. The 20 second round winners commenced operation in April 1993 and finished in March 1998. Tipton, Walsall and Birmingham fell into this category. Each City Challenge Partnership received £37.5 million over a five-year period, depending upon the satisfactory achievement of annually agreed targets and objectives. The programme was delivered through approved, annual Action Plans.

Each City Challenge local authority, together with its partners, was responsible for delivering an agreed programme for its area. The Partnerships set up a City Challenge Management Board, which included representatives of the various partners, to implement their programmes. In the case of 21 of the 31 Partnerships, companies limited by guarantee were established, the other 10 Partnerships remained unincorporated. The following paragraphs give examples of successful City Challenge projects.

Walsall City Challenge

Walsall City Challenge supported the particularly successful development of a new Art Gallery, which houses the Garman Ryan Collection and is located at the Town Wharf, adjacent to the town centre. Recently, the National Lottery

The new Walsall Art Gallery, rising above the canal,
houses a unique collection. It was funded by City Challenge and the National Lottery.

awarded one of the largest regional grants of £15.75 million to the new Gallery. Furthermore, the Government Office West Midlands has given conditional approval for Town Wharf Phase II, which will include further retail, office and leisure development. This project followed the developments by Chartwell at Town Wharf, which created 9,230 m² (100,000 sq. ft.) of retail, office and leisure opportunities, 151 new jobs and 83 new homes.

In addition to housing a unique art collection of national significance, an innovative Endowment Fund has been established, which will provide an income stream to safeguard the medium and long term future of the project. Resources from the Fund have been invested into gilt-edged stock for three years. The project has also been successful in terms of levering in additional resources and in terms of raising the profile of the City Challenge area, and beyond, by creating a major new visitor attraction.

Wolverhampton City Challenge

The largest single project within the Wolverhampton City Challenge area was the reclamation and servicing of land for a science park. The aim was to reclaim and bring forward the 16 hectare (40 acre) former gas works site on Stafford Road as a high quality business park. Some 3,000 m² (32,000 sq.ft.) of floor-space has been developed to date and key tenants include Wolverhampton University and business support agencies, such as Business Link.

Wolverhampton Science Park was the largest single regeneration project within the City Challenge area.

Stafford Road represented one of the largest and most derelict sites in the City Challenge area and a series of regeneration projects had failed in the past, primarily due to a lack of funding. At the same time, the company identified a demand for high quality commercial premises. Critical to the success of the project was the active engagement of the University, which not only became a development partner and the largest tenant in the scheme, but also took an over-arching head lease to enable development funding to be secured. Phase 1 of the scheme is now complete and let, with a waiting list, and Phase 2 is currently being reclaimed, with indications of significant developer interest.

The Challenge Company recognised that, in developing the project, it faced largely unknown ground conditions. As a result, the original plan was formulated to give flexibility to develop the project in phases – this phasing became a necessity. The active engagement of the University was an important catalyst in bringing forward the site. The creation of a joint management company between the local authority and the University will ensure that the long term management and sustainability of the park will be safeguarded.

A personal perspective from Chris Khamis, former Executive Director of Wolverhampton City Challenge:-

"I was Executive Director of Wolverhampton City Challenge from January 1992 to March 1996. It was genuinely one of the most exciting periods of my life. The creative energy generated by pulling together people from widely different backgrounds to deliver a 'joined up' regeneration programme which was owned by residents, businesses and agencies operating in the area was something achieved by few regeneration programmes before and after. From discussions with other City Challenges, this willingness to experiment, learn and achieve real change for deprived communities was a feature of many other City Challenges. Attempting to recapture this 'buzz' of City Challenge should be an objective of the joined up regeneration programmes currently being planned."

Newtown South Aston City Challenge

City Challenge funding was used to develop the St George's Post-16 Centre to provide a variety of educational and community facilities in Birmingham. It was supported by a wide partnership, including the Diocese of Birmingham, Birmingham City Council, Handsworth College, Aston Adult Education Fircroft College, the Newtown Ladywood Task Force, the TITAN Partnership, the College of Food and Tourism, Zen Shin Martial Arts and Fitness Company and various other community organisations. The main objectives of the initiative were to address the issues of low participation at schools and allow students a second chance to succeed at national examinations, thereby improving their chances of getting well-paid jobs. It was not part of the original Action Plan.

The St George's Centre attracted some 400 students during the life of the City Challenge, which led it to become self-sustaining well ahead of the target date. An innovative approach, which involved the identification and organisation of a large number of key partners, was central to the project's success.

Tipton City Challenge

Tipton provides a number of examples of successful City Challenge schemes. The creation of Tipton Urban Village was a key project. At its core is the Neptune Health Park, which provides state of the art health services for local communities, and the Stockdale Parade Shopping Centre by St Modwens Developments Ltd., which provides additional retail units and much needed vitality in the shopping core of Tipton. It was an early example of the implementation of the urban village concept.

The Neptune Health Park, a primary care-led health facility on the site of the former Neptune Works, was formally opened by HRH The Princess Royal on 12th July 1999. Its aims are to develop more integrated working between agencies, within agencies and between workers in Tipton; to increase local access to a number of services in one place; to create highly flexible primary care services; and to increase local ownership and involvement in health. The underlying philosophy of Neptune is integrated working between agencies, staff and the community. It will provide services which are highly flexible, multi-purpose and multi-agency, with shared resources, policies and development.

The Neptune Health Centre is Britain's first healthy living centre and provides an innovative response to health care in an area where life expectancy is well below average.

Neptune has been described as a 'one stop shop' where people will be able to see a health visitor, visit a voluntary group, obtain information, participate in an exercise class, walk around the garden or by the canal, or enjoy refreshments. No appointment will be needed to use many of its services, which will be open to everyone. The services to be provided will include outpatient services, such as X-ray, blood testing and outpatient clinics; community services, such as physiotherapy, chiropody and audiology; minor surgery using local anaesthetic; accommodation for the Black Country Family Practice; primary care surgery (emergency services); a public health information centre; a pharmacy; an optician; voluntary sector organisations, for example the Citizens Advice Bureau and Sandwell Advocacy; rooms for community use; and a cafe.

The partners in the Neptune project are Sandwell Healthcare NHS Trust, the Black Country Family Practice, Murray Hall Community Trust, the Citizens Advice Bureau, Murray's Chemist, Sandwell Metropolitan Borough Council, Tipton City Challenge and Sandwell Health Authority.

Another success was the six Multi-Agency Centres, established at primary schools to promote the benefits of an early start in raising educational attainment levels in pre-nursery children and to support and develop parents as first educators. The significant impact of this project has been widely recognised with, for example, the Regional Director of the Government Office for the West Midlands noting in his introduction to the 1995/96 Annual Report that "Tipton City Challenge's six school-based Multi Agency Centres are making a big difference to the culture of learning amongst parents and very young children locally."

The last example is the Tipton Youth Forum, set up by Tipton City Challenge in partnership with the local authority in 1993. The aim of the Forum is to get young people involved in the regeneration of Tipton and influence decisions affecting the town. Elections were held amongst young people, who voted 19 of their peers on to the Forum to be their representatives. The Chair of the Forum also sits on the Board of the City Challenge. There is also a development worker in place, whose job is to promote and enhance the role of the Forum around Tipton and to establish links elsewhere in the borough. At its inception, the Forum was an innovative development for a City Challenge organisation and it has since won a national award of £15,000 from the Civic Trust Regeneration Unit and J. Sainsbury plc for innovative work with young people. The Forum will continue to operate through resources made available from a successful Round 3 Single Regeneration Budget bid, which was based on giving young people an effective voice through techniques developed by the Tipton Youth Forum.

Some concluding comments based on the Tipton experience

Over the past five years, the Tipton Challenge Partnership has masterminded a £200 million programme which has led to a 50% reduction in local unemployment and a 20% drop in crime. The Partnership has championed community participation to new levels and helped pioneer a health-led approach to regeneration with the UK's first health park. In essence, it has transformed one of the poorest communities in Sandwell, which is the third most deprived Borough in Britain outside London.

The Urban Village symbolises Tipton's renaissance, with the old town centre completely redeveloped and local people rehoused in attractive new properties.

Since the City Challenge team was established in 1993, 800 jobs and 140 new businesses have been created in the Black Country town. Some 700 houses have also been built and 67 hectares (166 acres) of derelict land reclaimed. Why has it worked? In the first place, the programme was geographically specific and manageable in size, covering a population of 25,000 and around 200 businesses. Urban renewal exercises on this scale need a 15-20 year vision to facilitate a long term agenda for planning, as opposed to evolving the programme in response to a short term agenda. The initiative has to be seen in the context of a borough-wide strategy developed, understood and owned by the partners and setting ambitious, but achievable, targets. The programme is underpinned by an Action Plan, which sets clear milestones and output targets that are carefully monitored. Plans have to be flexible enough to drop projects which are not delivering and bring in replacements which can produce the required outcomes.

The team has taken a fine-grained approach to regeneration, with few obvious flagship projects. Linking projects across strategic objectives and the non-physical aspects of regeneration – education, training, safety, health and community development – are essential to sustainable revitalisation. Nobody has a monopoly of good ideas. City Challenge has stimulated local people to bring forward ideas, which the Partnership has been able to develop into real projects. This is what happened with the Tipton Sports Academy, which started as a £15,000 flood-lighting scheme and grew into a £5 million facility of regional significance.

Capacity building before any initiative gets under way allows local communities to participate more fully from the outset. Tipton benefited from a three-year community development pilot project, which spawned the Tipton Action Group, an umbrella organisation for the voluntary sector. To live up to demanding public expectations, it is crucial to 'hit the ground running' by delivering highly visible, often very simple projects almost immediately. It is important to let people know what is being achieved, particularly locally. An eye for non-traditional solutions pays dividends. The Neptune Health Park, an innovative response to health needs in an area where life expectancy is seven years below the national average, puts primary care services within reach of those who need it most.

The short-life nature of City Challenge means that, psychologically, every day counts for those involved in delivery. This does help to assist focus and drive. If sustainable regeneration is the key objective, it is important to consider the issue of succession at the outset and keep it high on the agenda for the duration of the programme. A ten-year vision and five-year Action Plan are now in place for the post-City Challenge period. A tapering end, rather than the 'sudden death' in resources when the five years were up would have been better, but the programme would have had nothing like the same impact without the scale of resources dedicated by the Government to pump prime it.

The lessons learnt from Tipton's experience are many and varied, but most of all they show how the public, private, voluntary and community sectors can work together to great effect. For the public sector organisations involved, it shows how productive working to a common vision and agenda can be.

The evaluation of City Challenge by the DETR concluded that "City Challenge is the most promising regeneration scheme so far attempted. There is widespread support from players across the range of sectors for most aspects of City Challenge's design. They see it as an advance on previous urban regeneration initiatives particularly because of its partnership basis, community and private sector involvement, strategic and targeted approach and its implementation by dedicated, multi-disciplinary teams."

The evidence collected as part of the Final Evaluation would suggest that the programme has had a significant impact upon the areas concerned and indicates that high levels of additionality were achieved. In the absence of the City Challenge programme, or other area based regeneration initiatives (*i.e.* a do nothing or counterfactual scenario), there was a very clear view expressed that these areas would have continued to decline. Overall, the Partnership approach appears to have contributed significantly to the programme's achievements. The programme has also benefited from positive changes in national economic performance.

The sum was certainly greater than the component parts. The key message is to ensure that the success of Tipton and other City Challenge initiatives is not a flash in the pan. If this approach to urban management works, why not more?

The Natural Environment

Graham Harrison

Man has modified the region's natural environment so much that little remaining habitat is semi-natural, let alone natural. Nevertheless, there is so much to be admired between the Peak District in the north and the Cotswolds in the south, or the Welsh marches in the west and the valleys of the Avon and Trent in the east.

So why is the natural environment not properly appreciated, with many people oblivious to its attractions? Partly this is because "to most people this is the region of motor cars, Spaghetti Junction and Birmingham." (Harrison, 1997). Partly it is because there are few physical features unique to the West Midlands. Instead, its prime natural assets are shared with the adjoining counties and regions, with which they are more often associated. Mention the Peak District, for example, and most people think of Derbyshire, the Cotswolds mean Gloucestershire, the meres and mosses Cheshire and the marches Wales. Yet significant parts of each lie within the West Midlands. So, whilst those living in the region turn to its countryside for leisure and recreation, tourism remains focused on the region's history, with its industrial heritage, wealth of historic towns and Shakespearian connections.

The Changing Environment

Only in the last decade have the region's inhabitants really begun to appreciate their priceless natural heritage. To understand why it has taken them so long, we must examine how attitudes have changed over the past fifty years. Although the 1947 Planning Act applied to both town and country, back in the 1950s development was the only perceived threat to the countryside. So long as this was controlled, no one expected the rural areas to change very much. The National Parks and Access to the Countryside Act, 1949 established National Parks, Areas of Outstanding Natural Beauty and Sites of Special Scientific Interest. These were all designated areas within which tighter planning controls were deemed necessary in order to protect the scenic beauty and wildlife from inappropriate development. Beyond that was 'white land', where existing uses were expected to remain undisturbed.

The Malvern Hills are one of several Areas of Outstanding Natural Beauty where visitor pressure causes erosion problems.

But this didn't happen. Fundamental changes occurred that were more insidious than development and mostly beyond planning control. Farming – the dominant land use throughout the region – changed out of all recognition. Three-quarters of the region is still farmed, yet agriculture has been transformed from a labour intensive to a highly mechanised, hi-technology industry. New machinery and the use of agro-chemicals have raised productivity, while successive governments, and more recently the European Union through its Common Agricultural Policy, have shaped the pattern of farming through subsidies and other financial mechanisms.

These changes have mostly run counter to sustaining the region's natural beauty and its wildlife and even though there have been some beneficial initiatives, such as set-aside and grants to support traditional ways of farming in Environmentally Sensitive Areas, much of our countryside has become a wildlife desert. Indeed, you can now often find a greater variety of fauna and flora in our towns and cities. Nor have the changes helped rural life. The lack of jobs caused many young people to drift from the countryside into the towns and cities during the 1950s and 1960s, while wealthy commuters and retired people were moving into the villages. Once there, they want to keep the countryside exactly as it is, creating the NIMBY (not in my back yard) syndrome. This changed the social structure and balance of many villages.

Farming

Climate, topography and soils determine the basic farming pattern of intensive market gardening, cropping and dairying in the lowlands and extensive stock rearing in the uplands. Fifty years ago, when communications were poor and refrigeration limited, proximity to the main towns and cities was also an advantage, but today farming in the urban fringe has significant disadvantages. Many urban fringe farms have consequently gone out of agricultural production and are now used as stables and paddocks for horses – the so-called 'horseyculture'.

The overall quality of the region's farmland is good, with a third of the land in Herefordshire and Worcestershire being of Grade 1 or 2 quality – a figure twice the national average (Carter and Winterflood, 1992). Again there have been changes over the years. Mechanisation has enabled cultivation of the heavier clay lands in the south, leading to the loss of much permanent grassland and the disappearance of over 90% of the flower-rich meadows in south Warwickshire and south Worcestershire. Miles of hedgerow have also been destroyed to create larger fields for cereal production, while nature herself dealt a devastating blow in the 1970s with Dutch elm disease, which in some parts killed half the hedgerow trees. The increasing use of fertilisers and pesticides has also caused concern as chemicals have found their way into watercourses and aquifers. Opposition to such changes was first voiced in the 1960s as the conservation movement grew. It has since steadily gathered momentum, especially during this decade when a series of food crises has really aroused public concern. Now, in the wake of the Bovine Spongiform Encephalitis (BSE) outbreak and the current controversy over genetically modified crops, we are seriously beginning to question the safety of the food we eat.

While changes in farming have fundamentally affected the region's natural environment, other factors have also had a significant impact. In particular, greenfield development has led to increased urbanisation and new roads have eaten into the countryside, causing pollution through emissions, noise and lighting. Today it is not easy to find the peace and tranquillity associated with the countryside of old.

Landscape, Leisure and Recreation

Leisure and recreation have increased too. Fifty years ago most people worked a six-day week, with two weeks holiday a year at most. Roads were poor and, for those Birmingham people without a car, a trip to Sutton Park, or the Clent or Lickey Hills, was a good day out. More leisure time, improved communications and wider car ownership have changed all that. More and more people are turning to the countryside for their recreation and are travelling to the remoter corners of the region, such as the Staffordshire moorlands or the Black Mountains, to find it. At some of the more popular spots, access restrictions have been introduced to reduce congestion and erosion. Following the 1968 Countryside Act, the Countryside Commission (now the Countryside Agency) began to promote country parks as focal points for recreation. The region now has a network of these, ranging in size from one of the country's largest, Cannock Chase, to some of smaller ones, such as Broadway Tower. A cluster of parks, varying from the hillsides of Waseley to the heaths of Highgate and the lakes of Kingsbury, encircles the conurbation. Others, such as Greenway Bank, do

Nationally Designated Landscape Areas

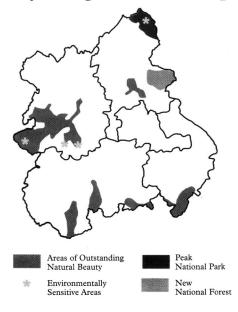

■	Areas of Outstanding Natural Beauty	■	Peak National Park
✳	Environmentally Sensitive Areas	■	New National Forest

likewise around the Potteries, while more distant from the cities are parks at Queenswood in Herefordshire and Ilam in the Peak District (Waugh, 1981). Several long distance footpaths and cycleways have also been created as more and more people visit the countryside for healthy exercise.

With people living so far from the sea, water is another popular attraction. Among the many rivers, the Wye – flowing through the region's only lowland Area of Outstanding Natural Beauty – must surely be one of Britain's loveliest, though stretches of the Avon, Severn and Trent are also locally popular. The extensive canal network is another asset, bringing tourists into the region. Enclosed waters, such as lakes, reservoirs and gravel pits, are much in demand for a range of recreational activities from quiet pursuits such as fishing to more active and noisy water sports such as water-skiing and power boat racing. Many of these frequently conflict with other interests, especially nature conservation. Examples include proposals to extend navigation rights on the rivers Avon and Severn, which would irreversibly alter their ecology.

Although primarily a lowland region, the West Midlands contains some fine upland landscapes, including parts of the Peak District National Park and five Areas of Outstanding Natural Beauty. Between them these cover 12% of the region and embrace such popular places as the jagged outcrops of the Roaches and Stiperstones; the windswept heather moor of the Long Mynd and Black Mountains; the grassy summits of the Cotswolds and Malvern Hills; and the

The potential conflicts between recreation and conservation loom large on Cannock Chase, which is an Area of Outstanding Natural Beauty, a Country Park and a Site of Special Scientific Interest.

heaths and forests of Cannock Chase. These nationally recognised designations help to protect such unique and scenically attractive areas from inappropriate development. Beyond them, a further 25% of the region's lowland landscapes have been designated in structure plans as of local importance.

However, the problem with applying designations to specific areas is that, by implication, the rest is less important and this can lead to a general deterioration in landscape character over large areas. Recognising this, the Countryside Commission (now the Countryside Agency) set up a project with Warwickshire County Council "to consider the unique and distinctive landscapes of the county and to develop a new methodology for landscape assessment tailored to the needs of lowland England." (Warwickshire County Council, 1993). Following on from this, the Commission and English Nature then published a map entitled *The character of England* in 1997. This states that "landscape character exist everywhere in equal measure even if we value it more in some areas than others." This approach to identifying countryside character was commended in *Planning Policy Guidance note 7* (DoE, 1997), which required a fundamental reassessment of local countryside designations, such as Special Landscape Areas. In taking this forward at the local level, Staffordshire County Council and Stoke-on-Trent City Council have claimed another regional first by producing *Planning for Landscape Change* (1999) as supplementary planning guidance to their structure plan review, pending its subsequent adoption in local plans.

Habitat Conservation

Attitudes towards wildlife have also evolved. Originally the emphasis was on protection, particularly of threatened species. Then it was realised that, to protect species, habitats must be protected too and the National Parks and Access to the Countryside Act, 1949 paved the way for this through the system of Sites of Special Scientific Interest (SSSIs). This system remains in place today, but is now reinforced by various European Directives and a network of nature reserves protected by bodies such as English Nature, the Royal Society for the Protection of Birds, the Wildlife Trusts and local authorities.

More significantly, at the UN Conference on Environment and Development in 1992, the Government made a commitment to conserve and enhance biodiversity as a key part of sustainable development (UK Parliament, 1994a). Crucially, this added a new dimension to nature conservation, which now embraces not just conservation of the most important semi-natural habitats, but wildlife in the 'wider countryside' as well. This is fundamentally important in the West Midlands, where habitats are so fragmented. National organisations have already joined forces to produce both habitat and species action plans and the same is now being done at the local level. These action plans will then feed into the statutory development plans. Informed by them, many local authorities are also producing their own nature conservation strategies.

So, after years of neglect and even destruction, there are at last signs that conservation and enhancement of the region's biodiversity is being taken seriously, not just because it gives us inspiration and enjoyment, but because it is a vital component of the healthy environment we need to sustain our economy and well being. The West Midlands has much worthy of conserving. The most important habitats are its woods, grasslands, wetlands, heaths and moors, each of which supports its own range of characteristic species. However, the rich diversity of wildlife in the region stems mostly from the intricate blend of habitats and the way in which they merge into the more extensive tracts of farmland and even penetrate our towns and cities.

Today roughly 6% of the region is wooded, which is about two-thirds the national average. Though much fragmented compared with fifty years ago, woodland is still widely distributed, especially in the west and north. The ancient, semi-natural broadleaved woods are the most important, particularly those on the lime-rich soils of the Lower Wye Valley, which have the greatest range of mature trees and shrubs to be found in Britain and are acknowledged to be of international importance. The Wyre Forest, too, contains an unusual range of woodland types and is a National Nature Reserve. More characteristic are the sessile oakwoods of the west and north, especially in the Churnet Valley, and the pedunculate oakwoods of the former Forests of Arden and Feckenham.

The woodlands of the spectacular Wye Valley are of international importance
for the richness of their wildlife.

Over the years our woodland has fundamentally changed. Coppicing has virtually ceased, allowing many of our broadleaved woods to develop into high forest. As a consequence, wild flowers have been shaded out and certain insects and birds have declined. More noticeably, alien conifers have replaced many broadleaved woods as well as being planted on our heaths and uplands. Notable examples are Cannock Chase and the Clun and Mortimer Forests of the Welsh Marches. Whilst nowhere near as rich in wildlife as broadleaved woods, these plantations do harbour a few specialist insects and birds. Of particular importance is the population of nightjars associated with the plantations and heaths of Cannock Chase.

In recent years, we have begun planting new forests, not just to improve landscapes and create habitats, but also for recreation and to stimulate economic regeneration. Indeed, the latter is a primary aim of the ambitious project to create a new National Forest in the Midlands, part of which will be in east Staffordshire. New community forests, promoted jointly by the then Countryside and Forestry Commissions, include the Black Country Urban Forest and the Forest of Mercia.

While forests expand, permanent grassland sadly contracts. Once such a familiar sight, it has disappeared alarmingly as yet more land has been brought into arable cultivation. That which was rich in wildflowers, grasses and sedges has vanished even more dramatically as intensive management has turned meadows into swards of just a few productive species. Without their larval food plants, butterflies and other insects have disappeared too. Nevertheless, Herefordshire and Worcestershire remain a national stronghold for lowland neutral grassland, with its rich assemblage of plants and insects, and a few examples can still be found elsewhere in the region. Also of national renown are the wild daffodil meadows along the M50 corridor. Calcareous grassland is even scarcer, though fragments can be found in most counties, and wet grassland also occurs sparingly, with the 'Flits' in mid-Herefordshire and the Stour marshes below Kidderminster being good examples. By far the largest tracts of 'unimproved' grassland to survive are those on the Black Mountains, the Peak District and the Malverns, but even here they are constantly under threat from improved drainage, over-stocking and erosion by visitors.

Among our natural wetlands, the meres and mosses of north Shropshire and Staffordshire are the most precious, with the Whixall-Fenn's Moss complex being the third largest example in Britain. Formed in hollows within the glacial drift, they are irreplaceable habitats and are the only wetlands in the region to receive international recognition under the Ramsar Convention. Rivers, streams and canals are another major ecological resource, with the Wye being of international importance and the Blythe national importance. Linear waterways such as these act as corridors along which wildlife can move between one area and another. Man-made reservoirs and gravel pits, many of them important habitats for plants, invertebrates and birds, have improved the diversity of our natural wetlands. Some indeed, notably Belvide and Blithfield Reservoirs and the former gravel pits along the Tame Valley, hold wintering waterfowl in nationally important numbers.

Frequently described in the past as 'wastes', lowland heath was until recently thought fit only for afforestation or development. Now it is recognised as one of Britain's most precious habitats and, in Cannock Chase, the West Midlands has a superlative example. Sutton Park, too, is outstanding, particularly for an urban area, and has recently been designated a National Nature Reserve (NNR). Another NNR is Hartlebury Common, one of a fine cluster of heaths around Kidderminster. At higher altitude, heather dominated moorland occurs on the Black Mountains, the Long Mynd, Clee Hills and the North Staffordshire Moors, where in each case it is threatened with drainage and over-stocking. The North Staffordshire Moors, especially, support a particularly important, but vulnerable population of birds.

Nature is not confined to the countryside, however, and a wealth of wildlife can be found even in the core of the conurbation. Indeed, it is here that many people, especially children, get their first, and sometimes only, contact with nature. In addition to Sutton Park, which is the largest urban open space in Europe, Wrens' Nest in Dudley is among the most notable geological sites in Britain. At a more local level, Saltwells Wood, Sandwell Valley (with its RSPB education centre) and Sheepwash Urban Park are all excellent wildlife oases, as is Park Hall in Stoke-on-Trent. The latter three were once derelict land – a pointed reminder in the pursuit of sustainable development not to regard all brownfield land as ripe for building. Certainly there is an undeniable logic in recycling land, but nature, too, does this through natural regeneration and succession and many of our most precious nature reserves were once industrial sites. Whilst no one would claim every brownfield site as a potential nature reserve, nor should it necessarily be a potential development site. That would be unsustainable and would deny future generations the enjoyment and educational opportunities that such sites can offer.

The Future

So what is the future for the region's remarkable natural environment? We expect a lot from our countryside. It has to be a giant food factory, a source of water and building materials, a repository for waste, a place to generate energy and somewhere for recreation. At the same time we expect it to look pleasant and abound with wildlife. For it to fulfil such an ambitious range of expectations, we need to nurture it very carefully. Only by finding the key to more sustainable forms of development can we expect it to absorb the pressures of global warming, climate change and acid rain along with our more humble demands for further development, increased recreation and more efficient farming.

Whether or not we understand our natural environment, we cannot escape the fact that we all depend upon it. It is the source of the air we breathe and the water we drink, while all our food and medicines are in some way derived from wild plants and animals. As Abraham Lincoln said, "If one day the cities disappear, the fields will survive. But if one day the fields disappear, the cities will not survive."

Regional Planning to the Fore

John Finney

The Beginnings

The 1990s will go down as the decade that saw the re-emergence of regional planning. The West Midlands was arguably, by the middle of the decade, in the vanguard. Central government and others involved with regional planning around the country alike became intrigued by its approach, one that would eventually be promoted as good practice. Why?

The earliest months of the decade saw local authorities in the region launching themselves into a new era of collaborative regional strategic thinking. Their efforts fed off thirty years of embryonic joint working. In the late 1950s and early 1960s, inter-authority overspill agreements were struck to accommodate population displaced by Birmingham's comprehensive redevelopment programme. The late 1960s and early 1970s saw the development of more formal plan making. Many will recall the Regional Study, described in an earlier chapter by Urlan Wannop, which was staffed by secondees from local and central government. Focus during the 1980s through the report of the Regional Study was on action and advocacy, for example to achieve Assisted Area status for the West Midlands. But change was on the horizon.

First Steps

Thus, as we entered the final decade of the Millennium the Department of the Environment charged local authorities in the English regions with giving it advice on the regional strategic planning policies that should be put in place as the strategic context for statutory development plans.

How would the planning authorities in the West Midlands respond? Would they throw themselves into this new challenge with vigour, or would they adopt what might be called a minimalist approach? So began a debate through the newly revamped West Midlands Regional Forum of Local Authorities (the Forum). It quickly became apparent that the issues facing the West Midlands were too serious and the opportunities too important to ignore. A half-hearted approach just would not do. It was, then, for the local authorities to dedicate officers from across the West Midlands to work alongside the Forum's small full-time secretariat. Critical would be their commitment to operate and think regionally.

Presenting the Issues

How would Forum decide to go about its business? Would it adopt the traditional survey, analysis, draft plan and consultation approach? No! A quality product that the majority wanted required something different. The answer was to undertake an initial overview of the West Midlands for sharing with partners across the region. Their commitment to the final agreed strategy necessitated their earliest possible involvement and engagement in the process.

The outcome, published in Regional Planning Guidance Consultation Report No 1 *Asking the Right Questions* (WMRF, 1991), presented the following key issues thought to be facing the West Midlands:

- Creating a sustainable environment;

- Regenerating and restructuring the economy;

- Addressing housing needs and requirements;

- Meeting the need for accessibility and mobility; and

- Analysing patterns of physical structure.

The focus was on forty questions about the choices that would have to be made about the kind of West Midlands stakeholders aspired to achieve. What and where were the greatest tensions and challenges? Were they between sustaining the environment whilst providing for economic and housing growth, and between improving accessibility and yet minimising the need for travel?

Of course, neither the local authorities, nor their strategic land use planners, had a monopoly of expertise and insight into these issues. Nor could they deliver the goods on their own. Hence *Asking The Right Questions* was put out to the widest possible consultation. So began a journey that would see the Forum leading, but not dictating, debate on the big issues facing the region.

Talking Triangles

Making The Right Choices, Regional Planning Guidance Consultation Report No 2 (WMRF, 1992) was imaginative and provocative in responding to views from across the region and in constructing the types of strategic choices that would probably have to be made. There appeared to be no better way to scope the range of choices than to construct strategy scenarios that majored exclusively on concern for either sustaining the environment or delivering market economy led policies.

These were by now familiar battlegrounds. But wait. There seemed to be something missing – people! More precisely, what about concern for the fortunes of people in areas of deprivation? What about their quality of life? The social dimension to regional strategic planning thus rather belatedly entered the fray.

So was 'squared' the environment/economic/social triangle. What was needed were three separate groups of enthusiasts to build and champion each of these approaches. The region had no difficulty in tracking them down and charging each group with developing its case and promoting its cause. Each found itself fiercely debating, promoting and defending its approach to rival groups. Debate by confrontation and cross-examination meant no hiding place for any aspect of our champions' arguments. This approach proved highly effective in exposing the strengths and weaknesses of each of the three scenarios.

The three sets of outcomes, warts and all, provided valuable raw material for the next, critical debate. How best to now stage discussions that were needed to edge the region towards decisions?

Circular Discussion

The answer was constructive face-to-face, round table dialogue between major stakeholders in the region. But some questioned whether all this was really necessary. Wasn't it going over the top? Were not the local authorities taking a sledge-hammer to crack a nut? And what about the risks? Were not the local authorities in danger of losing control? Events were to prove the brave decision to proceed to be inspired.

But how on earth should the round table conference be organised to best effect? The answer was to stage the conference under the stewardship of a neutral, knowledgeable and experienced chair: someone who commanded respect. So it was that the recently retired Department of the Environment Regional Planning Director, David Saunders, found himself chairing the West Midlands Regional Planning Guidance Conference from 8-19th February 1993 at the government's regional offices at Five Ways, Birmingham. Working to a programme he helped structure, the Chairman heard evidence from local authorities and partner organisations. He pushed, prodded and probed participants on their evidence and views.

Conference participants included representatives from the business community and other sectors which had long shown an interest in regional-scale issues. Others were drawn from newcomers to regional debate. Some health authorities and West Midlands Churches, for example, had become alerted to the significance of what was going on. The inclusiveness of the Conference embraced them into its midst. Their contribution provided new insights into the issues up for debate.

Working to 'a big issue a day' agenda, the Chairman set about synthesising discussion into areas of agreement, issues on which participants' views might be capable of coming together, and homed in on areas of outstanding disagreement. The Chairman's conclusions, published in May 1993, left the Forum with the relatively straightforward task of reflecting 'areas of *consensus*' in its recommended regional strategy, the less easy task of making decisions on 'areas of *less than consensus*', and focusing on 'areas of *difference*'.

The embryonic regional strategy was thereby borne out of consensus on the Forum's vision as follows:

- To develop and enhance the West Midlands as a prosperous, dynamic and attractive manufacturing region within Europe, with Birmingham as the international city at its heart;

- To pursue such policies and actions as to ensure the potential for all the citizens of the region to have a good home and a good job within an attractive environment; and

- To have regard to future generations by striving for a sustainable economy within a sustainable environment.

Some of the most significant issues on which *consensus* was achieved included valuing the distinctiveness of the sub-regions; celebrating 'la difference' and the interdependencies between urban and rural areas; highlighting the need for co-ordination and better provision of public transport; and making maximum use of existing transport infrastructure.

Areas of *less than consensus* included the need for Premium Industrial Sites to cater for large, single user 'footloose' industry; how best to handle social issues; making environmental sustainability a reality; and shifting the geographical focus of development from the M40/M42/Solihull sector north-westwards towards the Black Country/Telford axis and North Staffordshire.

Areas of *difference* that remained were levels of housing provision and the spatial distribution of growth; the 'transport corridor' concept (corridors of development versus corridors of movement); and the danger of linear, ribbon development and yet the potential for development concentrated in corridors of mass, high volume public transport.

Perhaps no one should have been surprised by this outcome. Disagreements on housing provision were predictable, whilst the region was clearly on a steep learning curve in investigating new concepts such as 'balanced communities' and growth along 'transport corridors'.

Sea Change

The Chairman offered pointers to help the Forum draw up its advice to Government:

"The bundle of planning policies that have been operating in the Region over recent decades:

- – urban containment using Green Belt,

- – selected peripheral growth,

- growth in freestanding towns in the Middle Ring, and

- regional growth points at Telford and Redditch New Towns

should be replaced with a sea change, a different mix, a different policy package to deliver the objectives of:

- economic revitalisation,

- urban regeneration and,

- environmental sustainability."

Finally, in setting the Forum on its way, he stated: "Several of these (above) points represent a significant step forward ...... Attitudes have changed and some convergence of thinking has taken place.... There is more consensus than has ever been publicly and openly expressed about the priorities for strategic planning in the West Midlands. The challenge is for Forum to pick up the outcome of the Conference process and convert it into draft Strategic Planning Guidance for the region."

But one particular difficulty just would not go away of its own accord; a sometimes fierce debate, largely between shire and metropolitan local authorities, as to whether new development should, in the main, be allocated within balanced communities beyond commuting range of the Birmingham/Black Country conurbation, or in public transport corridors.

Some of the array of documents produced by the West Midlands Regional Forum in setting the standard for good practice in regional planning.

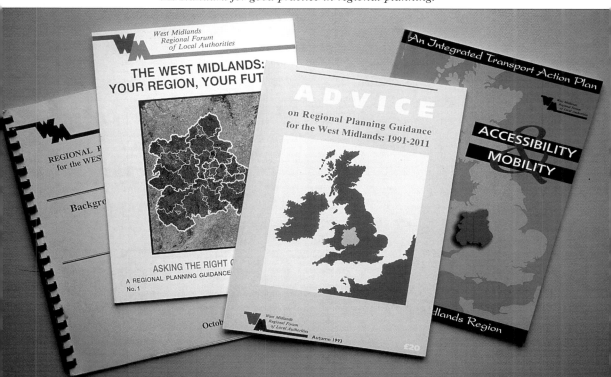

Eleventh hour discussion led to *Advice* (WMRF, 1993) advocating that "new development at suitable points in public transport corridors should be fully and carefully considered in the course of Development Plan preparation and in determining priorities for investment in transport infrastructure."

So it was that *Advice* was submitted to the Government in autumn 1993. The new agenda of sustainable development was embraced. Spatially, economic led development should, it said, be concentrated in the north and west of the region (rather than the south and east) to give emphasis to regeneration in sub-regions with less robust economies. Powerful dynamic forces, driving the region headlong towards decentralisation, should be reined in and renewed energy given to regenerating the major urban areas. Also, most significantly, *Advice* promoted a vision of the region that neither land use policies nor local government alone were in a position to deliver. What was needed was a comprehensive, cunning plan that gave direction to concerted action by partner organisations.

Draft Regional Planning Guidance was published for consultation by the Government in September 1994 and formal guidance (RPG 11: GOWM, 1995) a year later. Both largely reflected the advice offered by the Forum, because of widespread agreement on what was right for the West Midlands during this period of its evolution. Two pieces of additional homework were, however, given to the Forum. It was asked to work with its partners to identify major investment sites and to undertake a general review of housing provision.

Major Investment Sites

Regional Planning Guidance required the Forum to carry out a joint study with the Government Office for the West Midlands and the business community to identify suitable general locations to provide for up to two large sites of a minimum size of 50 hectares (125 acres), each for occupation by a single large multi-national industrial/commercial organisation. While the region had a good track record in attracting mobile inward investment, none of the larger new major investments attracted to the UK had located in the West Midlands. Indeed, since the 1980s, the Forum's own Regional Industrial Land Study (RILS) reports had consistently reported the region's land supply to be characterised by a dearth of readily available, high quality land for commercial investment. Land with potential for economic development had often suffered from problems of contamination and poor provision of support infrastructure. The West Midlands seemed incapable of competing with other UK and mainland European sites – unless action was taken.

So it was that a Major Investment Sites Project Team went about its business – in perhaps a rather unusual way. It decided to seek bids from across the region. Twenty-six proposals were submitted and evaluation by the Project Team led to the key recommendation to 'fast track' two sites for early availability, at Minworth and North of Wolverhampton. These suggestions, published in the

July 1996 Project Team Report, were subsequently taken up by the Forum and became subsumed in the revised RPG11, published in 1998. It was also for the statutory development plan system to address the still limited opportunities for bringing forward additional major investment sites. The study had highlighted the particular difficulties in identifying suitable locations in North Staffordshire. There was also the issue of how brownfield land could be brought forward to provide this type of development.

Review of Housing Provision

The Forum's second piece of homework would, it appeared, provide the ultimate test of partnership working. The task was for the local authorities to work with the House Builders Federation (HBF) and the Council for the Protection of Rural England (CPRE) to judge whether there was a need to revise housing provision figures in RPG11 in the light of new household projections. Although the HBF submitted a minority report, the Review Group's final report contained much that was commonly agreed. Some of its findings and recommendations, published in August 1996, were both unexpected and remarkable. They sparked debate across the land, not just regionally but nationally. Why?

The activities of the Group demonstrated, again, the value of painstaking partnership working and the importance of identifying areas of consensus between organisations with traditionally opposite perspectives. There was also a fascinating interface between planning and housing officers; the importance of both professions taking an active, joint interest in the regional housing agenda soon became apparent. These endeavours were to be shared with other English regions and were to be continued through into the activities of the West Midlands Local Government Association.

If the Group's conclusion "that there is no urgent need for review", as a direct consequence of the new household projections, appeared mundane, two components of 'the integrated policy package' it advocated were far from ordinary.

Social Housing

The Group made a fundamental distinction between the provision of 'affordable' and 'social' housing. The latter should, it said, be identified up front as an essential component (alongside market housing) of dwelling provision. Central to the commended definition was "Housing provided by an organisation – such as a local authority, housing association or local housing company – which allocates accommodation on the basis of need." Failure to specifically plan for the provision of this kind of housing would be to deny large sections of the regional community access to satisfactory housing. Overall housing provision targets would also go unmet. Consequently, of the total regional housing provision (1991-2011) of 330,000 dwellings, some 130,000 dwellings (39%) should be social housing. Sub-regional breakdowns were also given and advocated. The Forum embraced this approach and, although not accepted by Government, the social housing component stimulated immediate national interest. Social housing was very much on the agenda in reviews of statutory development plans in the West Midlands, so much so that the strength of the argument showed signs of finding favour with at least one Examination in Public Panel.

Green and Brownfield Housing

The Group was also keen to avoid housing land provision undermining efforts to use brownfield rather than greenfield sites and the move towards achieving sustainable development. It determined that land releases, especially in green-field locations, which could not be justified by specific housing requirements, should be avoided and that consequently: "Development Plans should provide for the phased release of greenfield land for new housing so that only when there is a need to make good any short fall in the five years supply of land, under the terms of PPG3 (DETR, 1999), would development on greenfield sites be allowed." Revolutionary stuff for regional strategic development planning. But that was not all. When there was more than a five years supply, development plans should provide for the release of allocated greenfield housing only if it secured the development of similar sized brownfield sites. There should be a fundamental policy distinction between the allocation and release of land.

Foundations for the Future

These accomplishments should stand the region in good stead as it faces the challenge of reviewing Regional Planning Guidance (RPG11). No doubt the West Midlands will go about its work in a way that keeps it ahead of the game. The need to address 'new' issues, such as social inclusion, and to embrace the implications of the European Spatial Development Perspective (ESDP), will demand an approach that builds on and develops, rather than replicates, the immediate past. New institutional structures involving Regional Chamber working and the strategies and action plans being fronted by Advantage West Midlands will alone keep it on its toes. Few should bet against the West Midlands coming up trumps again with the freshness that emerged in the 1990s.

West Midlands Planning Aid Service

Sheena Terrace

Planning Aid is the provision of free and independent town and country planning advice to groups or individuals who are unable to afford professional assistance. The planning system can have huge effects on people's lives and their environment and yet, although they may be consulted, the public often finds it difficult to participate in the planning process. Planning Aid was established to help this participation and complement the work of local planning authorities.

It began in the 1970s, following the Skeffington Report on public participation and the realisation of the huge impact of planning decisions on members of the public. Following a report to the Royal Town Planning Institute (RTPI) in May 1976, the West Midlands Planning Aid Group (WeMPAG) was started under the chairmanship of Harry Gardiner and run entirely by volunteers, initially on a county basis. It was not until 1989 that the West Midlands Branch of the RTPI decided to employ a member of staff to run and develop the service.

The Early Years

The first meeting of WeMPAG took place in July 1976 at the then City of Birmingham Polytechnic. There were twelve members of the Steering Group, one of which, Bill Bloxsome, is still a member, though he has had a break of several years. There were nineteen volunteers who came forward following a plea for help, including Sandra Newton who is now employed as a planning aid worker. In those days Planning Aid was perhaps seen as very new, almost revolutionary.

Urban renewal was an area of considerable Planning Aid activity; the types of cases included advising clients on the phasing and status of clearance proposals affecting their homes and on proposing General Improvement Areas, or Housing Improvement Areas, instead of clearance. Other cases involved carrying out negotiations and preparing detailed proposals for an adventure playground for a residents group and assisting clients opposed to a 'non-conforming' use in their area.

The Steering Group and volunteers struggled with codes of practice, conflicts of interest, indemnity insurance and indeed what is a planning aid case? These have been ongoing throughout the life of planning aid. Ian Hunter became Chair of the Co-ordinating Committee of the West Midlands Planning Aid Group and wrote to many different advice centres, including law centres, churches and community associations. Cases were referred to the Group by these centres and Ian then passed them on to the volunteers.

The service continued to be run on a voluntary basis until the late 1980s, when it was proving to be very time consuming for those involved. The RTPI

West Midlands Branch Executive commissioned a study on the feasibility of Planning Aid in the region, which was carried out by Mike Dando, who has since kept up his association with Planning Aid over the years and is now working for the Yorkshire Planning Aid Service on its Rural Project.

The re-launch and what followed

The Branch Executive was very keen that planning aid should continue in the West Midlands. As a result of the Feasibility Study, the West Midlands Planning Aid Service (WMPAS) was re-launched in September 1989, when I was appointed as a part-time co-ordinator. The Branch supported the service financially and received matched funding from the Paul S. Cadbury Trust. Community Networks, part of Birmingham Voluntary Service Council, provided a home for WMPAS at a very advantageous rent in order to help get the service up and running.

All planners in the West Midlands were contacted and a group of forty volunteers came forward to help the new service, with Clive Harridge chairing the Steering Group during this re-launch period. The service started to advertise and contacted advice centres, local authorities, neighbourhood offices and Citizens Advice Bureaux (CABx). To make the best use of its limited resources, its activities were focused on the conurbation. During this period the emphasis of our work began to change from one of primarily handling individual cases in response to enquiries, to pro-active approaches that helped people to participate more fully in the planning process. For example, as the metropolitan authorities were in the process of producing their first Unitary Development Plans (UDPs), two events were organised to help individuals and groups become more involved and influential in the UDP process.

Following the disbanding of Community Networks, it was decided to try and create a small Community Technical Aid Centre with WMPAS, the Digbeth Trust, Birmingham For People, West Midlands Regional Friends of the Earth and the Centre for Energy. It was intended that the group should join forces with other technical aid providers and form a 'one-stop' shop for clients. The group moved initially to Devonshire House and the Know-How Network was formed. Devonshire House is part of the Custard Factory, a former industrial building refurbished to provide office accommodation, studios, art galleries, restaurants and a theatre. Unfortunately the WMPAS office was in the un-refurbished part – conditions in the voluntary sector can be very difficult at times!

Funding for voluntary groups can be very uncertain and gradually members lost their funding and moved out. After two years in very poor office accommodation, WMPAS and the Digbeth Trust moved into the refurbished part of the accommodation, where they still are today in adjoining offices, but still sharing the photocopier and kettle!

During the 1990s the service developed from having one part-time worker to having full-time and part-time staff and two full-time project workers, with a growth in income from £6,000 in the first year to over £120,000 forecast for the year 2000. The Branch and the Paul S. Cadbury, now the Barrow Cadbury, Trust have generously supported the service over these years. More recently, some local authorities have also made grants to the service and the urban and rural projects mentioned later have attracted funding from the National Lotteries Charities Board, the Countryside Agency, the Herefordshire Chamber of Commerce and the Training and Enterprise Council (TEC) as well as local authorities in the rural project area. Indeed, WMPAS was the first Planning Aid service in the country to gain a National Lottery grant.

Initially the service reacted to requests from community groups or individuals who had come into contact with the planning system and needed help. It provided assistance in making planning applications and in responding both to applications and development plans. As the service has developed, it has become more proactive. This started initially in 1992 with the appointment of Ian Silvera as the inner city worker funded by the Birmingham City Council's Inner City Partnership Programme. Ian went out to community groups, local authorities and advice centres to promote planning aid and assist groups with such matters as community plans where the residents wanted to take the initiative. Ian also developed close working links with schools.

The service was awarded the West Midlands Branch Award for Planning Achievement in 1994 and the inaugural National Planning Aid Award for its work in the inner city areas of Birmingham and was commended by the Branch for its parish council training programme in 1998. It has become a model for other services and this has led to new projects in other parts of the country, *e.g.* Bradford, being established along similar lines to the Inner City Project.

WEST MIDLANDS

Providing Free and Independent Town Planning Advice

A GUIDE TO
PLANNING AID
IN THE
WEST MIDLANDS

Leaflet promoting the Planning Aid Service

Over the 1990s the trend has been for community capacity building, empowerment, greater participation and consultation, and 'best value' for local authorities. In this regard, Planning Aid assists both members of the public, by enabling them to participate in the process, and local authorities, by reducing staff time and public inquiry time. Cases have continued to be many and varied. Over the last few years nearly 500 cases per year have been dealt with and these have ranged in size and complexity. In one instance, a volunteer assisted a group of residents to oppose a 'sky park' which consisted of 65 luxury homes with 'hangarages' by their own runway. In other examples, residents have been assisted in appearing at public local inquiries into large industrial developments, superstores and housing developments. WMPAS has also helped a residents group with a 'Planning for Real' exercise, undertaken to find out how the local residents wanted the main road in their area improved.

Cases come to WMPAS from a variety of sources, including the Local Government Ombudsman, the Government Office for the West Midlands, local MP's, CABx and local authorities. The service has also been on the Ed Doolan radio show on Radio WM. This proved a nervous time for Ian Silvera and the then Chair, Peter Storrie, who answered questions live on air, but the publicity was very valuable and we still get calls from residents who heard that broadcast. In 1997 the Shell Better Britain Campaign commissioned WMPAS to write a series of articles on the planning system. These, and the general guide to Planning Aid in the West Midlands, have been widely distributed to local authorities, community groups and other interested parties.

Local Plan Projects

WMPAS has worked closely with central and local government agencies to facilitate participation in the preparation of local plans and the Government Office for the West Midlands paid for the production of a leaflet on these. The aim of the leaflet was to try and simplify the local plans process and the jargon of other formal publications and it has been widely welcomed by community groups, parish councils and others involved in the planning system.

Local authorities have asked Planning Aid to undertake work on consultation or provide advice on, for example, public local inquiries. WMPAS has run events with the then Wrekin Borough Council and Shrewsbury and Atcham Borough Council for individuals and community groups who had made comments on the local plans and were proposing to appear at the public local inquiry. It also ran workshops for the local authorities, which included a background to the local plan process and how to prepare evidence for the inquiry.

In January 1999, Walsall Metropolitan Borough Council invited WMPAS to run an event for community and interest groups on the issues to be looked at in the review of the UDP and about 80 people took part. Following a general introduction to the plan, the participants split up into topic groups to discuss such issues as housing, town centres, the environment and transport. We then prepared a report, which was presented to the Walsall Planning Committee. Building on this work, the service has been actively engaged in outreach work in the whole of the West Midlands Region and has subsequently developed two projects concentrating on two areas identified as having specific problems.

Rural Project

The Rural Project was established jointly with Yorkshire Planning Aid as a pilot project. In the West Midlands, it covers Herefordshire and Worcestershire. These two counties have special status under the Rural Development Agency and contain many isolated rural communities without access to advice centres or even the local authority offices. With a grant from the Herefordshire Chamber of Commerce and the TEC, the project also broadened the scope of planning aid to include helping small businesses, many of which get into difficulties when they are being run from home or are being started up. The general rules about eligibility still applied.

Planning Aid project worker Sakiba Gurda (second left) helping representatives of an action group.

The project started in July 1998 and was welcomed by the local authorities in the area. Herefordshire and Worcestershire had recently separated and new development plans were being prepared for each of the new councils. The project worker, Steve Hemming, in addition to making contacts with community groups, went out and talked to parish councils about the planning system and, in particular, the development plan process. In the second year, Andy Ford, seconded from the University of Central England, took over the project and was asked by the Neighbourhoods Initiative Foundation to help develop a new rural 'Planning for Real' pack. The Countryside Commission, later the Countryside Agency, had launched the idea of Village Design Statements (VDS) to promote local architecture and to prevent the growing suburbanisation of villages. The project has assisted several villages with producing their VDS, which, if agreed with the local planning authority, can become supplementary planning guidance.

Urban Project

The Urban Outreach Project, funded by the National Lottery Charities Board, started in July 1999 with the appointment of Sakiba Gurda as the project worker. The basic aims of the project were similar to those of the Rural Project in that disadvantaged groups in the West Midlands conurbation would be targeted and offered planning advice. Sakiba has established a Steering Group and is busy visiting all the local authorities to see where Planning Aid can assist. The UDPs are all being reviewed at present and the authorities are undertaking consultation with their residents. Sakiba has also started going out to groups and residents' associations to talk about planning in their area and how to get involved.

Planning Aid Nationally

Nationally, Planning Aid has become more prominent. It is now a core service of the RTPI and all its branches have to meet a minimum level of service. In October 1998, Ian Silvera was appointed as the first National Planning Aid co-ordinator. Ian, formerly with WMPAS, was employed to raise the profile of Planning Aid throughout the profession and beyond; to develop the smaller services; and to try and raise funds for all the services. The Planning Aid Panel is convened by the RTPI and sets policy for all the Planning Aid services, including the three independent ones in London, Wales and Scotland.

WMPAS is seen as a pioneer of branch services and has been called upon to help in the development of smaller services by sharing good practice and other procedures. In September 1999, I attended the Town and Country Planning Councillors' Summer School in Swansea to run two workshops for councillors. Many had never heard of Planning Aid and were very interested in the service.

The Future

WMPAS has been extremely fortunate to have the financial support of the Barrow Cadbury Trust for over 10 years and this funding has enabled it to grow and develop into the largest RTPI branch run service in the country. Also, since the funding was not tied to any particular area of work and the trustees were kept informed of our activities, there has been no onerous monitoring by them. However, this type of funding is now very rare and the new projects that have been established have specific aims and objectives as well as targets to be met. Their funding is 'ring fenced' and detailed reports on the work and the financial situations have to be made on a regular basis.

With core revenue funding very difficult to find, as most supporters want an identifiable project that can be monitored to see what they are getting for their money, future sources of funding are likely to be very heavily based on projects. Given the current emphasis on 'best value' and community capacity building, there is a role for Planning Aid to play in trying to achieve these two and other goals. A funding sub-group has been established to try and identify new sources of finance. In addition to charitable trusts, the service will be looking to the Single Regeneration Budget (SRB6) for funds and local authorities are also becoming more supportive as they recognise the value of the work carried out by the service.

The future is not secure; it never can be when Planning Aid is part of the voluntary sector. But being part of the voluntary sector is also its strength. The volunteers who give up their time to help clients not only provide a lot of financial support in kind, but also improve the public perception of planning and planners and help to achieve a better environment for all.

Chapter 6:

2000 onwards – The New Millennium
The most dynamic region in Europe?

Preview

David Chapman

The changes of the last fifty years have been great and it is doubtful if they could have been accurately predicted. We have moved from food rationing in the 1950s to agricultural 'set aside' in the 1990s. We have moved from parochial urban and rural district councils to integrated local authorities and potential regional government. Communications capabilities have mushroomed and we now have access to a global network. We have moved from 'world war,' through 'cold war' to a hoped for 'peace dividend.' But what changes will the next fifty years bring and how will they affect our region? Many forces can be expected to affect the prospects of the West Midlands, but there is enormous potential for the people of the region to shape their future. By reflection, creativity and hard work, it will be possible to address difficulties and take advantage of opportunities. But what will be needed for this? What values, attitudes and actions will give the greatest chance of success?

In looking towards the future, we have invited contributions towards these questions, not to answer them but to stimulate the debate. We believe that it is only if issues are continuously reviewed that we will be able to act responsibly and responsively. Sally Peeters, recently qualified from UCE; Trish Ingram, the Local Agenda 21 Coordinator for Nuneaton and Bedworth; John Acres, the former Chair of the Royal Town Planning Institute (RTPI) West Midlands Branch; and Kevin Murray, the President of the RTPI in the year 2000, all offer their ideas about the future. Their contributions consider the likely challenges we will face and what we can do to achieve a better, sustainable future for all of the people of the West Midlands. The views expressed reveal big issues and some conflicting priorities. We suggest that it is only through open and democratic debate that we will be able to move forward together. The chapter concludes with a reflection upon the main pointers for the future from the last fifty years, the likely issues facing planning practice and the key issues for the continued renaissance of the West Midlands region.

Planning into the new Millennium

Sally Peeters

Having spent the last five months travelling in Australia and New Zealand, with considerable time in Sydney and Auckland, I have seen the relative success of British green belt policies. Take Auckland for example, which has a population of 1.3 million, but is the fourth largest city in the world in geographical area. Terraced houses, tower blocks outside the city centre and housing estates are almost non-existent and dwellings are single storey set in their own plots. The city is a mass of urban sprawl.

How is this relevant to planning in the UK into the new millennium? As the pressure for development continues, I consider one of the major challenges for planning in the UK is to stand firm against releasing greenfield sites for development in order to prevent the kind of urban sprawl to which Auckland has been subjected. This would not only create more sustainable and viable urban areas, but also ensure the protection of the valuable countryside areas surrounding them. The question remains, however, how will planners meet the Government's housing targets and other development pressures without releasing these sites? In order to achieve this, Government and planners must focus on the existing urban areas and make brownfield sites a more attractive option, possibly the only one, if greenfield sites are simply not released for development. Another challenge remains as a result of tight green belt controls. What will happen to our countryside as the bottom falls out of agriculture? If this valuable countryside and farmland cannot be used for agriculture or development, what will it be used for? Farmers are already looking for alternative uses for their land, but how will the planning system respond?

It's not that easy though. The challenge for the future remains for planners to be able to market difficult brownfield sites and actively enable their development. In addition, it is not something that should be left to the planners, but should involve partnerships within the development process to consider the alternatives effectively. This may mean looking at different ideas and considering other options apart from brownfield sites. For example, how much land is wasted by open-air supermarket car parks? This then leads to another challenge – how to utilise this potential without town cramming. Although I accept the problems of the past, denser development designed sensitively should make public transport and local services more viable and therefore lead to a more sustainable way of living for the new millennium.

Linked in with this, I think that there are opportunities for planners to be more innovative. Although design is important, why has some development been refused because it does not fit within the 'existing street scene'? How important is 'street scene?' I consider that in areas that are not particularly sensitive, there are opportunities for development, if only the planner would allow more innovation.

In the new millennium, the planner needs to allow greater freedom and flexibility. Perhaps in this way, developers will be keener to look to develop within the existing urban area. All the players need to work together – planners and the Government working with, and not against, others in the development process. There are opportunities for stricter green belt controls which, combined with greater innovation, flexibility and freedom within the urban areas, could make our towns and cities more attractive options for development. This could then lead to more sustainable patterns of development in the new Millennium.

Sustainability for Real

Trish Ingram

Sustainability is about improving the quality of life, whilst ensuring that we live within the earth's scarce resources, and environmental issues are now being put ever more firmly on the policy making agenda. A key proposal of the World Commission on Environment and Development (Brundtland, 1987) was the "decentralisation of the management of local resources to local communities" (Elkin and McLaren, 1991) and the United Nation's Conference on Environment and Development (the 'Earth Summit') in Rio de Janeiro in 1992 powerfully reinforced the drive for equity and democracy, when 'Agenda 21' was signed by some 150 governments. This spelled out a range of steps that would need to be taken to bring the idea of sustainable development into reality by progressively balancing the social, economic and environmental factors that contribute to a sustainable quality of life. The idea of Sustainability for Real (SfR) originated in the West Midlands, with a small group of people involved in planning and environmental activities, and it is seen as a way of speeding the achievement of Agenda 21 objectives in reality. It is based on 'Planning for Real,' a technique developed by the Neighbourhood Initiatives Foundation, and is designed to put sustainability into practice on the ground. Planning for Real (PfR) was first used in Scotland in 1977 as a way of allowing residents to have a voice in the development of their local area without conflict. The technique makes use of a model, for example a three dimensional representation of the locality, which allows people a 'hands-on' experience. Cards are normally placed on the model to identify important issues and these are then prioritised into options that can be fed into decision-making. This allows people to have an increased level of involvement in defining local issues for action planning.

The concepts of sustainability have recently led to the Government's publication of a vision for *Sustainable Development* (DETR, 1999d). It seeks to promote:

- Social progress which recognises the needs of everyone

- Effective protection of the environment

- Prudent use of natural resources

- Maintenance of high and stable levels of economic growth.

These are objectives that harmonise well with our 'Sustainability for Real' principles.

A 'Sustainability for Real' project is designed to support a co-ordinated and comprehensive approach to be taken to a variety of issues in an area, for example waste management, energy management, land use planning, transport, health care, crime and the fear of crime. It is a concept that can be adapted for use with all community sectors. It aims to achieve sustainable development by balancing the pressures arising from economic development with the need for environmental protection and social inclusion. It seeks to achieve this through the involvement of local people, especially those most frequently excluded from decision making. The project allows communities to explore complex issues in relation to their own environment in an enjoyable, informative and practical way. Most importantly, its aim is to allow communities to make a genuine contribution to decision making within their own locality.

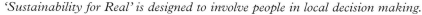

'Sustainability for Real' is designed to involve people in local decision making.

The Pilot Projects

There are initially five pilot projects and each will involve local communities in identifying and prioritising issues that affect their locality. Results from the projects will input into community strategies and support local and regional strategies relating to regeneration, environmental issues and local plans. Throughout the life of the project, the emphasis will be very firmly on community empowerment, community participation, community capacity building, consensus building, conflict resolution and sustainability. Good practice in community participation will be exchanged within the wider 'Sustainability for Real' partnership, with options to disseminate information at a national and international level at a later date. In the longer term it is hoped that the project will lead to a network of sustainable planning in practice.

The pilot projects are:

Building Community Participation in Rural Communities.
Here the West Midlands Planning Aid Service aims to enable community involvement in rural planning by introducing mechanisms for developing community consensus across the range of social, economic and environmental needs.

Education for Sustainability in Schools.
The University of Central England (UCE) School of Planning will promote SfR techniques to develop young people's awareness of sustainability issues and how they can become involved in the decision making process in the area of sustainable development. The aim will be to develop the skills necessary for young people to play their full role in shaping their future.

Community Participation in the Local Plan Review.
By using 'Sustainability for Real' techniques, Nuneaton and Bedworth Borough Council will seek to ensure sustainability issues are fully taken into consideration in an environmental appraisal.

Improving the Quality of Life by Empowering People.
Telford and Wrekin Council is seeking ways of enabling people to work together in their local communities to protect and enhance their environment. The Council is hoping to work with the Neighbourhood Initiatives Foundation in delivering this project.

Ward Action Service Plans (WASPs)
East Staffordshire Borough Council is promoting a Borough wide initiative that aims to improve responsiveness to local 'quality of life' issues and increase community involvement in local democracy. It provides a multi-agency approach to dealing with local issues.

The 'Sustainability for Real' pilot projects will run from April 2000 for an initial period of three years. A forward strategy is being produced to enable the continuation of the initiative indefinitely. People living in communities within the pilot areas are being enabled to work together to identify the issues within their locality that are of most relevance and concern to them. They will prioritise their preferences for the future of their area and explore solutions to the perceived problems. Progress of the project and its results will be monitored by a Project Co-ordinator and evaluated by staff of the Birmingham School of Planning, UCE. As good practice is developed, the experience will be disseminated through the SfR partnership by conferences, workshops, reports and further outreach projects. In this way we hope to achieve really sustainable communities and places.

Looking to the future – the next 50 years

John Acres

There is an old saying that life can only be lived forward, but can only be understood backwards. In other words, the only perfect vision is that of hindsight. The essence of planning is that it necessitates looking into the future, predicting and promoting change. Whilst planners may benefit from hindsight, they cannot afford the luxury of simply reacting to change. Nor can they rely on incrementalism. Planning, by its very nature, is about looking long term, making difficult and sometimes unpopular decisions and dealing with conflicting priorities. Planning is fundamentally a political process.

The new Millennium provides an opportunity to take stock, to look forward as well as back. Our history shows that the pace of change has accelerated and our society has changed more over the last century than it did in previous millennia. It may well change more in the next decade than it has in the last century. The last fifty years have seen some major challenges as well as some major changes to the planning system which have had a significant impact on the West Midlands. What began as a broadly *physical* planning process after the 1947 Town & Country Planning Act has gradually evolved into a more *holistic* planning system, encompassing not just physical, but also social, economic and environmental factors, and this is reflected in the consequences of planning in the region. The grandiose redevelopment schemes of the 1950s and 1960s in Birmingham and Coventry, for example, each with their ambitious and expensive 'motorway style' ring roads, have now been overtaken by more sensitive and arguably more 'sustainable' planning solutions, such as Brindleyplace in Birmingham and the

Coventry Canal Heritage Project, which was the 1999 winner of the Branch Award for Planning Achievement. The current concept of sustainable development is being pursued throughout the region, as local authorities and developers increasingly focus on urban areas and search out brownfield sites for development to try to satisfy Government policies and achieve change for the better.

Planning has changed from being *demand-led* in the 1980s to being *plan-led* in the 1990s and, finally, to being *capacity-led* in the new Millennium. This progression can easily be recognised in both development plan and development control policy in the region. As we look forward to the next fifty years, planners in both the private and public sectors will increasingly need to use their skills to *stimulate* and control change within towns and cities. They will need to be *facilitating* the complex process of redevelopment and regeneration, rather than simply *identifying* locations for development, or proposing land-use change. This will give the planning profession a much more critical role in the development process.

So what are the key pointers to the future? The most important change is likely to result from the information revolution. The use of the Internet seems likely to have a major potential impact on commercial life and social behaviour. This, coupled with the more liberal use of mobile phones, Fax machines, home and office computers, and video links, could give endless scope to re-order land uses, reduce the need for unnecessary travel and introduce genuinely more sustainable forms of development. Whether, of course, the desired positive effects materialise remains to be seen. Past experience suggests that new inventions and practices do not always have the hoped for consequences. The word processor replaced the typewriter, but it didn't save paper – it simply resulted in the production of more paper copies.

Similarly, whilst planners have focused their attention within the last few years on creating a better relationship between land uses to reduce the need for travel, in practice quicker, more efficient and more comfortable motor cars have meant that, on average, people have travelled more rather than less. We now drive longer distances to jobs, shops and leisure facilities. Somehow planners and politicians will need to promote a complete change in culture if people are to desert their cars in favour of walking, cycling or using public transport. The car offers great freedom and flexibility, so if public transport is to work, it must be better, safer, more convenient and above all quicker than private or personal transport.

The loosening of family ties and the emphasis on more informal relationships are also significant contemporary changes. This is something we must accommodate and plan for. Planning has always been concerned with the relationship of land uses. The desire to achieve a better configuration of land use and transport is nothing new. The design of Saltaire, in West Yorkshire, or Bournville, in Birmingham, over a hundred years ago (when society was very different) show marked similarities to the current vogue of 'urban villages'. If anything, the present precautionary attitude to new settlements displays a much less adventurous approach towards development and positive change than hitherto. The power of the public and the voice of the pressure group are now much more influential than in the past, but the precautionary approach should not be used as an excuse for the do-nothing option.

Concentration of development is the current watchword and building at higher density in mixed-use developments offers the scope for greater compactness, less need to travel and potentially more effective public transport. Urban capacity studies and the sequential approach are now designed to maximise the development of urban areas before land is developed on the urban periphery, or indeed, further afield. In those areas such as the Black Country with a loose knit urban fabric, or with a large proportion of derelict land or declining industry, urban capacity studies may serve a useful means of identifying development land – whether for housing, retail, leisure or employment. But at some point, and this may come sooner rather than later, many of our provincial towns and cities, such as Stafford and Worcester, are likely to become 'full up'. At this point the only options will be either to redevelop parts of the towns at higher densities, to enlarge them through peripheral development (in large new suburbs or along transport corridors), or to build entirely new settlements.

If development is to continue within the confines of towns and cities, we have to address the question of whether remodelling urban form, including replacing office buildings, factories and houses which still have a useful life, is a wise use of resources. Is it more sustainable to redevelop or reuse urban buildings if there are better and cheaper alternatives? Is it sustainable to convert old commercial buildings in town centres to residential flats if this means that commercial or industrial development is deflected onto greenfield sites on a by-pass? Is peripheral development the 'next best step' after the development of housing in urban areas?

Whatever happens, clear tensions are bound to emerge. How can the needs for longer term strategic planning and the desire for clarity and certainty (both amongst the private sector and the general public) be balanced against the need for flexibility? How can planners be sufficiently responsive to local needs when there is also a demand to satisfy national and regional objectives, whether for homes, jobs or transport? How can the understandable desire to contain the growth of towns and cities, in particular through tight green belt controls, be balanced against the wider concept of sustainable development, which tends to point towards development being focused in and around our towns and cities? This is a particularly relevant issue for the West Midlands.

We live in an era of rapid change. Just as the car has transformed the way of life for most people over the last fifty years, so too will the information and the telecommunications revolution over the next fifty years, possibly resulting in more people working from home. This may lead to more flexible working hours with different patterns of travel and energy use. It could also result in the need for larger, rather than smaller, homes. How will people respond to these changes? Will planners help to promote them; will they simply react to them; or will they even try to resist them?

For years planning has been both a *catalyst* for change in promoting growth and activity, and a mechanism for *control* of change. Arguably economic intervention, environmental protection and social change have always been at the heart of planning, but it is that delicate balance between promotion and protection, and between positive change and physical control, which will determine whether we move closer towards the ultimate goal of achieving sustainable development, whether in the West Midlands or nationwide.

Planning *real places* for *real people*

Kevin Murray

President 2000-2001, Royal Town Planning Institute

Congratulations to the West Midlands Branch on achieving its 50th Anniversary, particularly during a year which is giving us all extra cause to reflect on both the past and future.

This is a timely exercise for those of us involved in planning, because of the long timescales over which planning operates. Planning is not simply about short-term palliatives that fit with political and financial circumstances, although we have to learn how to play that game creatively at times. We need to retain our sights on the higher goals of achieving sustainable regions, towns and neighbourhoods over the long term. To do so, we need to have an appreciation of how dramatically change is occurring and how planners need to respond.

The changing context

The global economy is affecting every town and region in an increasingly interconnected way and the West Midlands is not free from this, particularly given its traditional strengths in manufacturing. The knowledge age is changing the economy away from an industrialised product-orientation towards information and services, while technological change is rapid and our take-up of new technology is at a much faster rate (compare the penetration of mobile phones and the Internet with radio and cars). The next wave of biotechnology will change the very nature of life itself.

Lifestyle change is taking place not only in the workplace, but also in how we live, how we spend our leisure and how we shop. All of this affects the very places with which planners deal. Do you remember when planners were fighting to keep financial services out of the High Street? Now, with branch closures and the advance of Automatic Telling Machines (ATMs) to dispense cash in the street, we are struggling to keep any in!

Regional and local government is changing constantly in size, scope and structure and this is not likely to stop just because we have reached 2000. Indeed, as the global economy bites everywhere, the pressure to reduce local tax burdens will intensify, putting even greater pressure on governance mechanisms and planning.

Response in planning

If planning is to meet its aspirations of securing sustainable development, we too need to rise to this challenge of constant, ever increasing change.

We need to question continually our own preconceptions of:

- the scope and definition of planning;

- the role of professionals;

- the role of the RTPI; and

- the knowledge and culture of planners.

Scope of planning

The RTPI is already leading a debate on the scope of planning and a range of key themes is emerging. For instance, planning is not merely about regulating land use as a minimalist function laid down by national or regional governments. As a global organisation with practitioners in over 90 countries, the RTPI cannot let governments define the scope so narrowly. We must take responsibility and create a definition of spatial planning which has a wider application. Other public sector functions are also important to planning, whether in the fields of transport, housing, economic development, education or health. Private sector bodies too, as the major investors in most development and infrastructure, are now a major part of our constituency. They are planning investments 5, 10 even 25 years ahead.

Planning is not just about systems, processes or policy either. Traffic Impact Assessments (TIAs), sequential tests and Planning Policy Guidance Notes (PPGs) all have their uses, but as *means* not *ends*. Our aim should be the creation of real, sustainable places at the different scales between trans-national, national, regional and settlement level.

Role of professionals

The role, and perhaps even the very existence, of the traditional professional needs to change because our community and client expectations are changing all the time. People expect more, they know more and they are less willing to be fobbed off by so called experts or gurus. There is pressure on our very legitimacy in such a complex, consumer oriented society, where we have no inalienable right to exist.

Our challenge is to demonstrate that we can bring added value wherever possible. We should illustrate this with positive outcomes in real places and not just hide behind regulatory processes. We should do all this in an appropriate style – learning and listening – because only through an ongoing process of intelligent collaboration with community stakeholders and other professionals will we manage to build up our credibility and respect in these important areas.

Role of the Institute

If the very nature of professionalism has to change in order to meet the changing world of planning, then so must the RTPI. We will not survive if we are about narrow, inward-looking professionalism. The RTPI needs to look outwards and provide a lead and focus for all planning interests – a broader constituency than at present. We should consider, for instance, different modes of membership that welcome in those who are not currently eligible, such as politicians.

In parallel, we should develop and enrich the One Institute concept – combining an outward looking attitude with an inclusive approach towards branches and panels and to individuals. We should embrace our regional and national diversity and develop our enormous international potential. We must be strongly knowledge based, with a research capability to generate up-to-date information and data capable of stimulating progressive ideas and serious debate. To do all this, we need to have a strong promotional role and advocacy mentality.

Knowledge & culture of planners

We cannot just be 'jack of all trade' generalists. We need to ensure planners build up a range of substantive specialisms and an ability to make the necessary connections between them. We already do this in so many areas, but fail to give ourselves due recognition. We must be strongly place-based and focus on delivering solutions in the real world. We therefore need to be integrative fixers, geared to converting 'joined up thinking' into 'joined up delivery'. This means a focus on follow through and delivery of real, sustainable places – something for which we are not widely enough recognised.

We therefore need good analytical *and* judgement skills. Ideally, we should all be *lobe jumpers* – capable of moving from the rational, deductive side of our brain to the more intuitive and spatial side. Our senses and qualitative response to place are as important as any rational interpretation. We need to be collaborative, because we do not have all the expertise and it would be arrogant to think otherwise. All of this needs to be done with an enthusiasm and commitment – even passion – for planning, which will carry others and stimulate our next generation.

Let us make a difference to the West Midlands over the next fifty years...by **planning *real places* for *real people*.**

Conclusions and reflections
Regional renaissance; myth or reality?

David Chapman

Where do these reflections of the last fifty years, and the speculations for the future, lead us? I believe that the future of the West Midlands will be shaped by local effort in response to the global challenges to society, economy and environment. But we must also reflect carefully upon the key challenges that may be identified internationally. We are now at a pivotal moment and, as Blowers and Evans (1997) assert; "...we have reached a defining moment in the relationship between the environment and society whereby changes in economic, political and cultural dimensions are occurring both in the response to environmental change and in order to prevent changes that may threaten survival." At the same time international economies and industries continue to exploit and pollute the world's physical and human resources. While much can be done at the local level, it may be only by curbing this globally that local communities can be 'sustainable for real.'

Powerful forces are at work in the burgeoning 'network society.' Massive opportunities are presented by ever speedier communication and data transfer, but there are also challenges. Castells (1996) suggests that "the development of electronic communication and information systems allows for an increasing disassociation between the spatial proximity and the performance of everyday life's functions: work, shopping, entertainment, healthcare, education, public services, governance and the like." Castells recognises that to date the impact of this potential disassociation has been slight, but it would be unwise to underestimate the longer-term consequences on society and spatial planning. Of more immediate concern, however, are the potential impacts of the 'information technology revolution' upon local democracy and local opportunity. Here Castells (1996) offers little comfort as he sees decision making becoming increasingly dominated by global 'managerial elites.' He sees local democracy and local communities becoming disenfranchised from decision making and at the mercy of global forces.

In the face of these sorts of pressure, will the West Midlands really be able to achieve a strong and sustained 'regional renaissance'? The following thoughts attempt to distil some of the key issues and challenges, if the ambition is to become reality.

Key pointers from the last 50 years

The earlier chapters of this book have given a very immediate, though necessarily partial, account of the way planning and planners have responded to the considerable challenges that have faced them. As explained in the introduction to this book, we have not been able to address many issues adequately and our accounts have had an urban and conurbation-centric bias. But there are some key pointers that transcend these inadequacies.

In the 1950s a whole new institutional and legal framework was set up and put into operation. This achievement has led much of the world in the development of planning systems and continues to do so. In the 1960s the wholesale re-planning and redevelopment of vast areas of our towns and cities was undertaken and new towns built. The scale of these achievements was enormous and shows the potential of public services where there is a real political commitment. The 1970s saw a backlash against the loss of cherished historic places and an upsurge in conservation work, and a new, more subtle, approach to integrated conservation and renewal was discovered. The 1980s revealed the profound dangers of abandoning strategic and regional planning, and the risks which can follow the abolition of strategic tiers of local government. But the decade also demonstrated the determination and flexibility of planners as they responded to the challenges of recession by supporting economic development and job creation projects, often in the face of Government's disregard. The problems resulting from the rejection of integrated land use and transport planning in this period are starkly revealed on the ground today. The 1990s could be regarded as a period of renaissance, with the return of a plan-led system and the fruition of many economic development, regeneration and heritage schemes. Most significantly, the emphasis became more and more people centred, although there is still much further to go.

The Future in Practice?

Kevin Murray has already provided an important insight into what planning practice might be like in the future from an RTPI perspective. Cliff Hague, a Past President of the RTPI, has also suggested that "attitudes and values are likely to become increasingly significant influences in the effectiveness of town-planning practice" (Hague, 1997). Blowers and Evans (1997) have claimed that planning "needs a vision, a rededication of its social purpose in a contemporary context." If so, what form will that rededication take?

I believe that the aims and objectives declared by any society provide a powerful signal of its values and the RTPI guidelines for initial professional education of planners may offer valuable insights into what might be needed. In addition to the acquisition of core knowledge, key skills and the ability to specialise, all planning students are required to reflect upon the diverse values and attitudes that must be appreciated and respected in practice. *The European Council of Town Planners Charter* (1998) also provides a valuable guide, saying that "Town Planning is not determinist. It seeks to establish balance and harmony. It draws attention to the possible options, it safeguards choice for the present and the future." It goes on to say that "Town Planning is rarely an independent process; it must take account of external decisions. It works through and negotiates with the decision-making mechanisms of society's political institutions and public and private sectors. Public participation is an indispensable element in the process. By virtue of its direct involvement with people and their day to day activities, Town Planning inevitably has strong political overtones." These statements have important implications for the future of planning practice and the development of inter-disciplinary relationships between people in the built environment professions.

At the turn of the century, there are several significant reports which may provide an insight into the future of our work and relationships in practice. For example, the Government's consultation *Modernising Planning* (DETR, 1999a) and the Urban Task Force's *Towards an Urban Renaissance* (DETR, 1999c) are worthy of note. Together they may contribute towards possible changes in the law, institutions and ethos of planning and the built environment. *Modernising Planning* highlights the "widely held desire to see the planning system play a positive and effective part in achieving the Government's aims of a better quality of life for all, economic growth and better public service." *Towards an Urban Renaissance* informs the first urban white paper for twenty years and makes a strong case for the development of a co-ordinated network of regional development centres, and also another network of design centres – something which the West Midlands has been promoting for the last decade!

The new Millennium already poses questions for both local and regional administration. How will planning be influenced by the emerging changes in the style of local government decision-making, the appointment of powerful 'mayors' and the adoption of cabinet style local government? What will be the implications for local democracy and what will be the impact on development plans and development control?

Earlier, Alan Cave reviewed the tensions that arose between district councils and the West Midlands County Council after its creation in 1974. He recorded the way those tensions were relieved and positive working relations established, only to reappear when abolition was proposed just a decade later. These experiences may have important lessons for us in the new century, when potential conflicts can be envisaged between the existing local government bodies, the Local Government Association and the new Regional Development Agency, Advantage West Midlands. Clearly, with good will and collaboration, much can be done to minimise the conflicts between, for example, economic growth and environmental protection. But can this be maintained without the benefit of a single regional forum or assembly? Experience has shown that if institutional structures are frequently revised or adjusted (as they have been) without a strategic decision making body, then priorities and focus can be confused and successor bodies either loose sight of strategic goals or repeatedly reinvent the wheel. There are already signs that Regional Development Agencies are developing economic strategies without drawing adequately upon the work and initiative which has already been undertaken over many years by existing bodies.

The changes currently being promoted in the style of local government decision making and the move to cabinet or mayoral decision making may have profound implications for future practice. For example, they are fostering proposals in some places to separate plan making and development control within local government. This apparently simple move could suggest much more profound changes in the UK's discretionary approach to planning. In the discretionary system great reliance is placed upon the development control process to interpret or define planning policies in site-specific ways, thus requiring them to be closely related. The alternative approach, more commonly found in mainland Europe, is the 'indicative' approach (CEC, 1997). In this approach development planning needs to be very prescriptive so that the exercise of development control is predominantly concerned with the technical application of plan policies. This has the benefit of minimising doubt in the minds of prospective developers and householders and reducing the scope for officer discretion and potential inconsistency of outcomes. The risk is that flexibility will be lost in the process. There is evidence (CEC, 1997) that these contrasting approaches are beginning to converge in some respects and it is possible that either approach could have appropriate application in different spatial and socio-economic contexts. Careful thought is required to ensure that the chosen process is closely related to the prevailing institutional context.

So, the future planning and development of the West Midlands in practice is still hard to predict. As observed by Gordon Cherry (1984) "town planning is governed by no fixed parameters; it changes over time and is shaped by various considerations including institutional, political and social, themselves very fluid." Planning institutions and practice may change as dramatically over the next fifty years as they did in the last. What is not in doubt is that the people and planners of the West Midlands will respond and that they will strive to overcome the challenges and to maximise the opportunities. Not for some abstract purpose, but to make the lives, industries and environment of the West Midlands better for everyone today and sustainable for future generations.

Key issues for the West Midlands region

Rising living standards over the last fifty years have provided many people with benefits and opportunities which would have been unimaginable to our grandparents. House ownership, car ownership and levels of disposable income have increased dramatically. But disparities and inequalities have also widened, socially and spatially. The inter-regional disparities, commonly described as the north-south divide, are matched by profound disparities within the region. Broad disparities between urban and rural communities are matched by extreme disparities within them. While many enjoy very high standards of living some live in poverty and homelessness. These inequalities are manifested within, as well as between, localities. Interestingly, some recent data from *Social Exclusion in Birmingham 98/99* (Killeen, 1999) shows that levels of young offenders are often higher in the wealthier wards than the poorer wards, possibly pointing to greater social cohesion in the most challenged localities. But will it be possible to eradicate poverty and disadvantage during the next fifty years, or will they persist? To have any real effect we must be dedicated to take consistent action, individually and collectively.

The transportation challenges facing the West Midlands are not unique, but they are profound. The region has made massive investment in its road system and, despite peak period congestion, there is a high level of mobility and access even directly into the urban centres. This mobility is gained at an increasing environmental and social cost and is dominated by the private car, with relatively poor public transport. Transportation noise and pollution now diminish the quality of life in both urban and rural areas. Air pollution alone could prevent the achievement of more compact and sustainable development patterns. The massive waste of space caused by the need to provide for cars and lorries, not just while moving but also when parked, represents a huge opportunity cost. Similarly, high levels of mobility also diminish local accessibility, especially for pedestrians. Increasing congestion on the roads and capacity limitations of the railways could seriously affect economic growth and limit the competitiveness of West Midland industry.

Previous contributors have asked what the impacts of the Information Technology (IT) revolution will have upon local life styles or movement patterns? Also, whether the potential that information technology has to facilitate integrated transport systems and controls will reduce or reverse the levels of traffic growth? These questions are intimately linked with the current debates concerning concentration or dispersal of settlement patterns. Whatever the answers and approaches adopted, the need for *integrated* transport and development planning is greater now than ever before.

Climate change and global warming present a set of problems that would have sounded unbelievable a few years ago. While tidal incursion is feared for coastal regions, there are real concerns about increased flooding, not just in the major river valleys, but also in major urban areas. The rate of development, especially hard surfacing, is reducing the natural permeability of ground conditions and increasing the levels of surface water run-off, thus contributing to more

The Millennium Point project in Birmingham (above)
and the Sky Blues Arena 2001 in Coventry (below) show that the West Midlands intends
"to set a new agenda for planning and development nationally and again play a leading
international role in social, economic and environmental sustainability. A true renaissance!"

frequent and widespread flooding. Action is needed to address and reverse this trend, partly through firmer development planning, and partly through more effective physical and biotechnological ways of slowing down surface water run off.

In reflecting upon the future development of the West Midlands region, we are not starting from a blank page. So much work has been done to lay the foundations for achieving success. For example, in January 1993, the New West Midlands Group, initiated by David Thew and Christian Kunz, published a little known, but influential report called *The West Midlands Beyond 2000*. Working in a range of topic groups, the report was finally drafted by the late Gordon Cherry. Graham Harrison represented the RTPI Branch on the group and chaired a topic group, which looked at development of urban form in the region. Many of the conclusions that the group came to are valid today.

Examples include the following statements:

- "We urge the strengthening of the institutional framework and strategic management capability at regional level.
- The importance of urban form for the Region must be recognised and (there is) a need to properly manage the deep-seated trends of dispersal and decentralisation.
- We believe that a coherent strategy to guide urban form should positively promote development, but in a way that is sustainable in environmental and social terms over the longer term.
- There is a need for space, (but) there is also the need to respect place.
- Whilst much of the emphasis here has been placed on questions of organisational and physical structure, we sincerely believe that the needs of people should always remain the central focus."
  (Cherry, 1993).

This report, and especially the background thinking, fed into debates on Regional Planning Guidance, providing a practical and aspirational foundation for subsequent work. I would particularly like to endorse the following remarks from *The West Midlands Beyond 2000* report (1993) as they seem to encapsulate the key needs for responsive and participative planning in the next century:

"The future of the West Midlands is not bound up with any 'flagship projects' for development, nor does it depend on the provisions of an ideal, utopian scheme of things into which people are supposed to fit into model environments devised by others. The future we sketch is incremental and open-ended. It relies on the way things are done, rather than specifying what things are done. It relies on the efforts of many rather than the insights of a few." (Cherry, 1993).

The West Midlands is one of the major industrialised regions of the European Union and Birmingham is an increasingly important international centre for financial and business services. In effect, the region is a major 'hub' in both the physical and the network worlds. Our lively and developing local and regional democracy could be used to harness and guide global decision-making. As an international centre for business-tourism and conferences the region can play an influential role, not just as a host, but as an opinion former. This would not be new and it is only necessary to look back one hundred years, to Joseph Chamberlain's time, when Birmingham was internationally known, and emulated, as the best governed city in the world. This region could now set a new agenda for planning and development nationally and again play a leading international role in social, economic and environmental sustainability.

A true renaissance!

Postscript

As we went to press the board of BMW decided (on 16th March 2000) that they would sell off Rover. This threatens the existence of Britain's largest car assembly plant, located at Longbridge on the southern edge of Birmingham. Thousands of jobs depend directly on the plant and many times more rely upon supporting the plant's supply chain, both in production and employee services. The news shocked the country and provoked an immediate response. There have been bitter recriminations between the UK Government and the BMW directors, an 80,000 strong protest march through Birmingham, and a rapid response by the West Midlands Regional Development Agency. Many questions arise. How much of the automobile manufacturing capacity can be saved? What new industries can be stimulated? How will relationships between global capital and regional democracies be affected? Already the three local planning authorities affected have declared that they will not approve the breaking up of the site, or changes of use to retailing or residential development. Hopefully legislators are already considering how obligations can be placed upon companies to work with national and regional bodies to devise humane and measured exit strategies when their commercial imperatives require it.

In an article entitled *How BMW wreaked Rover's revenge* (*The Times*, 16th March 2000) Anatole Kaletsky suggested that "creative destruction has always been a feature of dynamic capitalist economies." While the idea is not comforting, especially for those directly affected by the Rover sell off, the long-term benefits of restructuring West Midlands industry *could* help to create a more sustainable economy for future generations. It is not possible to predict today how this tragedy will eventually turn out. It will involve the loss of some of the older industries and embrace new and 'greener' technologies, but will also result in a stronger place, more able to overcome and transcend the challenges presented by global commercial interests. Without a doubt what can be predicted is that the people of the West Midlands will fight back, and once more planners will be called upon to help make sure of a stronger, more robust and sustainable future.

About the Authors ... ...

John Acres Dip TP, MSc Urban and Regional Planning is Senior Planning Manager for Redrow Homes. Previously he worked for the House Builders' Federation in the Midlands for ten years, and the GLC and Southwark. He is a former chair of the RTPI West Midlands Branch.

Michael Barker BA, DipTP, DMS, DipM, MSc, MRTPI is Head of Planning and Environment at Telford and Wrekin Council, which he joined in 1997. Prior to that he worked for West Midlands CC and Sandwell MBC, where he managed the project team for the award winning Sheepwash Urban Park. He is also a Director of the Town and Country Planning Summer School.

Alan Cave BA (Hons), DipTP, FRTPI, FRICS, FIMgt, FRSA is the National Head of Planning and Economics for Chesterton plc and was the Deputy County Planner and County Planner of the West Midlands County Council between 1982 and 1986.

Fiona Colville BA (Hons), MRTPI is a senior planning officer in the Department of Environment and Transport at Stoke-on-Trent City Council. She has worked on land reclamation programmes and projects for ten years.

John Cornell FRTPI, FIMgt, FRSA is the Director of Environment and Transport for Stoke-on-Trent City Council. He has witnessed dramatic changes in the North Staffordshire region over the past two and a half decades and has extensive experience in urban regeneration.

Ian Dickins PhD, MSc, BSc (Eng), MRTPI, FIHT, Cert Ed is Centro Principal Lecturer in the Birmingham School of Planning, at the University of Central England, where he has taught for 25 years. He has undertaken research and consultancy projects for Centro and other bodies and published a number of reports and articles about transport in the West Midlands.

Clive Dutton OBE, FRSA was appointed Head of Regeneration for Sandwell MBC in March 1996 after being Executive Director of Tipton City Challenge since 1993. He had previously worked with the Black Country Development Corporation and a number of local authorities. He was awarded the OBE in 1998 for his services to the regeneration of the West Midlands.

Martin Eade BA, DipTP, MRTPI has worked for Birmingham City Council since 1986. He is a member of the Strategy Team focusing on city-wide policy development and Birmingham's relationship with the rest of the West Midlands region. He has been closely involved with the preparation of the Birmingham Unitary Development Plan and Regional Planning Guidance.

John Finney BSc (Econ.), DipTP, MRTPI has experience ranging from urban renewal to regional planning. He held appointments with Wolverhampton Borough Council, Birmingham City Council and West Midlands County Council before joining the West Midlands Regional Forum of Local Authorities. He is currently Head of European and International Affairs with the West Midlands Local Government Association.

Alan Geeson, a former Chartered Town Planner, started his career with Chesterfield Regional Planning Committee in 1938. After a spell in the army, he moved to Mansfield and District Joint Planning Committee in 1946, to Coventry in 1949 and then to Birmingham as Chief Planning Assistant in 1957. He transferred to West Midlands County Council as Assistant County Planner in 1974 until retiring in 1981.

Terence W. Gregory OBE, Hon. MA, FRIBA, FRICS, FRTPI (retd.), FCIWEM was Coventry City Architect and Planning Officer from 1964-1973 and Chief Executive and Town Clerk from 1973-1983. He was on the London and Metropolitan Government Staff Commission (West Midlands) 1985-1992, various Government Advisory Bodies and was co-author of City Centre Redevelopment in 1974. He was also Chairman of the RTPI West Midlands Branch and a member of the RTPI Council.

John Holliday BA (Hons), FRTPI, FLI worked in the Durham and Kent County Planning Offices before moving to the Birmingham College of Art and then to Coventry Polytechnic, now the University, as head of the Department of Urban and Regional Planning. He has been a member of the Councils of the RTPI and the Town and Country Planning Association and has published several books.

Trish Ingram BA (Hons) Geography, DipTCP, Dip Environmental Decision Making, has fourteen years experience as a planning officer in local government, at Lichfield District Council and Cannock Chase Council. She has been the Local Agenda 21 co-ordinator for Nuneaton and Bedworth Borough Council since 1999 and has led the local Sustainability for Real project.

Lewis Jones DipArch (Hons.), DipTP, ARIBA, FRTPI had various appointments before moving to Worcestershire County Council in 1960. He joined the John Madin Design Group in 1963 and was a partner from 1975-1985, when he moved to Chesterton International plc. He is a consultant to Bigwood Associates and a member of the Birmingham City Council's Conservation Areas Advisory Committee.

Peter J Larkham BA, PhD Cert Ed is a geographer by background, but has lectured in planning at the University of Central England since 1991. He is now Reader in Planning and joint author of the RTPI's commissioned study on The Character of Conservation Areas; author of Conservation and the City (Routledge, 1996) and of numerous academic and professional journal articles.

Michael Law FRTPI (retd.) started his career in Northamptonshire in 1948 and arrived in Shropshire as County Planning Officer in 1969 after working in Nottinghamshire, Lindsey and East Suffolk. He retired as County Planning Officer in 1988 and from then until 1998 was a Member of the Lord Chancellor's Panel of Independent Inspectors. He is now fully retired.

John Lillywhite BA, MSc, DipTP, MRTPI came to Coventry City Council from Yorkshire in 1970. In 1975 he moved to the West Midlands County Council to work on the county structure plan. In 1986 he became a strategic planner with Wolverhampton Metropolitan Borough Council, which he has since represented at regional and sub-regional levels.

Kevin Murray BSc (Hons), DipTP, MSc, MRTPI is President of the Royal Town Planning Institute for 2000-2001 and a founder member of the Urban Design Alliance. He is a director of international consultancy EDAW and practices across the UK and overseas as well as writing and lecturing extensively. He was also involved in the influential Birmingham Urban Design Study.

Harry Noble OBE, MA, DipTP (Dist.), ARIBA, MRTPI moved from Yorkshire to Droitwich Town Development as Deputy Chief Architect in 1963. In 1967 he joined Birmingham as Assistant City Architect. In 1973 he moved to Coventry as the City Architect and Planning Officer and remained there until 1993, becoming Director of Economic Development and Planning in 1986. He now runs his own consultancy business. In 1993 he was awarded the OBE for 'services to local authority'.

Sally Peeters BSc (Hons) Environmental Planning, Dip TCP studied at the Birmingham School of Planning, UCE, and was awarded the Diploma in Town and Country Planning with Distinction in 1999. She also received the RTPI course prize. Since then she has been travelling and studying in Australia.

Graham Reddie MBE, ARIBA, MRTPI (retd.) joined Redditch Development Corporation in 1965 as Deputy Chief Architect and Planning Officer and became Chief in 1979 before retiring in 1982. In 1987 he co-founded and has since led the Midlands Amenity Societies' Association (MASA) and received the MBE for this voluntary work in 1999.

Colin Rodgers DipTP, MRTPI (retd.) joined Birmingham City Council in 1941 and worked for them until he retired in 1986, rising to Senior Assistant City Planning Officer in 1974. From 1957-1965 he led a multi-disciplinary team for the Central Redevelopment Areas. He was Chairman of the RTPI West Midlands Branch in 1976 and Secretary from 1969-1973.

Will Scott MA (Env. Plg.), BSc (Hons, Arch.), DipUD, RIBA, ARB, MRTPI, IHBC worked on urban design with Richmond-upon-Thames Borough Council before moving to Worcester City Council in 1978. Since 1986 he has been its Principal Conservation Officer with responsibility for historic buildings and areas.

Graham Shaylor OBE, FRTPI, FRSA worked in various local authorities before moving to Birmingham, where he was City Planning Officer from 1974-1986 and Director of Development and Deputy Chief Executive from 1986-1990. He was awarded the OBE in 1986 for his leadership in regenerating the city of Birmingham. Since 1990 he has run his own planning consultancy.

Alan Shrimpton MCIEH is the Development Director for Bournville Village Trust. He is a qualified Environmental Health Officer, who has specialised in housing and urban regeneration for over 35 years.

Sheena Terrace BA (Jt.Hons), DipTP, MRTPI has been the West Midlands Planning Aid Co-ordinator since 1989. Prior to this she worked for Birmingham and Leicester City Councils in both development control and on local plans.

Urlan Wannop OBE, MA, MCD, MRTPI worked initially in local government and for consultants planning five new towns. He then led the Coventry-Solihull-Warwickshire Sub-Regional Study from 1968-71 and directed the West Scotland Plan from 1972-74 before joining Strathclyde Regional Council. In 1981 he went to the University of Strathclyde as Professor of Urban and Regional Planning and is now Professor Emeritus. He is author of The Regional Imperative (Jessica Kingsley, 1995).

Colin Wood BSc (Hons) Geography, Dip TP, MA TCP is Postgraduate Programme Director of the Birmingham School of Planning at the University of Central England. He worked for Greater Manchester County Council from 1974-1986 and Manchester City Council from 1986-1988.

Peter Wright BSc (Hons) Town Planning, MBA (Public Service) is Team Leader Local Planning at Birmingham City Council, Department of Planning and Architecture. He is chair of the RTPI West Midlands Branch Environmental Education group and a member of the national RTPI panel.

... ... and the Editors and Picture Editor

David Chapman AADipl, RIBA, DipLD, ALI, DipTP, MRTPI, MIHBC, Cert Ed. is Professor and Head of the Birmingham School of Planning at the University of Central England. He worked for Nottinghamshire County Council from 1974-78 and Birmingham City Council from 1978-1988. He was a founding member of the Birmingham Design Initiative and is currently chair of the RTPI West Midlands Branch.

Clive Harridge BA (Hons), DipTP, MRTPI, DMS (Dist), MIMgt is a Director of the environmental and engineering consultancy Entec. His career in town planning began as a graduate trainee with West Midlands County Council in the late 1970s. He was Chairman of the RTPI West Midlands Branch in 1995 and has been a member of the RTPI Council since 1998.

Graham Harrison DipTP, DipLA, FRTPI was Head of Policy Development and an Assistant Director of Planning and Transport with Warwickshire County Council before retiring in 1997. Prior to that he worked for Birmingham, Redditch and the Coventry-Solihull-Warwickshire Sub-regional study. He was RTPI West Midlands Branch Chairman in 1987 and its representative on Council from 1989-1994.

Janet Harrison DipTP, MRTPI is now retired. From 1955-74 she worked firstly in the redevelopment section of Birmingham City Council and then as shopping consultant for the West Midlands Regional Study. She was RTPI West Midlands Branch Junior Section Chairman in 1967. After a break, she then made a new career in photography and natural history.

Bob Stokes DipTP, DipEnvMan, FRTPI is a town planning consultant with extensive experience in plan-making and development planning in West Midlands local authorities. Before retiring from full-time employment he held management positions with Warwickshire County Council. He was RTPI West Midlands Branch Chairman in 1990.

Sandra Newton BA (Hons), DMS, MRTPI is employed by the RTPI as West Midlands Planning Aid worker. She was previously Planning Control Group Leader with Coventry City Council where she worked for 23 years. Sandra was a member of the national RTPI Equal Opportunities (Women's Panel) 1992-94.

References

Adams, D. (1994), *Urban Planning and the Development Process*, UCL Press, London.

Adams, E. & Ingham, S (1998), *Changing Places – Children's participation in Environmental Planning*, The Children's Society, London.

Aldous, T. (1975), *Goodbye Britain?*, Sidgwick and Jackson, London.

Architecture West Midlands (1970s), particularly special issues on conservation in 1971 (issue 5), 1973 (issue 15) and on European Architectural Heritage Year, 1976 (issue 23).

Barlow Report (1940), *Report of the Royal Commission on the Distribution of the Industrial Population*, Cmd. 6153, HMSO, London.

Baugh, G.C. (Ed.) (1985). *A History of Shropshire: Vol XI, Telford*. OUP, Oxford.

BCDC (1989), *Corporate Plan 1989*, Black Country Development Corporation, Sandwell.

BCDC (Black Country Development Corporation) (1995), *1994-1995 Annual Report and Accounts*, Black Country Development Corporation, Sandwell, 12th May.

Beveridge Report (1942), *Social Insurance and Allied Services*, Cmd. 6404, HMSO, London.

Birmingham City Council (1952), *City of Birmingham Development Plan*, City Council, Birmingham.

Birmingham City Council (1973), *The City of Birmingham Structure Plan*, City Council Birmingham.

Birmingham City Council (1986), *City Centre Local Plan*, City Council, Birmingham.

Birmingham City Council (1987), *City Centre Strategy*, City Council, Birmingham.

Birmingham City Council (1988), *East Birmingham Development Agency – adoption of revised development strategy*, Report of Director of Development, July.

Birmingham City Council (1989), *Developing Birmingham; 100 years of City Planning*, City Council, Birmingham.

Birmingham City Council (1993), *Birmingham Unitary Development Plan*, City Council, Birmingham.

Birmingham City Council (1998), *Regeneration through Conservation*, City Council, Birmingham.

Birmingham Evening Mail (1965), *The Motorway Maze*, page 1, June 1st.

Bishop, A. (1992), *Birmingham Heartlands Limited: progress over four years*, unpublished paper.

Blowers, A. & Evans, B. (Eds.) (1997), *Town Planning into the 21st Century*, Routledge, London.

Borg, N. (1973), Birmingham, in *City Centre Redevelopment*, J. Holliday (Ed.), Charles Knight, London.

Bournville Village Trust (1941), *When we build again*, Allen and Unwin, London.

Bournville Village Trust (1955?), *Bournville Village Trust 1900-1955*, BVT, Birmingham.

Brundtland, G.H. (1987), *Our Common Future: Report of the World Commission on Environment and Development*, Oxford University Press, Oxford.

Buchanan Report (1963), *Traffic in Towns*, HMSO, London.

Cadbury, G. (Jnr.) (1915), *Town Planning with special reference to the Birmingham Schemes*, Longmans, Green & Co, London.

Carter, C. & Winterflood, S (Eds.) (1992), *Regional Planning Guidance for the West Midlands Region: Background Technical Report 1: Sustainable Environment*, West Midlands Regional Forum, Stafford.

Castells, M. (1996), *The Information Age: Economy, Society and Culture, Vol 1, The Rise of the Network Society*, Blackwell, Oxford.

CEC (Commission of European Communities) (1997), *The EU Compendium of Spatial Planning Systems and Policies*, Office for Official Publications of the European Community, Brussels.

Centre for Environmental Studies (1973), *Education for Planning*, Pergamon Press, Oxford.

Cherry, G. (1984), Town planning: an overview, in Bruton, M.J. (1984) *The Spirit and Purpose of Planning*, 2nd Edn., Hutchinson, London. p170.

Cherry, G. (Ed.) (1993), *The West Midlands Beyond 2000*, Birmingham Settlement, Birmingham.

Cherry, G. (1994), *Birmingham; a study in geography, history and planning*, Wiley, Chichester.

Church of England, Archbishop's Commission on Urban Priority Areas, (1985) *Faith in the City*, Church House Publishing, London.

Church of England, Archbishop's Commission on Rural Areas, (1990) *Faith in the Countryside*, Churchman Publishing, Worthing.

Civic Trust, annual announcement of Civic Trust Awards.

Commission for the European Communities (COM) (1997), *The EU compendium of spatial planning systems and policies*, Office for Official Publications of the European Communities, Brussels.

Community Development Project (CDP)(1977), *Gilding the Ghetto*, CDP Inter-Project Team, London.

Cook, A. (1999), *Partnership in Action: A Critical Evaluation of Birmingham's Fourth Generation Urban Development Corporation*, unpublished PhD thesis, University of Central England.

Countryside Commission & English Nature (1997), *The character of England*, CC, Cheltenham/EN, Peterborough.

Coventry City Council (1951), *Coventry City Development Plan 1951*, City Council, Coventry.

Coventry City Council (1966), *Coventry 1966 Review of the Development Plan*, City Council, Coventry.

Coventry City Council (1970), *Coventry into the '70s – Planning and Development*. City Council, Coventry.

Coventry City Council (1973), *Coventry Structure Plan*, City Council, Coventry.

Coventry, Solihull, Warwickshire Sub-regional Study (1971), *Coventry-Solihull-Warwickshire: a Strategy for the Sub-Region*, Coventry City Council, Solihull County Borough Council and Warwickshire County Council, Coventry.

Cullingworth, J.B. & Nadin, V. (Twelfth Edn. 1997), *Town and Country Planning in the UK*, Routledge, London.

de Soissons, M. (1991), *Telford, the Making of the Shropshire New Town*, Swan Hill Press, Shrewsbury.

DEA (Department of Economic Affairs) (1965), *The West Midlands – A regional study*, HMSO, London.

DETR (Department of the Environment, Transport and Regions) (1997) *Planning Policy Guidance Note 1: General Policy and Principles*, HMSO, London.

DETR (1998), *Planning for the Communities of the Future*, HMSO, London.

DETR (1999), *Revision of Planning Policy Guidance Note 3: Housing*, Public consultation draft, HMSO, London.

DETR (1999a), *Modernising Planning: a progress report,* Department of the Environment, Transport and the Regions, London. p1.

DETR (1999b), *Planning Policy Guidance Note 12: Development Plans,* HMSO, London.

DETR (1999c), *Towards an Urban Renaissance.* Final Report of the Urban Task Force, HMSO, London.

DETR (1999d), *A Better Quality of Life: A Strategy for Sustainable Development for the United Kingdom,* HMSO, London.

Diocese of Birmingham Commission (1988), *Faith in the City of Birmingham,* Paternoster Press, Exeter.

DoE (Department of the Environment) (1973), Circular 5/73 *Public Passenger Transport,* HMSO, London.

DoE (1973a) Circular 104/73 *Local Transport Grants,* HMSO, London.

DoE & DTp (Department of Transport) (1977), *Design Bulletin 32: Residential Roads and Footpaths; Layout Considerations,* HMSO, London.

DoE (1980), Circular 22/80 *Development Control – Policy and Practice,* HMSO, London.

DoE (1988), *Planning Policy Guidance Note 6: Major Retail Development,* HMSO, London.

DoE (1990), *This Common Inheritance. Britain's Environmental Strategy,* HMSO, London.

DoE (1992), *Planning Policy Guidance Note 12: Development Plans,* HMSO, London.

DoE (1994), *Planning Policy Guidance Note 13: Transport,* HMSO, London.

DoE (1995), *Planning Policy Guidance Note 2: Green Belts,* HMSO, London.

DoE (1997), *Planning Policy Guidance Note 7: The Countryside – Environmental Quality and Economic and Social Development,* HMSO, London.

Ecotec (1987), *The Black Country Development Corporation: A Strategy for Development,* Ecotec, Birmingham.

Ecotec (1998), *Future Trends in Office Development,* Birmingham City Council, Birmingham.

Elkin, T. & McLaren, D. (1991), *Reviving the City,* Friends of the Earth, London.

European Council of Town Planners (1998), *European Council of Town Planners Charter,* appendix A.

GB Central Housing Advisory Committee (1944), *Design of Dwellings,* Design of Dwellings Sub-committee, HMSO, London.

GOWM (Government Office for the West Midlands) (1995), *RPG11: Regional Planning Guidance for the West Midlands Region,* HMSO, London.

Hague, C. (1997), Diverse Worlds and Common Themes, in Blowers, A. & Evans, B. (Eds.) *Town Planning into the 21st Century.* Routledge, London.

Hall, P. (Ed.) (1975). *Urban and Regional Planning.* Penguin, Harmondsworth.

Hall, P. & Ward, C. (1998), *Sociable Cities – the Legacy of Ebenzer Howard,* Wiley, Chichester.

Harrison, G.R. & Sankey, J (1997), *Where to Watch Birds in Herefordshire, Shropshire, Staffordshire, Warwickshire, Worcestershire and the former West Midlands County,* Christopher Helm/A&C Black, London.

Heald, H. (Ed.) (1992), *Chronicle of Britain,* Jacques Legrand, Paris and Chronicle Communications Ltd., Farnborough.

Henslowe, P. (1984), *Ninety Years On – an account of the Bournville Village Trust,* BVT, Birmingham.

Holliday, J. (Ed.) (1973), *City Centre Redevelopment.* Charles Knight, London.

House of Commons Expenditure Committee (1972), *Urban Transport Planning,* HMSO, London.

Howe, G. (1979), *Throw the Inner Cities Wide Open to Initiative,* Estates Times, 14th Sept., pp. 10-11.

Jones, Laing, Wootton Eds. (1999), *Shopping Centre and Retail Directory*, William Reed Directories, Reading.

Killeen, N. (1999), *Social Exclusion in Birmingham 98/99*, Birmingham City Council, Birmingham.

KPMG Peat Marwick (1993), *The economic impact of the International Convention Centre, the National Indoor Arena, Symphony Hall and the National Exhibition Centre on Birmingham and the West Midlands*, KPMG Peat Marwick, Birmingham.

Larkham P.J. (1986), *Conservation, planning and morphology in West Midlands Conservation Areas*. Unpublished PhD thesis, Department of Geography, University of Birmingham.

LDR/HLN Consultancy (1988), *Pedestrian Movement and Open Space Study*, prepared for Birmingham City Action Team, City Council, Birmingham.

Llewellyn-Davies & Associates (1977), *Unequal City*, Final Report of the Birmingham Inner Area Study, London, HMSO.

Loftman, P. (1990), *A Tale of Two Cities: Birmingham the Convention and Unequal City*, Research Paper No. 6, Birmingham Polytechnic, Birmingham.

MacMorran, J.L. (1973), *Municipal Public Works and Planning in Birmingham 1852-1972*, City Council, Birmingham.

Marriott, O. (1967), *The Property Boom*, Hamish Hamilton Ltd., London.

Marwick, A. (2nd Ed.1990). *British Society since 1945*, Penguin, London.

MHLG (Ministry of Housing and Local Government) (1955), Circular 42/55, *Green Belts*, HMSO, London.

Millennium Point Trust (2000), Web-site www.millenniumpoint.org.uk

Ministry of Health (1944), *Housing Manual*, HMSO, London.

Modern Railways (1971), *Rail looks best for Birmingham*, pp112-115.

MVA (1989), *Birmingham Integrated Transportation Study*, final report, MVA Consultancy, Woking.

Nevin, B. (1993), *Developer-Led Land Use Strategies: The Black Country Development Corporation* in Imrie R. & Thomas, H. *British Urban Policy and the Urban Development Corporations*, London, Paul Chapman Publishing.

Ove Arup (1988 and 1989), *City Centre Traffic Studies*, Birmingham City Council, Birmingham.

Oxenham, J.R. (1966), *Reclaiming Derelict Land*, Faber and Faber, London.

PAG (Planning Advisory Group) (1965), *The Future of Development Plans*, MHLG & Ministry of Transport, HMSO, London.

P.E.P. Broadsheet (Political and Economic Planning) (1970), *Changing Manpower Needs*, PEP, London.

Reade, E. (1997) Planning in the Future, in *Town Planning into the 21st Century*, A. Blowers & B. Evans (Eds.), Routledge, London.

Robson, *et al* (1994), *Assessing the Impact of Urban Policy*, for the Department of the Environment, London, HMSO.

RTPI (Royal Town Planning Institute) (1979), *The Role of the Planner in Environmental Education*, RTPI, London.

RTPI, West Midlands Branch (1977), *Predicting Shopping Requirements 2*, RTPI West Midlands Branch, Birmingham.

RTPI, West Midlands Branch (1981), *Environmental Education – Resources available from Planning Authorities in the West Midlands Region*, RTPI West Midlands Branch, Birmingham.

RTPI, West Midlands Branch (1986), *Environmental Education Resource Registers*, 5 vols., RTPI West Midlands Branch, Birmingham.

RTPI, West Midlands Branch & National Association for Environmental Education (NAEE) (1995), *The Local Environment in the School Curriculum using Planning Issues: A Guide for Teachers and Planners*, RTPI/NAEE, Wolverhampton.

Schaffer, F. (1972), *The New Towns Story*, Paladin, London.

Skeffington Report (1969), *People and Planning*: Report of the Committee on Public Participation in Planning, HMSO, London.

Social Exclusion Unit (1998), *Bringing Britain Together: a national strategy for neighbourhood renewal*, HMSO, London.

Solihull CBC (1972), *Solihull Structure Plan*, Solihull County Borough Council.

Staffordshire County Council & Stoke-on-Trent City Council (1999), A Summary of *Planning for Landscape Change: Supplementary Planning Guidance to the Staffordshire and Stoke-on-Trent Structure Plan 1996-2011*, SCC, Stafford.

Sutcliffe, A. & Smith, R. (1974), *Birmingham 1939-1970*, OU Press, Oxford.

Taylor, N. (1967), The Failure of Housing, in *Architectural Review*, November.

Taylor, R., Cox, M. & Dickins, I. Eds. (1975), *Britain's Planning Heritage*, Croom Helm, London.

Thew, D., Holliday, J. & Roberts, P. (1982), *West Midlands Futures Study*, West Midlands County Council/Managing the Metropolis Group, Birmingham.

Thornley, A. (1991), *Urban Planning Under Thatcherism: The Challenge of the Market*, Routledge, London.

Tibbalds, Colbourne, Karski, Williams (1990), *City Centre Design Strategy: Birmingham Urban Design Study; Stage 1*, Birmingham City Council, Birmingham.

TPI (Town Planning Institute), **West Midlands Branch** (1967), *Predicting Shopping Requirements*, Birmingham.

Tym, R. & Partners (1988), *Birmingham Heartlands: development strategy for East Birmingham*, Final Report, January.

Tym, R. & Partners (1993), *Merry Hill Impact Study*, in association with Colquhoun Transportation Planning, HMSO, London.

UK Parliament (1994) *Sustainable Development: The UK Strategy*, Cm2426, HMSO, London.

UK Parliament (1994a), *Biodiversity: The UK Action Plan*, Cm2428, HMSO, London.

Urban Task Force (1999), *Towards an Urban Renaissance*, Routledge, London.

URBED/DEGW (1988), *The Highbury Initiative; City Centre Challenge Symposium*, Birmingham City Council, Birmingham.

Uthwatt Report (1942), *Report of the Expert Committee on Compensation and Betterment*, Cmd. 6386, HMSO, London.

Walsall CBC (1973), *Walsall Structure Plan*, Walsall County Borough Council.

Ward, S. (1994), *Planning and Urban Change*, Paul Chapman, London.

Warwickshire County Council (1993), *Warwickshire Landscapes Guidelines*, WCC, Warwick.

Waugh, M. (1981), *The Shell Book of Country Parks*, David and Charles, Newton Abbot.

West Midland Group, The (1948), *Conurbation: A Survey of Birmingham and the Black Country*, The Architectural Press, London.

West Midlands Regional Study (1971), *A Developing Strategy for the West Midlands*, West Midlands Planning Authorities' Conference, Birmingham.

White Paper (1969), *In Place of Strife*, HMSO, London.

White Paper (1977), *Policy for the Inner Cities*, HMSO, London.

White Paper (1977a), Cmnd. 6836 *Transport Policy*, HMSO, London.

Wilson, H. & Womersley, L. (1966), *Redditch New Town: Report on Planning Proposals*, Development Corporation, Redditch.

WMCC (West Midlands County Council) (1975), *Transport Policies and Programme*, West Midlands County Council, Birmingham.

WMCC (1980), *West Midlands County Structure Plan*, West Midlands County Council, Birmingham.

WMCC (1986), *West Midlands County Structure Plan: Proposals for Alterations*, West Midlands County Council, Birmingham.

WMRF (West Midlands Regional Forum) (1991), Regional Planning Guidance Consultation Report No 1 *Asking the Right Questions*, West Midlands Regional Forum of Local Authorities, Stafford.

WMRF (1992), Regional Planning Guidance Consultation Report No 2 *Making the Right Choices*, West Midlands Regional Forum of Local Authorities, Stafford.

WMRF (1993), *Advice on Regional Planning for the West Midlands: 1991-2011*, West Midlands Regional Forum of Local Authorities, Stafford.

WMRS (West Midlands Regional Study) (1971), *A Developing Strategy for the West Midlands*, West Midland Planning Authorities' Conference, Birmingham.

Wolverhampton CBC (1967), *A Black Country Rapid Transit System*, memorandum to the Technical Committee of the West Midlands Transport Study, Wolverhampton County Borough Council.

Wolverhampton CBC (1969), *A Telford and Black Country Transit System*, Memorandum to the Technical Officers' Panel, West Midlands Planning Conference, Wolverhampton County Borough Council.

Wolverhampton CBC (1973), *Wolverhampton Structure Plan*, Wolverhampton County Borough Council.

Wood, C. (1994), *Local Urban Regeneration Initiatives: Birmingham 'Heartlands'*, Cities, Vol. 11, No. 1, pp. 48-58.

Subscribers

Jonathan Abbott
John Acres
Daveleen Alder
G.J. Ball
Michael Barker
Bigwood Group plc
M.G. Bishop
Hannah Blake
cds Development Services Ltd.
David Chapman
Richard Cobb
Peter Cornfield
Coventry City Council City Development Directorate
Phil Crabtree
Mrs J. Crampton
Rodney Crossley
John Dring
Keith P. Durrant
Entec UK Ltd.
Judith Etchells-Sturley
Andrew Ford
Andrew S. Freeman
David Giles
George Goodall
Terence Gregory

Sue Griffith-Jones
Sakiba Gurda
Bill Hanna
Judith Harridge
Clive Harridge
Paul Harris
Graham Harrison
Janet Harrison
Herefordshire Council
Liz Hill
Heidi L. Hollins
David Horne
Tony Horton
Ian Hunter
Conrad James
Peter Lindsell
Christina Mannering
Dr Alison Millward
A. Murie
Sandra Newton
Michael O'Connell
Phillips Planning Services Ltd.
Stephen J. Pratt
M.W. Price
Quinton Meadows Action Group
Graham Reddie

Colin Rodgers
Sandwell MBC, Department of Environment & Development Services
Shropshire County Council
Barbara M.D. Smith
Bob Stokes
Peter Storrie
John Symons
Sheena Terrace
David Thew
Grant Thornton
Christopher E. Timothy
Colin Totney
Shirley Trafford
Frank Walmsley
Julie Warwick
Warwickshire County Council Dept. of Planning, Transport & Economic Strategy
West Midlands Local Government Association
Andrew Wharton
Woodgate Valley Conservation Group
City of Worcester Development Services Department

Index